Pilgrimage in the Marketplace

The study of pilgrimage often centres itself around miracles and spontaneous populist activities. Although some of these activities and stories may play an important role in the emergence of potential pilgrimage sites and in helping create wider interest in them, this book demonstrates that the dynamics of the marketplace, including marketing and promotional activities by priests and secular interest groups, create the very consumerist markets through which pilgrimages become established and successful—and through which the sacred as a category can be sustained.

By drawing on examples from several contexts, including Japan, India, China, Vietnam, Europe, and the Muslim world, author Ian Reader evaluates how pilgrimages may be invented, shaped and promoted by various interest groups. In so doing, he draws attention to the competitive nature of the pilgrimage market, revealing that there are rivalries, borrowed ideas, and alliances with commercial and civil agencies to promote pilgrimages. The importance of consumerism is demonstrated, both in terms of consumer goods/souvenirs and pilgrimage site selection, rather than the usual depictions of consumerism as tawdry disjunctions on the sacred. As such, this book reorients studies of pilgrimage by highlighting not just the pilgrims who so often dominate the literature, but also the various other interest groups and agencies without whom pilgrimage as a phenomenon would not exist.

Ian Reader is Professor of Religious Studies at Lancaster University. He was previously Professor of Japanese Studies at the University of Manchester and has worked at academic institutions in Japan, the United Kingdom, Denmark and Hawaii. His main research interests are pilgrimage and religion in the modern world.

Routledge Studies in Religion, Travel, and Tourism

1 **Pilgrimage to the National Parks**
 Religion and Nature in the United States
 Lynn Ross-Bryant

2 **Pilgrimage in the Marketplace**
 Ian Reader

Pilgrimage in the Marketplace

Ian Reader

LONDON AND NEW YORK

First published 2014
by Routledge

Published 2016 by Routledge

711 Third Avenue, New York, NY 10017

Simultaneously published in the UK
by Routledge
2 Park Square, Milton Park, Abingdon, Oxon OX14 4RN

*Routledge is an imprint of the Taylor & Francis Group,
an informa business*

First issued in paperback 2015

© 2014 Taylor & Francis

The right of Ian Reader to be identified as author of this work has been asserted in accordance with sections 77 and 78 of the Copyright, Designs and Patents Act 1988.

All rights reserved. No part of this book may be reprinted or reproduced or utilized in any form or by any electronic, mechanical, or other means, now known or hereafter invented, including photocopying and recording, or in any information storage or retrieval system, without permission in writing from the publishers.

Trademark Notice: Product or corporate names may be trademarks or registered trademarks, and are used only for identification and explanation without intent to infringe.

Library of Congress Cataloging-in-Publication Data

Reader, Ian, 1949–
Pilgrimage in the marketplace / by Ian Reader. — 1 [edition].
   pages cm. — (Routledge studies in religion, travel, and tourism ; 2)
   Includes bibliographical references and index.
  1. Pilgrims and pilgrimages—Japan. 2. Tourism—Religious aspects—Japan. 3. Japan—Religious life and customs. I. Title.
   BL2211.P5R43 2013
   203'.50952—dc23
   2013013335

ISBN: 978-0-415-70919-4 (hbk)
ISBN: 978-1-318-64776-3 (pbk)

Typeset in Sabon
by Apex CoVantage, LLC

To Keith

Contents

List of Figures ix
Conventions xi
Acknowledgements xiii

1 Pilgrimages in Department Stores and Airport Malls:
   Modernity, Commerce and the Marketplace 1

2 Of Swans, Lakes and Constructions of the Sacred 28

3 Religious Authorities and the Promotion of Pilgrimages 61

4 Merchants, Transport, Guidebooks and the Democratisation
   of Pilgrimage 83

5 Pilgrims in the Marketplace: Shaping, Producing and
   Consuming Pilgrimage 112

6 Scrolls, Singing Toilet-Paper Roll Holders, Martin Luther's Socks
   and Other Sacred Goods of the Marketplace 141

7 Strawberries, Camel Coolers and Luxury Hotels: Heritage,
   Hiking, Holidays and the Consumer Rebranding of Pilgrimage 169

8 Concluding Comments 194

Notes 197
References 209
Index 221

Figures

1.1 *Sunafumi* Saikoku pilgrimage at a department store in Osaka, September 1987.   3
1.2 People getting scrolls and books stamped at the temporary temple office for the Saikoku temple Enkyōji in Kintetsu department store (Osaka, September 1987).   4
2.1 Poster at Coutances Cathedral, France listing the pilgrimages offered by the cathedral's office for 2004.   51
2.2 Replica Lourdes grotto at Cleator Moor, Cumbria, England.   53
3.1 Statue of Kōbō Daishi as a mendicant wandering monk.   64
3.2 Statue of the *boke fūji* Kannon at Ima Kumano Temple, Kyoto.   68
4.1 Poster advertising the Japan Rail/Saikoku pilgrimage campaign.   92
4.2 Pilgrim accommodation in Knock.   97
4.3 Roadside advertisement by a travel firm in Shōdoshima offering pilgrimage and tourist bus tours.   103
5.1 Rosary sculpture at Knock shrine with beads indicating other Marian pilgrimage sites.   124
5.2 Pilgrimage party in Shikoku washing hands before entering a temple.   128
6.1 'Holy water from Knock. I prayed for you at Knock'.   145
6.2 Souvenir shop window in Knock (including assorted Marys and Padre Pio).   146
6.3 Temple official inscribing calligraphy on a Japanese pilgrim's book at a Saikoku temple.   153
6.4 Completed Saikoku pilgrimage scroll.   155
6.5 Poster advertising the *Juzu junrei* pilgrimage.   164
7.1 Xubi, the 2010 Holy Year pilgrimage mascot, along with other pilgrim badges in a shop window in Santiago de Compostela.   176
7.2 Poster from the Shikoku campaign to gain recognition as a UNESCO World Heritage site.   181

Conventions

Japanese names are given in standard Japanese order (i.e., family name followed by given name). I use the modified Hepburn system when romanising Japanese words and use macrons to indicate long vowel sounds in words such as *kaichō* and *shūkyō*. I have omitted macrons from Japanese names and words widely used in English contexts without their long vowel signs, such as Shinto, Tokyo, Kyoto and Kyushu.

A number of Japanese words and terms related to pilgrimage appear in the text and have been put in italics to show that they are non-English terms. In the first case of usage, I provide an explanation for the term and thereafter may use it as a Japanese term in italics. Thus, *kaichō* (the term for displaying for public view Buddhist icons normally kept hidden) occurs in Chapter 1 and in other chapters besides. In Chapter 1, I explain the term and what it conveys, and in later chapters, I use the term *kaichō* in the text when referring to such events and likewise with *sendatsu* (pilgrimage guide in Shikoku) and so on.

I use the standard mode of referring to religious institutions in Japan in that Shinto ones are called 'shrines' and Buddhist ones 'temples'.

I refer when first mentioning major pilgrimages in Japan to the Japanese term used for them (so in the first chapter I introduce the *Saikoku junrei*, or Saikoku pilgrimage, and the *Shikoku henro*, Shikoku pilgrimage). Thereafter, I refer always to them as 'pilgrimage' using the English term.

When I have quoted directly from Japanese materials, I give my own translation followed by the Japanese words. However, I have as a rule avoided translating and have paraphrased or summarised what is said in Japanese.

JAPANESE ERAS

Japanese history is divided into eras and I make reference to some of these in the text (notably the Tokugawa era, 1603–1867, and the Heian era, 794–1185, and the Kamakura, 1185–1333). When the era is first mentioned in the text, I give its dates but not thereafter.

Acknowledgements

In Japan, numerous people have helped me over the years, notably priests from a number of pilgrimage sites around the country, whose temples I have visited on a regular basis over more than a quarter of a century and who have shared with me and allowed me to use information related to their pilgrimages, ranging from statistics of pilgrim numbers to strategies adopted by their temples. In particular, I would like to thank Fukuhara Shōgen from Shōdoshima, Hayashi Kakujū from Sasaguri, Hirahata Ryōyū from Manganji in Chiba, Tsutsumi Kakusei and Aramaki Jikai from Fukuoka, Kawanishi Ekai from Suō Ōshima and Oyamada Kenshō from Shikoku. Shimoyasuba Yoshiharu and Miyazaki Tateki, both of whom passed away in recent years, were helpful and generous with their time in discussing their activities in terms of pilgrimage promotion. In Shikoku, I also benefited from the help given by many people involved in the World Heritage campaign discussed in Chapter 7, notably Matsuki Shūji, Matsuoka Hirofumi and Ninomiya Hiroyuki, along with officials from the Iyo Tetsu and other bus companies on the island over a period of many years. Miyauchi Kensuke and Okumura Maki of NHK were also helpful in answering questions on NHK's programmes and publications about the Shikoku pilgrimage.

Sakata Masaaki of Waseda University has been both a very good friend and a very kind source of introductions to relevant people in Shikoku, as well as a prolific source of information on pilgrimages in Japan. Mori Masato of Mie University also has been of great assistance. John Shultz has helped me in many ways, introducing me to new materials on contemporary pilgrimage in Japan, and he and Ritsu have always been wonderful hosts when I have been passing through the Kansai.

I would like to thank Dr. Birgit Staemmler of the Japanology Department at Tübingen University in Germany and editor of that department's online series of academic papers Beiträge des Arbeitskreises Japanische Religionen, for encouraging me to write for that publication and allowing me to draw on the section in it on the Shikoku heritage application discussed in Chapter 7.

I acknowledge the support of the British Academy, whose research grant R105159 in 2007 enabled me to visit Japan in the spring of 2008 and Ireland later that year to conduct fieldwork and gather research materials that have been, and the Daiwa Anglo-Japanese Foundation, which awarded me a grant in 2006 that supported a visit to Japan in spring 2007 to carry out research at a number of regional and small-scale pilgrimage locations there.

John Eade, Alana Harris and Ellen Badone are thanked for the stimulating discussions we have had on pilgrimage over the years and for their comments and encouragement as I have worked on this book. Various people who invited me to give talks on aspects of this study and have thus allowed me to try out many of the ideas within it are also to be thanked, including Ute Huesken of the University of Oslo, Norway, and Mark Rowe of McMaster University, Canada. Ruben Lois Gonzalez of the University of Santiago de Compostela has helped me understand aspects of the Santiago pilgrimage in the present day. Mara Patessio of the University of Manchester has always been ready to answer my questions on Japanese history. Many thanks also to George and Willa Tanabe, now retired from the University of Hawaii, whose support and friendship has been so valuable over the years.

My family, as ever, have been a source of support and have put up with my involvement in the research for this book. Rosie and Phil have both accompanied me on trips around Japan visiting temples, and Dorothy has, as always, been a source of strength, stability and sanity. Finally, my brother Keith has not just been around all my life but has also been the closest friend one could wish for. Thanks, Keith—it is to him that this book is dedicated.

1 Pilgrimages in Department Stores and Airport Malls
Modernity, Commerce and the Marketplace

INTRODUCTION: A PILGRIMAGE IN A DEPARTMENT STORE

During 1987 the Saikoku Reijōkai—the association of temples that together form one of Japan's oldest and most popular pilgrimages, the *Saikoku junrei*[1] or pilgrimage to the thirty-three temples of Saikoku—commemorated the 1,000th anniversary of the founding of their pilgrimage. In reality, what they commemorated was the anniversary of its legendary founding in 987, when the retired[2] emperor Kazan, who had withdrawn from court life to take the Buddhist tonsure, is said to have set out on a pilgrimage to thirty-three temples enshrining Kannon, the Buddhist bodhisattva of mercy. The temples were all in the Saikoku (western Japan) region that includes the ancient capitals of Nara and Kyoto, as well as Kumano, a region with deep connections to Japanese founding myths and religious traditions. Kazan's pilgrimage, according to this story, replicated an earlier legendary journey by the eighth century Buddhist priest Tokudō, who had a vision in which he was taken on a tour of the Buddhist hells by Enma, the Buddhist guardian of the hells, who showed him how sinners suffered in the afterlife. Enma then took Tokudō on a visionary pilgrimage to thirty-three Saikoku temples and informed him that through the pilgrimage one could eradicate bad karma and avoid such hellish fates. Such stories and their message that doing the pilgrimage could eradicate one's sins and ensure a better rebirth became a central attraction of the Saikoku pilgrimage for generations of pilgrims (Hayami 1983, Foard 1981: 236).

However, neither Tokudō's visionary journey pilgrimage nor Kazan's later pilgrimage are historically valid. Kazan did visit a number of pilgrimage sites in 986 (Hayami 1983: 235, MacWilliams 2004: 42), but there is no record of him doing the Saikoku pilgrimage. Indeed, not all of Saikoku's thirty-three were extant in 986 (Hayami 1980: 268). Likewise, there is no record of Tokudō making such a journey in the eighth century, when fewer still of the Saikoku temples existed (Satō 2004: 23–24). The earliest realistic documentation of the Saikoku pilgrimage comes from 1161, when a priest from the prominent Buddhist temple Onjōji (popularly known as Miidera) is recorded as having made a pilgrimage to thirty-three temples dedicated to Kannon (Hayami 1983: 281).

Historical accuracy, however, is not necessarily the most pressing concern of those who oversee and publicise pilgrimage sites or of those who visit them. Legends redolent with miraculous promises of liberation in the afterlife and that link the pilgrimage to retired emperors and Buddhist guardians of the underworld are far more conducive to making the pilgrimage attractive than are mere historical narratives. Such legendary histories have certainly been a prominent means through which the Saikoku temples have promoted themselves over the ages. The 1,000th anniversary of Kazan's (legendary) pilgrimage was used to this end by the Saikoku temples during 1987 with an extensive publicity campaign involving ceremonies, rituals, public displays of normally secret icons, and exhibitions of the temples' art treasures. This campaign and its related exhibitions were supported and cosponsored by various commercial concerns and interest groups including national and private railway companies that serviced the areas through which the pilgrimage ran, media agencies (including newspapers and broadcasters), and department stores. The campaign was successful in that, although the 1980s were a period of general pilgrimage growth for the Saikoku temples, 1987 proved to be its apex, with pilgrim numbers reaching a peak never reached since (Satō 2004: 142–143).

One of the 1987 events was an exhibition cosponsored by the pilgrimage temples in conjunction with NHK, the Japanese national television and media broadcasting corporation; two newspapers, the *Kyoto Shinbun* and the *Nihon Keizai Shinbun*; and commercial firms including the Kintetsu private railway company and department store conglomerate. The Saikoku exhibition took place during August and September 1987 at several Kintetsu department stores in cities in the Saikoku region such as Osaka, Kyoto and Gifu. I attended the event held at Kintetsu's Abenobashi department store in Osaka; the publicity materials I acquired from the Kyoto and Gifu exhibitions indicate that the same pattern occurred at each location.

The exhibition, which took up one whole floor of the store, consisted of three parts. One was a *junrei ichi* ('pilgrimage market') consisting of stalls manned by workers dressed as market vendors from the Tokugawa (1603–1867) era and decorated with banners and selling 'traditional' Japanese foodstuffs and artefacts special, as signs informed visitors, to the Saikoku region. The second was an exhibition of paintings by the artist Maruyama Iwane, depicting the Kannon images of the Saikoku temples. The third was a *sunafumi* (literally, 'stepping on the soil') miniature version of the Saikoku pilgrimage in which statues representing each of the thirty-three temples had been ranged around the floor in a circuit. On the ground before each icon was a sack of soil taken from the courtyard of the temple; by stepping on the soil of each temple in turn and praying before each icon, participants could do the pilgrimage in microcosm.

Alongside this miniature pilgrimage were two *nōkyōjo* (temple offices for the stamping of pilgrimage scrolls and books), each representing one of the temples on the route; pilgrims in Saikoku, as on other multisite Japanese pilgrimages, normally carry either special books or scrolls that are stamped at each temple they visit. Although pilgrims have to visit each site to complete

Figure 1.1 Sunafumi Saikoku pilgrimage at a department store in Osaka, September 1987.

such multisite pilgrimages, they need not do so in any fixed order, and it is common for them to do such pilgrimages in stages, over an extended time, rather in one go, and in any order they choose (Reader and Swanson 1997: 238–242). The completed book or scroll is not just evidence that one has completed the pilgrimage. It also serves as a commemoration and souvenir of the journey (see the following and Chapter 6), as a ritual object in memorial services for the spirits of the dead and, in popular pilgrimage lore, as a 'passport' to the Buddhist Pure Land and as a sign that one has avoided the hells visualised by Enma and Tokudō (Shinno 1980: 52). During the exhibition, five temples, including some of the most distant and least readily accessed from Osaka, were represented in this way. As a result, people could conveniently 'visit' at least two (and as many as five if they came every day) of the temples on the route and thus complete part of the Saikoku pilgrimage while enjoying the exhibition and doing some shopping. Many were clearly happy to take advantage of this ready-made access to distant temples, as was evident by the lines of those with books and scrolls to be stamped. People also had the opportunity to start their pilgrimages at the exhibition, for blank pilgrims' books and scrolls were on sale and several people took advantage of this to buy them and then 'visit' the temples represented there. Priests associated with the pilgrimage with whom I spoke emphasised that one aim of the event was to encourage people to 'sign up' as pilgrims in such ways.

It was by no means a singular event. Japanese pilgrimage temples have a long history of publicity and marketing campaigns that include exhibitions

4 *Pilgrimage in the Marketplace*

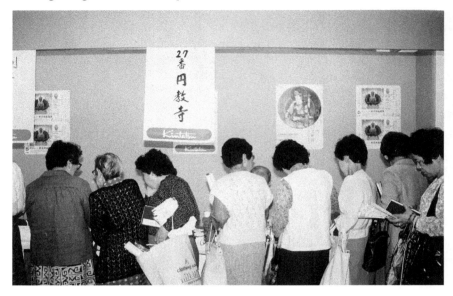

Figure 1.2 People getting scrolls and books stamped at the temporary temple office for the Saikoku temple Enkyōji in Kintetsu department store (Osaka, September 1987).

and public displays in order to heighten their profiles and attract pilgrims. The practice of *kaichō* ('opening the curtain') in which normally secret and hidden Buddhist icons (kept from public view because they are believed to be endowed with esoteric powers and are seen as especially powerful because they are hidden) are temporarily or periodically opened to public view, has for centuries been a stratagem used by many Buddhist temples to attract crowds of worshippers and to raise funds via the offerings and donations made at such events.[3] A variant form of such displays, known as *degaichō*, in which icons and images of specific temples or pilgrimage routes are put on display at distant places to draw attention to the sites concerned and to drum up custom, has been widely used to similar ends (McCallum 1994: 170–171, 191–192, Yamanoi 1987: 240–246). Satō Hisamitsu (2004) has shown how such events have commonly been successful, by focusing on the Chichibu pilgrimage, a thirty-four temple route centred on Kannon,[4] that is readily accessible from Tokyo and that has long drawn its clientele mainly from the Tokyo region. During the Tokugawa era, the Chichibu temples organised numerous campaigns to attract pilgrims from Edo (present day Tokyo), including both *kaichō* campaigns and *degaichō* events held in the city itself, that helped boost pilgrim numbers in Chichibu on a regular basis (Satō 2004: 135, 148). Such *degaichō* events were normally in Tokugawa Japan held in the grounds of Buddhist temples such as Ekōin, which hosted 166 such events in Edo (Tokyo) between 1676 and the mid-nineteenth century; in all, some 741 *degaichō* and 841 *kaichō* events were held in the city between 1650 and 1850, largely to raise funds for temple restorations and to attract new devotees and pilgrims. Such events were not simply centred on icons and reverence but were infused with street entertainment, souvenirs and all manner of visual diversion (Kornicki 1994: 178–179). They were part of a wider development of popular entertainment and tourism, and during these events, temple grounds

> were transformed into a pleasure district crowded with vendors and attractions of all sorts, even including freak shows . . . performances by strong men and female horseback riders were extremely popular. (Ishimori 1995: 15)

In more recent times, however, *degaichō* have often taken place not in temple courtyards but in seemingly more 'secular' locations such as the department store mentioned earlier. In part, this is because department stores in Japan have, since their development in the nineteenth century, assumed a prominent role as settings for public displays and cultural exhibitions and because, located in the centres of cities, they can readily draw in large crowds of people (Young 1999, Mori 2005: 19–20). Such secular settings also facilitate the representation of pilgrimage as a cultural and artistic phenomenon while often downplaying any overt religious connections to broaden their appeal. This is especially so in the contemporary Japanese context, where secularising tendencies are evident, religious affiliation is declining (Reader 2012a) and where Buddhist temples have been struggling to sustain themselves as a result (Reader 2011a, Nelson 2012). This has led them to seek out new ways of engaging with the public, a point that was made to me in 2008 by the representative of a public relations agency that had been retained by a leading Buddhist pilgrimage temple to publicise it via a series of exhibitions similar to the Saikoku event described previously. With increasing competition from elsewhere—not just other pilgrimages but from tourist places nationally and internationally—Japanese pilgrimage sites, he said, had to market themselves in such ways if they were going to be still attract visitors.[5]

Kaichō and such exhibitions thus remain important strategies for pilgrimage temples today. The Saikoku pilgrimage temples held a new *kaichō* campaign from September 2008 until summer 2010 in which each temple displayed, for a limited period, their hidden icons, some of which had not been seen for more than a century and many of which are normally only put on display at very lengthy intervals, but which on this occasion were displayed far ahead of their normal display schedules.[6] The Chichibu pilgrimage temples also held an out-of-sequence *kaichō* in 2008. Normally the Chichibu icons are displayed every twelve years, but this event happened just five years after the previous *kaichō* in 2003. Many other exhibitions with pilgrimage themes also occurred around the same time, including an exhibition of Saikoku pilgrimage temple treasures at the national museum in the ancient capital, Nara, cosponsored by the temples, NHK, the Yomiuri

6   *Pilgrimage in the Marketplace*

newspaper company and a number of Shikoku-pilgrimage-related exhibitions and events were also sponsored in part by NHK (Reader 2007a). Other pilgrimage routes also have used this strategy in recent years, including the temples on the thirty-three-stage Mogami Kannon pilgrimage route in Yamagata prefecture, which also held a *kaichō* for similar reasons in 2008.

The Saikoku and Chichibu *kaichō* of 2008 and the 1987 Saikoku department store exhibition are aspects of this same phenomenon, of displays and events intended to publicise pilgrimages and increase their clientele. They also indicate a point central to this book: that pilgrimages cannot rely on a continual flow of pilgrims and that those who oversee them need to engage in publicity activities in order to ensure that their sites continue to attract pilgrims and flourish. They also underline another important aspect of pilgrimage: that pilgrimages can wax and wane in popularity over the ages. The Saikoku and Chichibu cases confirm this. The 1987 event cited above occurred at a time when there was widespread talk of a 'pilgrimage boom' (*junrei būmu*[7]) in Japan. Satō's aforementioned study indicates that pilgrim numbers were rising in Saikoku and buoyant in Chichibu at the time. By the early 2000s, pilgrim numbers in Saikoku and Chichibu were falling significantly, down to about 22,000 in Chichibu in 2002. In the *kaichō* year of 2003, however, and testament to how such events could boost pilgrimages, Chichibu numbers rose dramatically to over 78,000 (Satō 2004: 143–154). The following years, according to temple officials in Chichibu, saw a sharp decline again; Saikoku priests also said much the same. The irregular *kaichō* events the pilgrimage temples put on in that year, which included displaying icons that, if the normal schedule of display had been followed, would not have been seen for many years or in the lifetime of many people, were specifically designed to boost flagging numbers.[8]

PILGRIMAGE IN AN AIRPORT MALL

Twenty years after the apparent Japanese pilgrimage 'boom' of the 1980s, pilgrim numbers had, by the early 2000s, fallen on many routes in Japan. Priests in Saikoku and Chichibu were not the only ones to feel perturbed by this fluctuation, as numerous events designed to rectify the situation occurred throughout Japan. One such event took place from August 27 through 31, 2008, in the shopping mall at Centrair, the recently developed international airport outside Nagoya in Japan. This involved replicas of three of Japan's better-known regional pilgrimage routes—the Sasaguri, Chita Hantō and Shōdoshima eighty-eight-stage pilgrimages, all of which are modelled on perhaps Japan's best-known pilgrimage, the eighty-eight-temple Shikoku pilgrimage. It involved a *sunafumi* replication of the three routes, using soil from each of the sites to construct a miniature version of the pilgrimages, and local products from all three areas were on sale along with exhibits highlighting the attractions of the areas involved. The event was organised by the Sasaguri, Chita Hantō and Shōdoshima pilgrimage temple associations along with the Centrair airport authorities. Similar to the Saikoku exhibition cited earlier, it was also supported by commercial and media agencies, in this case including the Chūnichi newspaper company based in Nagoya and the tourist branch of Meitetsu, a major private rail company in the Chūbu area that, like the aforementioned Kintetsu company, also owns department stores and travel agencies.

Similar to the 2008 Saikoku and Chichibu *kaichō*, this event was spurred by the worries of priests on the Sasaguri, Shōdoshima and Chita Hantō routes that pilgrim numbers were declining; in Shōdoshima alone, for example, they had fallen regularly through the 1990s and 2000s, from about 32,000 in the late 1980s to just 12,500 in 2007, and falling by about 1,500 per year in the 2000s.[9] The priests, worried that such decline could threaten the very existence of their routes, felt that new modes of publicity were needed to rectify the situation. Whereas they had previously relied on pamphlets, posters and guidebooks, along with word of mouth, to publicise their pilgrimages, they had, by 2008, realised this alone was not enough; they had to heighten their profile by taking the pilgrimage to the people by putting on exhibitions in contemporary public gathering places. On this occasion, they chose not a temple or even a department store for the event but one of the most common, consumerist, transient and 'secular' of gathering places, a shopping mall in an airport. According to priests involved in the event, people are no longer visiting temples and shrines in their leisure time, but instead are going to other, consumer-oriented attractions such as shopping malls. If temples wanted to make people aware of their existence what they have to offer, they had to go into such places themselves, rather than waiting and hoping that people would come to them.[10]

The exhibition also fitted with the agenda of the Centrair authorities, who were seeking to attract visitors to the airport and to make it into a competitor for Japan's major air hubs (Narita and Kansai International). Their plans involved making it into a major visitor attraction, in which (in a manner successfully used in Japan by department stores) its extensive shopping malls could be projected both as consumer centres and as cultural entrepôts holding exhibitions and related events. They saw the pilgrimage exhibition as one such means of doing this, and various shops within the mall also joined the act by selling special commemorative *bentō* (lunches) and other such goods for participants. The event thus allowed participants to perform the pilgrimage in miniature while enjoying a day out shopping and eating at the mall (or while waiting for their flight). This combination of consumerism and pilgrimage proved remarkably successful in that around 50,000 people took part in the event over the five-day period, with long queues of people to perform the miniature pilgrimages, giving the priests hope that their pilgrimages might benefit as a result. This encouraged them to plan future publicity exhibitions, the next of which was held in Fukuoka (the largest city of southern Japan, and near to Sasaguri) in 2011. According to the head of

8 *Pilgrimage in the Marketplace*

the Shōdoshima pilgrimage temples, there was a slight increase in pilgrims there in the aftermath of the event, which he attributed to the interest and publicity generated by the airport exhibition.[11]

AN INVENTED PILGRIMAGE IN KOREA

In 2008, the same year as the Centair airport event and the Saikoku and Chichibu out-of-normal-sequence displays of their hidden icons, a new thirty-three-stage Kannon pilgrimage route was inaugurated in Korea. It had been developed through cooperation between the Korean National Tourist Office and Korea's main Buddhist sectarian organisation, the Jogye sect. Unlike Japan, Korea has no tradition of thirty-three-temple Kannon pilgrimages, so the new route was very much an innovation, one aimed, according to the Korean National Tourist Organisation, not at Koreans but at the Japanese pilgrimage market. It was primarily promoted through Korean National Tourist Organisation's offices in Japan, its publicity materials were in Japanese, and Japanese pilgrimage tour groups were the first to undertake the pilgrimage in 2008. The target number of pilgrims for its first year was 3,000 in 2008, increasing to 10,000 by 2010. Because, according to Korean tourist officials, the temples were widely spread across Korea, pilgrims would probably need to make five or six trips there to complete the route, thereby benefiting the tourist infrastructure greatly.[12] Promoting tourism via pilgrimage is a strategy widely mooted in Korea at present, and this cooperative venture has been flagged up as a prime example of how Korea could boost its tourist industry by developing a 'new kind of religious-pilgrimage tourism in Korea' (Mason 2010). The Korean Kannon pilgrimage was not the first such pilgrimage focused on pilgrims from overseas in East Asia, for in 2001, Taiwanese and Japanese Buddhist priests had worked together to create a thirty-three-stage Kannon pilgrimage in Taiwan—again, like Korea, a country with no tradition of such pilgrimages—similarly aimed at Japanese visitors (Morikawa 2005: 97).

THE MARKETPLACE AND ITS DISCONTENTS

These events take us to the core themes of this book, which draws attention to how pilgrimages are embedded in a context of markets, consumer activity, publicity and promotion, and how they operate not just in the marketplace but through it. The events described, however, may also appear to jar with common perceptions of pilgrimage as something associated with the realms of the sacred, with hardship and journeys to distant places, and as originating in spontaneous outpourings of populist faith that occur because of dramatic manifestations of sacred figures and/or miraculous events, in which pilgrims 'vote with their feet' (Turner and Turner 1978: 25) and are drawn to pilgrimage sites because they somehow possess a special quality that is depicted as being 'sacred' or possessing 'spiritually magnetism' (Preston 1992). The aforementioned exhibitions and events, with their market stalls, consumer items, accessibility of normally distant temples and ready embracing of the marketplace through their use of department stores and airport malls, seem to fly in the face of such images. So, too, does the idea of pilgrimage as something invented as part of a tourist promotional campaign, rather than as something spontaneous and faith driven. These events might even, to some, appear to signify the degradation of pilgrimage into little more than an easily accessible, modern consumerist commodity.

Certainly there have been plentiful complaints, in media accounts, guidebooks and popular and academic writings alike, that modern consumerism and commercialism are disjunctive and corrosive forces undermining pilgrimage's 'true', 'authentic' and 'sacred' nature. The U.S. author Oliver Statler (1984: 299), in his poetic but romanticised account of the Shikoku pilgrimage, is clear that the development of bus pilgrimage tours, and the use of motorised by transport by pilgrims, are 'travesties' causing the pilgrimage's true meaning to be lost. Such views are replicated in different pilgrimage contexts beyond Japan, with frequent complaints that the modern consumer and commercial era has—as with Shikoku's bus pilgrimage tours—made a travesty of what pilgrimages 'ought' to be like. Thus, an article in a Sri Lankan newspaper in 1991 (now available online) bewails the 'commercialisation' of Kataragama, the Sri Lankan pilgrimage site sacred to Hindus, Buddhists and Muslims, and paints a picture of a site that was once pristine, sacred and serenely unsullied by modernisation, where nature reigned, where elephants roamed, and where all pilgrims were devout. Now, it complains, there are 'vendors' around the shrine while modernisation, commercialisation, and good transport links have enabled people to get to and from Kataragama in no time, leading to mass tourism, in which people expect all manner of creature comforts and in which the sanctity of the site has been destroyed:

> What a contrast Kataragama is today! Attractive village belles in cloth and jacket seated in 'Aappa kades' put up in the town area use their charms to inveigle young men to sell hoppers. The right 'connections' could even produce liquor at anytime of the day or night in this holy sanctuary. It would not be surprising if a range of drugs was also available.[13]

Guidebooks and travel websites alike often stress similar mages of commercial destruction at once apparently sacred and tranquil locations. The *Rough Guide to France*, although emphasising that people flock from all over the world to Lourdes in France because of its status as a pilgrimage site associated with miracles and apparitions of the Virgin Mary, warns visitors that the town has but one function: 'exploiting them' through the 'sale of indescribable religious kitsch' (Bailie and Salmon 2001: 706). In a now-defunct website entry for Knock on its travel guide website, the budget airline bmibaby bemoaned the commercialisation of the Irish Catholic pilgrimage centre of Knock (while overlooking the irony that cheap flights might be part of the reason why such a trade has grown up there) as follows:

> As with many places of pilgrimage, Knock has also fallen victim to the tacky trade industry that always seems to pop up at sacred sites. The main 'drag' is lined with stalls competing for Euros: offering imaginatively decorated Catholic icons and paraphernalia favoured by the Catholic religion or lovers of kitsch. The green fluorescent Virgin Marys with pump tears are a favourite, together with over-priced bottles of 'genuine holy water', but this doesn't distract from the magic surrounding the shrine.[14]

Pilgrims, too, may similarly complain of commercial pollution scarring the sanctity of the places they visit. The Moroccan Muslim academic Abdellah Hammoudi (2005: 81–82) writes about how, in his hajj pilgrimage, he expected to see the 'old town' of 'Medina the Radiant'. Instead, he records his disappointment at finding an endless modern city landscape of 'concrete cubes', satellite dishes and markets where he was harassed by merchants trying to sell him consumer goods. Robert Bianchi (2004: 15) similarly complains of how aspects of the hajj have become intolerable due to the masses that now, thanks to modern transport systems, throng to Mecca each year and of how Muzdalifa, where pilgrims rest before engaging in the essential hajj stoning ritual at Mina, has become little more than a huge asphalt parking lot full of thousands of air-conditioned buses. Japanese pilgrims on foot in Shikoku—a pilgrimage widely portrayed in the public imagination as involving peaceful footpaths in sylvan settings—have complained about the fact that more than 90 per cent of the pilgrimage even for walkers is along asphalt roads, and about the disjunction they feel after walking quietly along small roads and through forests only to arrive at some of the Shikoku temples thronged with stalls, noise, parking lots and buses disgorging tour parties of pilgrims (Takada 1985: 42, Harada 1999: 45–49, Hirota 1999: 26). Nancy Frey comments similarly on the feelings of pilgrims who walk the pilgrimage to Santiago de Compostela in Spain. Many, she writes, are hit with a sense of 'dismay at the encroachment of what appears to be thoughtless modernity imposing its crude development on the sacred medieval Camino' as they enter the city of Santiago and find themselves enveloped by its suburbs and by the everyday aspects of the modern commercial urban environment (Frey 1998: 150).

Underlying such comments are assumptions that pilgrimage has a 'sacred', 'true' and 'authentic' nature that is despoiled and undermined by modern commercialism. Frey's study draws attention to the ways in which walkers on the Santiago route disparage those who travel by modern conveyances such as cars or buses as 'inauthentic', and she speaks of a 'cult of authenticity' among foot pilgrims (Frey 1998: 125–136). Walkers on the Camino often appear to underline this point in their denunciations of those who do not walk.

Lee Hoinacki (1996: 216), for example, writes disparagingly of those who make the pilgrimage to Santiago by car, bus and cycle, reserving special condemnation for cyclists, who 'all behave in exactly the same way'. He also repeatedly castigates them for talking too much in pilgrim hostels, displaying arrogance and incivility, and even for having 'fancy clothing' and high-tech bicycles (Hoinacki 1996: 68–69, 145, 158). Foot pilgrims in Shikoku, too, have often been highly critical of anyone who goes by any other means (e.g., Kagita 1962, Statler 1984). People in the mass media, too, sometimes appear to be swayed by the notion that pilgrimage used to be 'authentic' but has now descended into a modern morass of easy travel, materialism and commercial exploitation. Thus, when, in 2007, I took part in a BBC radio programme about 'spiritual tourism' and pilgrimage, the interviewer's questions revolved around the view that 'in the past', pilgrimage was all about hardship and purity of purpose, whereas in the modern day, creature comforts and tourism had crept in, eroding the purity of pilgrimage and turning it into a modern commercial affair.[15]

ACADEMIC STUDIES AND PROBLEMATIC ASSUMPTIONS

Academic studies have shown how such notions of past purity and modern corruption are at the very least oversimplifications, in that complaints about the intrusion of market forces and their impact have been evident in numerous historical accounts of pilgrimage accounts. Judith Adler (2002: 27) draws attention to complaints being raised about the presence of markets around Christian pilgrimage sites in the period from the fourth to seventh centuries CE, and the corruption evident in them. One can find numerous other historical examples of such complaints and criticisms by pilgrims (see, for example, the following and Chapter 5) to counter any notion that it is solely in modern times that pilgrimage has become tied in to the world of commerce or that any supposed degradation of pilgrimage is simply a product of the modern world. Such complaints indicate that the interweaving of commerce and pilgrimage has been a recurrent theme from early times, as well as one that has evoked much criticism. However, this interweaving has not been as widely assessed in academic studies of pilgrimage as it might have been. Rather, there has been a frequent tendency to treat the commercial dimensions of pilgrimage and its involvement with the marketplace as little other than disjunctions from the core issues in the field. Examples abound of how academic studies have portrayed the commercial, promotional and material domains of pilgrimage, especially in the modern day, as somehow contradictory to the 'true' nature of pilgrimage. In his study of relics, shrines and pilgrimages, for example, David Sox (1985: xv) suggests that as a result of modern commercial forces, it has become almost impossible for people nowadays to be pilgrims 'in the old sense of the word'. He then speaks of the 'unpleasant shock' visitors to Lourdes may receive at seeing 'endless rows of stalls selling what must be the most outrageously garish and tasteless 'religious objects' in the world' (Sox

1985: 195). Michael York (2002: 139) even uses the term 'true pilgrimage', which he claims entails transformation as well as danger—an innate element, according to York, in the pilgrim's 'sacred journey' and one that marks it out from modern tourism. James J. Preston (1992) seemingly endorses this view, citing Indian temple priests who complain that many shrines nowadays have attenuated rituals in order to cater for the increasing numbers of pilgrims travelling by organised bus pilgrimage tours, which run on tight schedules and are full of people (whom Preston calls 'tourist pilgrims') who are 'soft' and cannot endure tough rituals. As such, he suggests that 'such busloads of "tourist pilgrims" . . . have negative effects on the spiritual magnetism of pilgrimage shrines' (Preston: 1992: 36). Peter van der Veer (1988: 187) also appears to regard the 'development of a pilgrimage market' as something modern and contradictory to the true nature of pilgrimage, speaking as he does of a 'striking contradiction' between 'the pilgrimage market on the one hand and the fact of pilgrimage with its aims of acquiring merit, purification and expiation on the other'.

These comments reflect a wider problem in studies of religion in general, which have often displayed a tendency or perhaps a *wish* to make demarcations between what is perceived of as pertaining to religion—which thereby becomes conceived of in idealised terms and placed in a special category of the 'sacred—and the everyday realities of existence. I look further at some underlying reasons why such demarcations have come about in the field in Chapter 2. Here I will draw attention to the seeming widespread wish among those involved in the study of religion to set it apart from the everyday. Robert Orsi (1997) has argued that such a tendency remains strong in the present day, which he illustrates with a fascinating account of how his university students reacted when he took them to St. Lucy's church in the Bronx in New York, which has a replica Lourdes grotto in its grounds, along with 'holy water' ('holy' because it is from the grotto, although it actually comes from a New York water main pipe). Orsi reports that the students were 'offended' by the practices there, could not accept them as 'religious' and were especially taken aback when devotees used the grotto's 'holy water' for seemingly 'secular' purposes such as putting in their car radiators. According to Orsi, what his students studying 'religion' appeared to want (or perhaps one might suggest are conditioned to want) was the maintenance of distinct categories such as sacred–profane and spirit–matter—in other words, to construct barriers that set 'religion' apart from the mundane world in which people might use water that is deemed 'holy' for practical purposes (Orsi 1997, Sullivan 2005: 140–141). My teaching experiences suggest that Orsi's students are representative rather than otherwise and that they reflect a wider wish among many scholars, too, to maintain distinct categories of the religious and the secular and between the sacred and the profane. They indicate also a recurrent tendency in the study of religion to view any manifestation of the material and commercial as somehow antithetical to the true and authentic nature of religion and, by association, of pilgrimage. In such ways, they also reflect the aforementioned attitudes of pilgrims and others who seek 'authenticity' and who decry modern transport and the presence of modernity, marketplace phenomena and commercial enterprises.

The images evident earlier, in which pilgrimage is associated predominantly with notions of the sacred (and hence set apart from normative activities and from the worlds of everyday behaviour and commerce), are frequent in academic attempts to define and categorise pilgrimage and to develop analytical frameworks through which to interpret the phenomenon. Thus, for example, Christopher McKevitt (1991: 78) states that it is 'axiomatic that a pilgrimage is a journey to a sacred place which lies beyond the mundane realm of the pilgrim's daily experience,' whereas William Swatos and Luigi Tomasi (2002: 207) state that pilgrimage is

> a journey undertaken for religious purposes that culminates in a visit to a 'holy place', one considered to be the locus of supernatural forces and where divine intervention may be more easily forthcoming.

Recently Peter Jan Margry (2008: 36) has defined pilgrimage as

> a journey undertaken by individuals or groups, based on a religious or spiritual inspiration, to a place that is regarded as more sacred or salutary than the environment of everyday life, to seek a transcendental encounter with a specific cult object, for the purpose of acquiring spiritual, emotional or physical healing or benefit. A pilgrimage must therefore entail interaction between the sacred or the religious, an element of personal transition, and the existence of a cult object.

Both Alan Morinis (1984, 1992) and Nancy Frey (1998) have similarly portrayed pilgrimage as an individual process centred on personal experience, spiritual journeys and narratives. This does not mean that all studies of pilgrimage have focused so explicitly on notions of separating pilgrimage out into some special realm framed by idealised images of the sacred. Although the early influential (yet highly critiqued) work of Victor and Edith Turner (1978), for example, attributed the origins of pilgrimage primarily to manifestations of miracle and apparitions and to spontaneous displays of faith by pilgrims, they were also particularly concerned with the social flows of pilgrimage, with how social structures formed around and reshaped the initial spontaneity, as they saw it, of pilgrimage and gave rise to antistructural responses through which ordinary people were able to create a sense of nonhierarchical bonding, which they termed 'communitas'. They also drew attention to the wider links between pilgrimage and the market, especially in the context of the potential tourist dimensions of pilgrimage (Turner and Turner 1978). John Eade and Michael Sallnow (1991), whose critique of Turnerian analysis has been highly influential, especially in the study of Christian pilgrimages, have argued that pilgrimage was grounded in a sense of contest and should be analysed as a

14 *Pilgrimage in the Marketplace*

field of competing market relations—a theme evident also in Philip Taylor's (2004) excellent study of Vietnamese pilgrimage.

Other approaches that have opened up new dimensions in the study of pilgrimage include Ruth Harris's (1999) study of Lourdes, which identified miracles, healing, the body and suffering as crucial themes in the pilgrimage process, and Jill Dubisch's (1995) work on Tinos in Greece, which shows how understandings of pilgrimage as a process and a practice can be enhanced by examining it via the field of gender relations. Recently, too, Simon Coleman and John Eade (2005) have highlighted the importance of movement as a key analytical frame for pilgrimage, whereas Martyn Smith (2008) has drawn attention to the critical role of narratives and stories in the construction of pilgrimage sites. A recurrent theme in pilgrimage studies has been the relationship between pilgrimage and other forms of travel (notably tourism, but recently with subcategories such as 'pilgrimage tourism' and 'religious tourism') and the extent to which pilgrimage and tourism may overlap and be seen as potentially contradictory modes of behaviour (e.g., Cohen 1992) or be seen as indistinguishable from each other (Naquin and Yu 1992: 22, Reader 2005: 37). Unsurprisingly, much of the focus has been on the pilgrims not just as participants in the pilgrimage process but also as creators of pilgrimage (as with the Turners' notion of pilgrims 'voting with their feet'), a view emphasised, for example, by Jill Dubisch (1995: 36) in her statement that 'by going in large numbers to a place believed to be sacred, devotees in effect *create* [her italics] a pilgrimage site.' Pilgrims, however, are not the only interested agencies in the wider framework of pilgrimage, a point recognised by some studies that have focused on the concept of place and that have discussed the notion of 'placemaking' and how this—and the role of various actors including not just pilgrims but also religious authorities and officials—may give rise to and produce pilgrimages.[16]

Yet often, even as such studies have helped develop and enhance the study of pilgrimage, they have continued to focus primarily on notions such as the sacred, and/or on particular categories (pilgrims, place) while not infrequently omitting discussion of the issues I have highlighted earlier, such as the commercial and the promotional activities of pilgrimage authorities and of external and secular agents. In such terms, discussions of the making of place (and its attractiveness to pilgrims) often continue to revolve around concepts such as the prior existence of the sacred as a special category and notions that journeys made to such places thus are set apart from normative everyday routines and the mundane world.

AIMS AND INTENTIONS

A key aim of this book is to challenge the tendency in pilgrimage studies to portray the dynamics of the marketplace as disjunctions from pilgrimage's 'true' and sacred nature. By contrast, I argue that—as the examples outlined at the start of this chapter indicate—the dynamics of the marketplace, with its themes of pilgrimages being promoted, reshaped, invented and exhibited to increase their custom, along with issues of consumerism and the acquisition of material goods and souvenirs, are not antithetical to pilgrimage (or to 'religion'), but crucial to its successful functioning, development, appeal and nature. The point that pilgrimages can go into decline and lose support means that those in charge of sites may have to take action to attract new custom if they are not going to disappear completely, as indicated by the attempts of Japanese priests to revitalise interest in their pilgrimages. Market engagement—by, for instance, taking exhibitions of pilgrimages to places such as shopping malls where people gather—may be essential for the survival, let alone the success, of a pilgrimage. It is an essential characteristic of pilgrimage, without which the pilgrimage places and routes that are famed and successful around the world, would not have attained the status and preeminence that they have and would not be able to maintain them. Implicitly (and often, as will be evident in later chapters, explicitly), such market engagement and the ways in which those involved with pilgrimage sites may need to promote them in order to maintain their survival and success mean that pilgrimage sites may compete with each other for custom. Yet such issues—of the importance of market engagement and of competition as a theme in pilgrimage—have been paid relatively little attention in the literature thus far. This book is an attempt to address such lacunae in the field.

The interweaving of the market and the sacred—and hence the impracticability of trying to separate out the religious from the wider realms of existence—is in effect recognised in linguistic terms in Japan, where the Japanese word *ennichi* conveys meanings related to both. An *ennichi* is a day (*nichi*) when special *en* (karmic connections) operate; as such, *ennichi* are special festive or holy days when a particular holy figure or icon at a shrine or temple is believed to be specially open to dispensing its benefits and powers to supplicants. Thus, the *ennichi* of Kannon is on the eighteenth day of the month, at which times she is considered to be more open than usual to petitions. Temples devoted to Kannon might, therefore, have special prayer services and rituals on that day, whereas Kannon statues that are normally kept hidden may be opened to public view. Temples and shrines often provided the context in premodern Japan for markets to develop on a regular basis, linked to the religious calendar of festivals and prayer days; the coming together of crowds who came to gain Kannon's blessing (or that of other figures whose *ennichi* it was) provided an occasion for the selling of goods and the convening of markets. In Japanese, *ennichi* also means a market—a term that continues to be used in this manner in the present day. The events described earlier, such as the pilgrimage promotion event complete with stalls selling goods in the Osaka department store, are basically a form of *ennichi* and an example of a widespread Japanese process that combines fairs, markets and special religious days together. The *kaichō* and *degaichō* events held in places such as Edo mentioned earlier are also examples of this.

A similar link can be discerned in Western contexts, as is evident in Diana Webb's (2002: 33) and Jonathan Sumption's (1975: 211) comments about how markets in medieval Europe developed in the vicinity of churches and were especially held on such churches' feast days. One can also see a similar coalescence of meanings inherent in the term *ennichi*, in the English terms *holy day* and *holiday*, which have common roots and meanings in which the celebration of the holy (e.g. saints' days) provided often the only opportunity in feudal times for having time off (holidays; Davies and Davies 1982).

The inseparability of the sacred and the marketplace, and of the worldly and the holy, is something I have discussed in previous work, and here I develop themes outlined in an earlier book coauthored with George Tanabe in which we argued, with regard to Buddhism in general and to religion in Japan in particular, that it is highly problematic to separate the worldly from the religious or worldly concerns and the commercial dimensions of life from the so-called religious and spiritual; they are crucially bound together (Reader and Tanabe 1998). Similar themes have emerged more recently also, in some studies of pilgrimage, notably in Suzanne Kaufman's (2004) study of Lourdes in France. Kaufman states that depictions of Lourdes have commonly counterposed two aspects of Lourdes as distinct yet opposing entities: faith and healing, on one hand, and commercialism (illustrated by the trinkets and bottles of Lourdes water on sale there), on the other, with the second commonly portrayed as debasing the first—a perspective that Kaufman attributes to a scholarly bias against commercialised religion. However, Kaufman argues, such a bias and a dichotomy between the spiritual and the commercial is false, for commercialisation has been key to Lourdes's emergence as a viable and vibrant shrine. As such, she states, '[T]he notion that real spirituality resides beyond the dross of the marketplace needs to be challenged' (Kaufman 2004: 7). Other recent studies that have identified how pilgrimages develop and may be shaped through a set of social, economic and commercial themes include Mart Bax's (1995) study of the Croatian Catholic pilgrimage site of Medjugorje; James G. Lochtefeld's (2010) study about how the Hindu site of Hardwar rose to prominence in the twentieth century; Sarah Thal's (2005) account of how priests at Konpira, a prominent Shinto shrine in Japan, repeatedly innovated and sought new ways to maintain the shrine's status as a popular pilgrim destination meeting the needs and interests of potential pilgrims over many centuries; and my (2005), Mori Masato's (2005), and Asakawa Yasuhiro's (2008) studies of the Shikoku pilgrimage.

Bax, indeed, complains that studies of pilgrimage frequently begin from the assumption that a place is sacred, and pay little attention to how it came to be seen as such. However, as he indicates, Medjugorje's emergence as a sacred site cannot be divorced from a number of linked factors, such as local politics and the privileging, by local religious authorities, of one set of claimed apparitions (at Medjugorje) over rival claims elsewhere (Bax 1995: 67). Lochtefeld (2010: 4), in his study of Hardwar, argues that any place is in essence an *idea* (his italics) that is 'consciously and deliberately constructed, propagated, ascribed to, and imposed on the physical landscape . . . of a space'. Pilgrimage places such as Hardwar are, thus, in one sense, ideas that are constructed, and Lochtefeld shows that in understanding how this process occurs one needs to pay attention not just to pilgrims but to those whom he calls their 'providers': those who live at, administer and promote religious centres such as Hardwar, including priests, guides, professional pilgrimage agents who organise pilgrimage groups in the town and merchants and others who help create and spread the stories that enthuse pilgrims and provide the services on which they are dependent. Thus, one needs to take account both of pilgrims and providers and of their constant interactions in order to see how pilgrimage places function; it is through such interactions that pilgrimage places such as Hardwar (and by implication other pilgrimage sites) retain their continuing vitality (Lochtefeld 2010: 9).

My intention is thus to build on the studies of scholars such as Bax, Kaufman, Lochetefeld and Thal in order to help move the field on beyond the simplistic explanations that have so often been allowed to serve as explanations for the emergence or existence and attraction of pilgrimage sites. I accept that (for example) particular places may be considered especially significant in the minds of some because they believe that a particular figure (for example, Mary in the Catholic tradition or Kannon in Japanese Buddhism) has manifested there and because, for devotees, such spiritual interventions might be believed to produce miraculous events and/or offer the hope that the sick may be healed there. Similarly, I accept that important narratives often endow certain places with special significance—for example, because they are projected as places where seminal figures from a particular religious tradition once lived, walked and engaged in significant acts relevant to their tradition's narratives—that their followers wish to tap into by being there. However, I do not think it viable to explain the emergence, popularity and sustainability of pilgrimage sites in general by focusing only on such notions of special sanctity, miraculous events and the like; by distancing such events and places from the material world of the marketplace; or even by focusing just on the multiple motives of those (the pilgrims) who visit pilgrimage sites. Stories of miracles and apparitions may well be a factor in the development and success of pilgrimage sites, but this does not mean that every place where a miracle or apparition is rumoured to have occurred will necessarily become a successful spot on the pilgrimage map; as will be seen in the next chapter, some may succeed but others may well fall by the wayside.

One of the themes of this book is to ask why this is so. Why and by what means do some places attain prominence as pilgrimage sites? There are, as I show in Chapter 2, a multiplicity of potential pilgrimage places that pilgrims can choose from if they want to go on pilgrimage. Not all such places will attract crowds of pilgrims, and some may lose out to nearby competing shrines. Moreover, as I have noted already, pilgrimages can fluctuate in popularity; just because Saikoku was doing well in the 1980s did not mean it

18 *Pilgrimage in the Marketplace*

would necessarily continue to do so, and as I have noted earlier, by the current century it was losing custom. One factor in such changing patterns may be the dominance of particular pilgrimage centres that effectively draw custom away from others. William B. Taylor (2005: 947), using a U.S. supermarket analogy, has spoken of the potential of producing a 'Wal-Mart-style history' of pilgrimage in Mexico 'in which other shrines fell away in the face of the irresistible attraction and relentless promotion of one dominant symbol', namely the Marian shrine of Our Lady of Guadalupe, which as Taylor notes, was in the mid-nineteenth century 'not much more appealing' than several other shrines in its region but which later rose to become the country's most powerful and successful pilgrimage centre.[17] In Japanese terms, at present, it would be possible to look at how the success of one pilgrimage (Shikoku) has in part been at the expense of other routes—including those mentioned above, such as Shōdoshima, that have been losing custom in recent times—to the extent that if one can suggest there talk of a 'Wal-Martisation' of pilgrimage in Central America, one might similarly use the term *Shikoku-isation* in Japan. This is not just in terms of this one pilgrimage achieving such success that it may be drawing people away from other routes but also in terms of how this pilgrimage has become a dominant model in terms of image and publicity that is having an impact on and is influencing how those overseeing or involved with other pilgrimages are seeking to project and publicise them in the face of massive competition from Shikoku. Similar phenomena occur elsewhere too, as I indicate in Chapter 2, where I look at how Shri Mata Vaishno Devi Shrine, one of a group of seven goddess shrines known as the 'Seven Sisters' in the Jammu and Kashmir province in India, has become such a mass pilgrimage phenomenon in recent times that it has conclusively outstripped its six 'sisters'.

The prominence of massively popular pilgrimage sites such as Guadalupe in Mexico or Shikoku in Japan has the potential to capture the attention of academics in ways that can present an unbalanced picture of pilgrimage at any given moment. Perhaps unsurprisingly, for example, the Shikoku pilgrimage has been afforded far more academic attention in recent times than has any other pilgrimage in Japan.[18] Its apparent success (to be discussed more in later chapters) too, has given rise to the view widely expressed in the media and in academic contexts, that pilgrimage in general is growing in Japan in the modern day—a perception that I have also fostered in the past (see Reader 2007b). Yet such tendencies may in reality be distorting the wider picture; although Shikoku pilgrim numbers have grown in recent years, several other Japanese pilgrimages, as I have already indicated, are not doing so well. To that extent, in Japan at least there may be either an overall decline or redistribution of numbers between different pilgrimages, rather than general growth.

Again, these are issues that this book seeks to engage with. The tendency to assume that pilgrimage is blossoming in the modern world is one that has been readily accepted in the field. The evident popularity of some major pilgrimage sites, such as Santiago de Compostela, Lourdes and San Giovanni del Rotondo in Europe; Shikoku in Japan; and Mecca and Medina in the Muslim world, does not necessarily mean that all pilgrimage sites are similarly flourishing. My argument is that the picture is more variegated than this simplistic assumption of growth. If we are to develop more sophisticated understandings of pilgrimage and gain a properly global awareness of pilgrimage as a phenomenon, we need to pay greater attention to the issues raised here, such as how (some) pilgrimages become major mass events and attract crowds, whereas others seem less able to do so or may be facing decline. We need to include at the centre of our studies an examination of the circumstances and phenomena that make pilgrimages successful or not, and we need to think more carefully about how the image of the sacred itself is produced, developed and sustained or otherwise. This necessitates a recognition that the consumerist dynamics of success and/or failure are integral to the ways in which pilgrimages function and an understanding that such phenomena (which include the engagement of commercial interest groups, media publicity and promotional activities by pilgrimage sites and commercial, government and secular agencies associated with the places concerned) may be essential and intrinsic features of pilgrimage, rather than intrusive external disjunctions to it.

PILGRIMAGE, JAPAN AND THE MODERN WORLD

There are a number of general points that I need to make here. The first is that I use the term *pilgrimage* in a broad generic sense, treating it as a virtually universal phenomenon, found in most (if not all) cultures and religious contexts. Studies of pilgrimage have largely accepted this point and have tended towards a comparative framework and a recognition that, whatever the specific cultural and religious context, there is some commonality and universality to pilgrimage as a practice, concept and phenomenon. Although the English word *pilgrimage* derives initially, via Latin and French, from Christian contexts and associations with (Christian) travel, search and prayer, this does not mean that the Christian tradition has any monopoly on such ideas or concepts. There are numerous terms in other Western and non-Western languages alike that resonate with and contain broadly the same nuances and meanings as are normally associated with it. In Japanese alone, for example, there are more than a dozen terms that contain within them notions of travelling, visiting religious sites and performing acts of worship and prayer and that broadly accord with and are most conveniently translated by the English word *pilgrimage* (Reader and Swanson 1997: 232–237, Reader 2005: 32–33), whereas other languages, too, have similarly complex vocabularies relating to such contexts and practices (Dubisch 1995: 46). Nonetheless, although various languages and cultural contexts thus point to a complex array of modes of travel and practice related to religious institutions, *pilgrimage* is the most useful referent through which to translate them and through which to convey the similarities that are found cross-culturally and that show that although the word *pilgrimage* itself may have originated in one religious context, it points to a phenomenon that is global in nature.

My interpretation of pilgrimage does not limit it to a narrow set of parameters focused just on ideas of travel, of the acts of those who make special journeys or, indeed, of the shrines, icons and sites of pilgrimage and of prayers associated with them. Although many definitions of pilgrimage, such as some I have cited previously, have centred on the notions of a journey and of a sacred place (or places), I see pilgrimage as a broader phenomenon encompassing not just journeys and (so-called) sacred places but also the wider context within which those places are located and those journeys are carried out. I use the term *encompassing* because it involves not just the journeys of pilgrims and their visits to special places; whereas pilgrimage may be about people who travel to visit (and return from) places that are deemed sacred and it is most often associated with religious phenomena and traditions, it incorporates much more besides. Neither journey nor practitioner operate or exist in a vacuum; the places pilgrims visit are shaped by various forces, as with, for example, the motives of officials who might invent new miracle tales, develop new displays, create new buildings, icons, spectacles and events to attract pilgrims or the prevailing transport and economic conditions of the time that facilitate (or otherwise) travel. Along with the motives and journeys of individual pilgrims and the views and intentions of those who oversee pilgrimage sites, and who have their particular interests in and reasons for presenting the site(s) as they do, one needs to take note of the social dynamics within which pilgrimage sites are framed and promoted and the interactions between various parties with interests in the functioning of the places being visited. The activities of pilgrims themselves occur in an arena in which various others have vested interests, including religious authorities, commercial enterprises, local populaces, merchants, lodge keepers and others who provide pilgrims with ways of getting to and staying at and around pilgrimage sites. They may be shaped or framed by historical patterns as well as by legends and narratives that have helped construct the pilgrimage in the ways that pilgrims experience and encounter it. Pilgrims, site officials, places, stories, the pilgrimage 'service industry' (M. Bowman 1993: 49) and the various manifestations of material culture (from souvenirs to promotional materials) intersect in the wider rubric of making, manufacturing and shaping pilgrimage. It is important to consider this wider rubric in order to understand what it is that produces the places and environments that people visit, what it is that facilitates and persuades them to make such visits, and what it is that enables pilgrimage centres to develop and maintain (or try to maintain or revive) their popularity over extended periods of time.

In treating pilgrimage as a generic phenomenon, I do not suggest that one can readily fit every pilgrimage or pilgrimage phenomenon into exactly the same box, or that a pilgrimage site in (say) Japan will manifest exactly the same dynamics and phenomena as one in Spain or India- or that a well-known pilgrimage route in Japan will necessarily display the same contours and patterns as every other Japanese pilgrimage. Local, regional and phenomenological differences will exist across the complex diversity of pilgrimages, and so, as has already been noted, will their degrees of success. Nonetheless, enough generic similarity exists to enable one to make generalised comments and to posit theoretical and analytical commonalities that may be applicable across the broad swath of pilgrimage contexts. As I have already noted, scholars in the field have commonly recognised this and have often recognised that the specific pilgrimage(s) they may be studying in one cultural and religious context and tradition, may also be better understood when placed in a broader context and discussed within the framework of a universal category.

Indeed, familiarity about pilgrimage sites can transcend localities and traditions. James Lochtefeld realised this when he visited the Catholic pilgrimage site of Assisi in Italy. He had spent years studying the Indian pilgrimage site of Hardwar and had not previously been to Assisi. Yet when he arrived there, he found himself thinking, 'I've never been here, so why does this feel so familiar?' (Lochtefeld 2010: 19). He quickly realised what that familiarity was. Assisi may have had its particular unique circumstances, but structurally it manifested patterns and characteristics found also at Hardwar. I have often felt the same. My first visits to pilgrimage centres were in India—places such as Amarnath, Varanasi and Bodh Gaya—but much of what I saw there made my first visits to Japanese pilgrimage sites, and later to Catholic sites in Europe, seem very familiar indeed. At Varanasi, I was struck by the juxtaposition of the bathing ghats, where pilgrims came for their purifying baths; the temples where they worshipped; and the places where pilgrims could eat, shop and do business. Bodh Gaya may be Buddhism's holiest site, but when I stayed there in 1978 and later in 1983, clustered around the main temple where pilgrims—notably Tibetans—prostrated, meditated and said their devotions, were numerous tea shops to which the pilgrims readily repaired for sustenance and relaxation and stalls selling beads, where the pilgrims spent plentiful time as well as money. They appeared complementary aspects of a comprehensive whole. In the summer of 1971, I walked, along with groups of Hindu devotees, to the cave temple pilgrimage site of Amarnath in Kashmir, and my observations (described further in Chapter 4) of the markets that sprang up around this remote mountain site during the pilgrimage season, opened my eyes to how the supposedly secular merchants bringing commercial concerns to the pilgrimage were, rather than somehow 'polluting' its purity, playing a critical role in making the pilgrimage possible and in shaping its very dynamic by helping increase pilgrim numbers in ways that made the pilgrimage feel more vibrant and captivating. Thus, when I first went to Japan in the 1980s and began visiting pilgrimage sites there, I was hardly surprised by the same admixture of prayer, rituals, markets, and bus tours I saw. I certainly did not feel (to use the words of the bmibaby website cited earlier) that these sacred sites (or indeed Knock itself, which I visited in 2009) had 'fallen victim' to and been betrayed by commercialism. Likewise, I felt on familiar territory when I started visiting Catholic pilgrimage locations such as Knock in Ireland and Einsiedeln in Switzerland, and encountered their particular interweavings of piety, play and purchasing.

Although I focus in this book on pilgrimage as a generic, largely universal phenomenon, however, I pay particular attention to Japanese pilgrimages, as this chapter has already indicated. There are significant reasons for this. One is that my main area of research has been on Japan, and during the past three decades, I have spent much time examining the pilgrimage culture of that country. That has provided me with a base of familiarity from which to examine other cultures and pilgrimage phenomena and with insights that I feel can be utilised in the analysis of other pilgrimage cultures. Another is that Japan has a remarkable pilgrimage culture, with numerous routes and sites, from prominent pilgrimages such as Shikoku that have begun to attract an international dimension; to ones that have been deeply associated with themes of Japanese artistic, cultural and political heritage; to regional and local routes that have struggled to put themselves on the map and that, such as Shōdoshima and the others mentioned earlier, need to generate new clienteles if they are to survive. Many of the themes and phenomena that I indicate as signs or manifestations of the modern(ising) dynamic of pilgrimage are evident in Japan and are—as is suggested in later chapters—perhaps more pronounced there at present than anywhere else. As such, Japan might also be a pointer to the ways in which pilgrimage in the modern world is developing.

A further reason for focusing particularly on Japan is that, given my preceding argument about pilgrimage as a generic phenomenon with relevance across cultures, it naturally follows that utilising one particular area or context of pilgrimage is a viable means of developing broader analyses of the whole. Although scholars of pilgrimage may use specific case studies to posit potentially more universally applicable theoretical discussions of pilgrimage, thus far, there has been a particular tendency for the field to privilege Western, Christian pilgrimage contexts in this respect while paying less attention than ought to have been the case to seminal studies of pilgrimage in other (for example, Asian) contexts. Although this point was made some time back about the general lack of attention paid to Japanese pilgrimages by scholars outside the Japanese field (Reader and Swanson 1997: 226), it remains much the same in the present, as Paolo Barbaro (2013: 44–45) has recently noted. Many of the theories that have commanded attention and have helped stimulate research into pilgrimages have been grounded in studies of Christian pilgrimages. The aforementioned studies of Turner and Turner (1978) and of Eade and Sallnow (1991), for instance, sought to develop universal theories around pilgrimage while basing themselves almost wholly in Christian (and mainly Western) examples. More-recent contributions to pilgrimage theory, such as those by Swatos and Tomasi

(2002) and Coleman and Eade (2005), also have a predominantly Western orientation, even as they talk about pilgrimage as a generic phenomenon.[19]

I do not question the use of a particular area or religious tradition when developing general model and theories, but a logical extension of this is that other cultural contexts and religious traditions beyond the Western and Christian should be equally valid and useful for extrapolating general theories about pilgrimage. It is time to break the hegemony of Western Christian-based pilgrimage studies and make the field more properly universal in nature. If pilgrimage as a generic phenomenon does have universal dimensions then one would expect that examples and studies from other contexts beyond the Western Christian domain could—and should—be utilised. As will become clear in this book, one can find striking similarities in terms of pilgrimage creation, production and marketing between, for example, Western Catholicism and Japanese Buddhist pilgrimages (as well as with pilgrimages in other countries and religious traditions). This does not mean that the West necessarily therefore provides the universal theoretical model for the rest, so much as that it can be accommodated and can be seen to comply with models and theories developed primarily from a Japanese context—just as Japanese examples can be used in conjunction with and help complement and develop studies based more on Western Christian models. Thus, although I draw examples from a number of contexts, I make Japan my main focus in terms of examples and data.

The final point to make is that my main focus is on the modern era, a period I loosely define as starting in the mid-nineteenth century (the time frame most commonly used with regard to Japan) with the rise of mass transportation systems and mass media outlets that have been significant in the (re)shaping of pilgrimage since their development. This is not because I view the commercial aspects of pilgrimage as a modern phenomenon or view the onset of the modern world as a particularly disjunctive element in the context of pilgrimage. As is indicated throughout, my view is that the modern world and the forces that have come to the fore in it have by and large intensified and enhanced some of the potential commercial dynamics of pilgrimages rather than having brought them into play for the first time. To that extent, also, and contrary to some earlier studies that associated pilgrimage especially with premodern societies, I view pilgrimage as being in tune with, and essentially a product of, its times. It accords with and follows the contours and variegations of the age and, as such, fits in well with the developments of modernity—a point emphasised also by Philip Taylor's (2004) study of how the pilgrimage to the shrine of Bà Chúa Xú (the Lady of the Realm) has developed in conjunction with modernising patterns in contemporary Vietnamese society.

However, I focus primarily on the modern world both because this is the period on which I have done most of my research and because it has been in conjunction with many of the phenomena associated with modernity and the modern era, such as the rise of mass transport systems and of the mass media, that the pilgrimages that I pay particular attention to in this book, such as Shikoku in Japan, have developed in the ways they have. To that degree, I do argue that modernity has facilitated, hastened and intensified particular patterns that potentially heighten the commercial and consumerist tendencies of pilgrimage. However, I do not claim that the 'modern' has specifically altered the nature of pilgrimage so much as it has helped intensify dynamics that have historically been embedded in it.

THE STRUCTURE OF THIS BOOK

In order to do this, in Chapter 2, I look more closely at some of the themes outlined here, notably looking critically at 'explanations' about why people make pilgrimages to particular places and why places have become pilgrimage sites. Arguing that the concept of the sacred and associated terms, such as that of 'spiritual magnetism', are too fraught with problems to be useful modes of analysis in pilgrimage, I suggest that what is vital in understanding how and why places develop as pilgrimage sites are questions such as why do people choose to visit certain places (and implicitly, not others). Claims of miraculous events and apparitions, for instance, may help attract people to potential pilgrimage sites, but they alone are unlikely to sustain them. Something more, such as substantial support structures and promotional activities, are required to make them stand out from other places where perhaps similar miraculous events or apparitions might be claimed. In discussing this issue, I also pay attention to issues of competition among pilgrimages. The supply of pilgrims is not infinite, and sites have to repeatedly compete to ensure that they, and not some other, perhaps nearby or similar site or route, are the ones that pilgrims go to. Nor—despite frequent assumptions to this end—should we fall into the trap of thinking that pilgrimage is to do with the remote and the ascetic or with separation from the mundane world; far more important are issues of access, proximity, convenience, the presence of the marketplace, noise and other such factors. Pilgrims, as Chapter 2 shows, are more likely to flock to places because they are popular, noisy, crowded and promoted as such, not because they are distant and shrouded in silence and an aura of otherworldliness.

In Chapter 3, I look at a frequent driving force behind the creation and promotion of pilgrimage sites: the religious specialists and officials—often priestly entrepreneurs—who so often play an inventive role in creating, promoting and sustaining the popularity of pilgrimages. In focusing on such figures, I provide further evidence for my argument, outlined in Chapter 2, that the notion of pilgrimage spontaneously arising out of miracles and populist flows is overstated and problematic. Rather, pilgrimages (and the stories underpinning them) can very well be carefully cultivated and created by religious and other authorities, whether through the promotion of miracle stories, through the acquisition (or theft) of objects such as icons or relics that are claimed to be holy or through simple processes of invention along the lines outlined in the Korean example mentioned earlier. Religious authorities not only invent but also assiduously promote sites, often through using the very commercial and entertainment-oriented mechanisms that are deemed in some literature to be antithetical to the nature of pilgrimage. Such examples indicate that, far from being necessarily grounded in populism, pilgrimage often involves a top-down process of creation and promotion that may be critical to its success and development, and that the changing vicissitudes of the pilgrimage marketplace at any given era may be to a great degree because of the activities of such religious entrepreneurs. I draw further attention also to the competitive dimensions of pilgrimage by showing how Japanese temples and priests may be on the lookout for new ideas and ways of bolstering their pilgrimages, often seeking to borrow ideas from rival pilgrimages as they do while keeping an eye on market flows.

In Chapter 4, I extend this discussion by examining other active agencies in the pilgrimage market. Some are closely associated with specific sites, such as civic and regional authorities, including tourist offices, that want to promote local or major pilgrimages primarily for local economic reasons. Others may be commercially driven because of the nature of their businesses, such as travel companies that benefit from organising pilgrimage tours and that have helped promote pilgrimage sites accordingly, and mass transport systems, such as the national rail systems that developed in Japan and India and that promoted pilgrimages in order to popularise their services. In so doing, they have reshaped the ways people perform pilgrimages, increased the potential clientele of sites and enabled (some) pilgrimage places to acquire national and international profiles. In this chapter, I also examine some of the apparent accoutrements of the pilgrimage industry—such as guidebooks—that have made pilgrimage increasingly accessible while having an impact on the ways in which pilgrims perform pilgrimages and on what they see or wish to see as they travel. In this context, I also draw attention to the mass media and to various ways in which projections of pilgrimage in and by the media, and often replicated by other agencies such as tourist offices, have—especially in very recent times through television and other modern media forms—helped create new images that influenced the ways in which pilgrims view pilgrimage sites, an issue I discuss particularly with regard to recent Japanese contexts.

In this process, one should not forget the role of pilgrims themselves. Although pilgrims may often be projected in the literature as the primary shapers of pilgrimage, they are also at times depicted as being focused solely on the sacred and disturbed by the intrusions of the mercantile world intent solely on exploiting them and separating them from their money. However, in Chapters 5 and 6, I counter this perception by showing just how readily pilgrims engage in pilgrimage consumerism and how they play their part in shaping the pilgrimage market. As I note in Chapter 5, rather than seeking out quiet pilgrimage places untouched by crowds, they flock to those that are noisy and full of other pilgrims, and they bring with them expectations of the sites they visit and of the things they want to see, such as fine buildings that confirm to them the importance and special nature of the places they visit. They also want efficient and speedy services to help them get to and fro, comfortable and convenient places to stay, good food to eat, plentiful things to buy as souvenirs and, frequently, also tourist attractions as well. Rather than hoping for shrines free of commercial goods, they seek out shops selling pilgrimage items and souvenirs that they can take home as reminders, mementoes and rewards for their journeys and as presents for others. By readily embracing such things, pilgrims also help foment a marketplace ethic and a sense of competition at and around sites, as well as amongst them. They also are consumers in another way for, as I show by citing examples from my fieldwork, many pilgrims do not make just one pilgrimage journey in their lives. They are very often frequent travellers, with aspirations and desires to visit numerous pilgrimage places and to gain status through their travels. More commonly, certainly in modern times as travel facilities have improved and people have generally been better off and more able to travel, they may well go on several pilgrimages or make repeated pilgrimages to the same place. In so doing, they may (as is discussed in Chapter 6) expect and demand new things to buy on each trip. By traveling repeatedly, too, they help stimulate the commercial aspects of pilgrimage, encourage the proliferation of pilgrimage sites, and play a role in the development of new places of potential pilgrimage interest. The invented pilgrimage in Korea mentioned earlier, for instance, is an example of a pilgrimage developed because of the modern tendency of some older Japanese to go on several pilgrimages in their retirement years.

Pilgrims not only consume pilgrimages; they also buy souvenirs and take back items that are deemed holy (including objects that are seen as relics) from the sites and places they visit. While such items—especially souvenirs sold at shops in the town(s) around famous shrines—have often been derided as gross and unseemly scars on the spiritual face of pilgrimage, I argue in Chapter 6 that we should view them in a very different light, as seminal and central facets of pilgrimages. If one is going to claim (as has so often been the case) that pilgrimage is about the sacred, I suggest, then one has to include the souvenirs it is associated with as parts of that sacredness, not as distortions of or disjunctions from it. Such goods are intrinsic to the appeal of pilgrimage and motivating elements that bring pilgrims to sites. As such, they exemplify how problematic the entire conceptualisation of a binary opposition between the sacred and the profane is. In discussing this issue, I look more closely at a number of types of pilgrimage souvenir, a category in which I include the idea of relics (both physical and digital), and examine how they may be used and how they can play a crucial role not only in the performance of pilgrimages but in encouraging people to become pilgrims and in the development of successful pilgrimage sites.

In Chapter 7, I further discuss some of the ways in which pilgrimages in the present day may be reshaped in order to continue to attract a following.

Although recent developments in Shikoku form one key element in this discussion, I also show how they reflect and in some aspects are drawn from other pilgrimage examples worldwide. As I discuss in this chapter, people involved in promoting the Shikoku pilgrimage draw on the example of the Santiago de Compostela in their most recent campaign to enhance the standing and potential clientele of Shikoku. This not only reinforces the point made earlier about how those involved in running and promoting pilgrimage sites may be on the look out to borrow ideas from other pilgrimages, but it also suggests how pilgrimages are nowadays being marketed in ways that involve a form of rebranding for the modern day. This process, I suggest, tends to privilege certain (usually richer) pilgrims, while at the same time marginalising practices that are seen as out of step with modern consumerist pilgrimage dynamics. I examine, in this context, how pilgrimages such as Shikoku are becoming increasingly depicted through a lens of heritage that helps sanitise pilgrimage and make it into an ever-more amenable consumer commodity. Related to such processes, too, is the appearance of pilgrimage theme parks and of a heritage and tourist industry that nowadays may depict pilgrimages as a modern form of holiday. In drawing attention to such issues, I ask whether this represents a convergence of pilgrimage and tourism and whether such a convergence (or indeed an emphasis on tourism) might be a natural development following on from the inextricable associations of pilgrimage and the marketplace. After this, I add a short set of concluding comments that refer back to the main themes of the book and to the prevailing arguments in it.

2 Of Swans, Lakes and Constructions of the Sacred

> If there is a lake, the swans would go there.
>
> —Sixteenth Karmapa, head of the Tibetan Kagyu Buddhist lineage, on visiting America in 1976

INTRODUCTION: THE IMAGE OF THE SACRED AND OF SPIRITUAL MAGNETISM

Popular lore and literature frequently portray pilgrimage places as manifestly sacred and possessing special magnetic powers to draw in pilgrims. Lourdes developed, in popular imagination and, according to Catholic popular literature and Lourdes-related guidebooks and websites, because it was there in 1858 that the Virgin Mary appeared on several occasions to the fourteen-year-old Bernadette Soubirous, after which a spring miraculously appeared at the grotto where the apparitions occurred. People came, drawn by such stories, miracles occurred, people were healed, and Lourdes naturally—as a sacred place of miracles where Mary's intercessionary grace was manifest—became a major pilgrimage site attracting pilgrims from far and wide.[1] Such explanations work well in marking out Lourdes as a sacred realm of faith, hope and potential healing and in ensuring that it retains an allure for millions of pilgrims every year. Similarly, the visions of a group of young Croatians who claimed to have seen the Virgin Mary (the Gospa) from the early 1980s onwards, mark out Medjugorje as a sacred place where Mary is manifest, while subsequent reports of miracles and graces bestowed by her on the faithful reaffirm this sanctity. As such, Medjugorje, particularly after the end of the wars and upheavals that tore apart the Balkan region in the 1990s, has drawn in huge crowds of pilgrims from across the globe.

Japanese pilgrimages likewise have stories imbuing them with the aura of the sacred and that offer pilgrims similar hopes of miracle, grace and intercession. A key Shikoku founding story, for example, says that the holy Buddhist miracle worker Kōbō Daishi established the pilgrimage in 815 as a way of enabling pilgrims to travel spiritually with him along the path of enlightenment and eradicate bad fortune in their lives. Another related foundation tale has Kōbō Daishi granting liberation from past bad deeds to a penitent pilgrim, and promising that all pilgrims will meet Kōbō Daishi if they do the pilgrimage.[2] As was seen in Chapter 1, the Saikoku pilgrimage, whose thirty-three temples all claim miraculous apparitions of Kannon, also has founding stories marking it out as a specially sacred journey enabling pilgrims to follow in the footsteps of prominent figures, wipe away their sins and attain rebirth in higher realms. Popular Japanese pilgrimage literature regularly repeats such stories and commonly portrays such pilgrimages as grounded in such (legendary) stories that mark them and their temples out as sacred terrain imbued with the presence of holy beings.

Such stories and popular literature present a simplistic explanation of why pilgrimage places exist or develop, emphasising their holy dimensions, dissociating them from mundane concerns and suggesting that their continuing popularity remains grounded in this nexus of the sacred and the miraculous. This implies that much of what is seen at and associated with popular pilgrimage sites—from souvenir shops to hotels and other places catering to the pilgrim trade—is little more than a post hoc commercial cashing in on, and an aftermath of, these manifestations of the miraculous and sacred, rather than being a factor in their very popularity. However, although such images and representations may work well in popular literature and although hopes of grace, healing and spiritual advancement may well play a significant part in attracting pilgrims, they do not provide either a complete or a reliable account of how and why sites develop or what sustains them.

Yet such questions about why certain places achieve prominence as pilgrimage sites (and others not) have not been asked as often as they should be in studies of pilgrimage, a point evident in Mart Bax's (1995: 67) complaint, cited in the previous chapter, about academic studies of pilgrimage too often starting with the assumption that places are sacred, rather than asking why and how they come to be seen as such. Although academic studies of pilgrimage may not follow the narratives of pilgrimage websites and guidebooks by simply repeating legends and tales of miracle without question, they too often appear grounded in a somewhat unquestioning acceptance of the sacred as a category explaining the existence of pilgrimage sites and in an assumption that such sites are popular because of their special sanctity.

Such academic tendencies are grounded in long-standing conceptualisations of the world as existing in a binary divide between the sacred and the profane—concepts that in different ways have underpinned much of the study of religion in general and the sociological analysis of religion in particular from the eras of Emile Durkheim and Max Weber onwards. However, the work of Mircea Eliade (e.g., 1957, 1971) has especially made the notion of a sacred domain standing in contradistinction to the profane, everyday world, so prevalent in the study of religion, and has influenced many interpretations of pilgrimage. This contradistinction between the sacred and the profane with its potent binary divide has also underpinned the ways in which the 'worldly' domain of souvenirs and commerce has been portrayed as a gross intrusion into the sacred realm of pilgrimage. Eliade's concept of the sacred is central, for example, to Erik Cohen's (1992: 50) discussion of the relationship between tourism and pilgrimage, in which Cohen posits conceptual differences between pilgrimage and tourist sites, with the former being grounded in the sacred in contrast to the latter.

Eliade's concept of the sacred was not merely binary, however. He also claimed that certain places were specially imbued with the potency of the sacred, using the term *hierophany* to describe such places where, he argues, the sacred world protrudes into the mundane world. For Eliade, all hierophanies are similar; they are 'axis mundi', special pivotal places imbued with spiritual power, that are not created by people but that are discovered by them (Eliade 1957, Naquin and Yu 1992: 8). Thus, pilgrimage places are in a sense preordained, their identification as such owing to their inherent nature as hierophanies. Miracles or apparitions are thus events that enable humans to realise the innate sacred power and status of such places and are demonstrations of their status as hierophanies. Eliade's notions of hierophanies and the sacred, in effect, underline the popular conceptualisations inherent in popular pilgirmage literature and its associated stories of miracle and holy apparitions.

A closely related idea is James J. Preston's (1992) concept of 'spiritual magnetism', which has been widely cited to 'explain' why certain places have become pilgrimage sites. Preston identified four elements that, he argued, contributed to or created such magnetism: the emergence of miraculous cures, apparitions of supernatural beings (including saints), sacred geography, and difficulty of access—the last of which helps set a place apart from the wider world and endows it with a special magnetic aura. Not every element needs to be present, and just one of the four may be sufficient to produce the magnetism that draws in pilgrims. Preston recognises that 'spiritual magnetism' is not intrinsic to a place, and as such, he does not fully endorse Eliade's notion of hierophanies. Rather, he says, magnetism derives 'from human concepts and values via historical, geographical, social and other forces that coalesce in a sacred center' (Preston 1992: 33). However, despite identifying these parameters, he does not ask whether any of these elements might be manufactured and pays little attention to pragmatic issues such as the wishes of religious officials and local authorities to attract people to their sites and regions. He similarly disregards anything related to the worlds of markets and economics, except through his comments, cited in the previous chapter, suggesting that the levels of popularity that made pilgrimage sites into mass phenomena and drew in 'busloads of tourists' were detrimental to the sites' spiritual magnetism. Magnetism in Preston's terms appears grounded entirely in sacred manifestations, miracles and remoteness and, on the notion of the sacred as a special category and power, separate from, or standing in contradistinction to, the profane world. This again inclines towards an idealised notion of what 'authentic' pilgrimage is, while portraying the mundane world as something that mars its sacred aura.

Preston's notion of 'spiritual magnetism' has certainly been widely embraced as a means of 'explaining' why places of pilgrimage flourish. Nancy Frey (1998: 211) uses it to suggest why the pilgrim's way to Santiago continues to attract pilgrims as does Curtis Coats (2009) when discussing the growing popularity of Sedona, a Native Amerindian site that has been transformed into a New Age pilgrimage centre attracting what he calls 'New Age pilgrim-tourists', in the southwestern United States. The reason why they flock there, he states, is because of Sedona's 'spiritual magnetism' (Coats 2009: 383–389). Jill Dubisch (1995: 35) also affirms the concept as follows:

> pilgrimage is based in the belief that certain places are different from other places, specifically, that they are in some sense more powerful and extraordinary—what Preston (1992) calls 'spiritual magnetism'.

PROBLEMATIC ASSUMPTIONS AND MAGNETIC CONSTRUCTIONS

I do not disagree that devotees may regard the places they visit as being specially marked out in this way. Places with deep historical connections to great religious narratives and figures at the heart of religious traditions may well be seen by their followers to possess some especially potent (and therefore sacred and magnetic) nature. The sites of the Christian Holy Land, for instance, naturally hold a special significance for believers because they provide a link to the Biblical narratives of Jesus. Likewise, the region around Mecca and Medina is special for Muslims because of its role as the crucible of Islamic faith, its associations with Islam's Prophet Muhammad, with the revelation of its most sacred text and with the formation of its tradition. For Buddhists, sites such as Bodh Gaya, in northern India, where the Buddha attained enlightenment, appear to be natural centres of pilgrimage, sacred and spiritually magnetic because of the events said to have happened there that are so central to the teachings of the religious tradition itself. Other religious centres associated with founders, prophets and leaders may be viewed similarly by their followers.

However, does this mean that such places are *innately* sacred and magnetic? Bodh Gaya, for example, is a place where a historical figure stopped on his mendicant travels, meditated and attained enlightenment; as such it is the foundational place of a major religious tradition. However, there is nothing in Buddhist narratives to say it was innately sacred before the Buddha stopped there or that he had to be in *that* place to achieve enlightenment. It certainly does not fit into Preston's frameworks of having dramatic geography or being especially remote, for Bodh Gaya sits amidst the flat north Indian plains which have long been populated, and its immediate environment differs little from the surrounding region. Yet it certainly has an allure in my mind. When I first visited Bodh Gaya in 1978, I was struck by its visual potency, by the towering Mahabodhi Temple that was later built at the spot where the Buddha is said to have meditated, and by the ambiance of the town with its numerous temples, pilgrims and monks from different Buddhist traditions and countries. Arriving there, I felt I had come to a truly special place where something significant—the beginning of a great religion—had happened. I have walked to Bodh Gaya from the nearest major town, Gaya, around eleven kilometres to the north, several times and every time have felt a sense of excitement and of reaching somewhere special as the Mahabodhi temple tower has come into view towering up amidst the flat plains ahead of me and as I have entered the town. Yet I am also very much aware that I was reading my own emotions into the place, rather than engaging in a historically grounded analysis of its nature. The reality is that no matter what visitors such as me or Buddhist pilgrims going there might feel about the Bodh Gaya they encounter, they are responding to a modern (re)invention and (re)construction. Whereas in the early days of Buddhism Bodh Gaya did attract pilgrims, it had for many centuries thereafter, as Buddhism became marginalised and then (from around the twelfth century) virtually defunct in the land of its origin, become disused as a Buddhist pilgrimage centre until being rediscovered and transformed into a living pilgrimage site by Buddhists from outside India from the late nineteenth century on.

As Toni Huber (2008: 251–293) shows, during the nineteenth century, while India was under British rule, a series of archaeological discoveries led to a 'rebirth' of Buddhist India—a process that included the reclamation by Buddhist pressure groups from outside India of long neglected sites such as Bodh Gaya. The British poet Edwin Arnold, whose 1879 poem *The Light of Asia*, helped bring Buddhism and the Buddha, until then little known in Europe, to wider notice, visited Bodh Gaya in 1885 and spoke of it as having a similar religious significance to Jerusalem or Mecca. Arnold's words were a boost to the campaign being waged at the time by the Sri Lankan monk Dharmapāla, for Bodh Gaya (then supervised by Hindus) to be placed under Buddhist control. Dharmapāla was joined in this campaign by the Mahabodhi Society, a Buddhist organisation with Sri Lankan roots, and together they sought to reinvent Bodh Gaya as a pilgrimage centre and to furnish it with appropriate markers of sanctity, such as a temple and other monuments to give the site a degree of architectural splendour. By turning it into a major pilgrimage centre, they aimed for a way to press the British authorities into transferring Bodh Gaya to Buddhist control. Controlling the site was also a key tactic in their strategic goal of making the Mahabodhi Society a key arbiter and authority on Buddhism in the modern world. Promoting Bodh Gaya as a pilgrimage centre thus served to advance the society's religious and political agendas.

Because Buddhism had died out centuries earlier in India, the society was reliant on attracting pilgrims from outside to fulfil this aim. Hence, it engaged in international campaigns to promote Bodh Gaya as a pilgrimage centre, advocated pilgrimage as an 'authentic' practice with roots deeply embedded in Buddhist tradition and sought to create 'an archaeologically recovered and discursively redefined Buddhist holy land' of places that pilgrims could visit (Huber 2008: 293–295). The Mahabodhi Society's promotional activities included printing commemorative certificates for pilgrims who visited Bodh Gaya, arranging archaeological tours of north Indian Buddhist sites and developing links with Indian Railways to offer cheap transport for pilgrims not just to Bodh Gaya but to Sarnath and other Buddhist sites (Huber 2008: 304). The society was influential in helping Buddhist interests gain control of Bodh Gaya, renovate its main temple, build several other Buddhist temples and develop a growing infrastructure as the once-defunct site was rebuilt into a thriving pilgrimage centre. Thus, although Bodh Gaya may have a deep historical resonance and magnetic qualities for Buddhist pilgrims today, such qualities are very much a product of the activities of nineteenth- and early-twentieth-century reformist Buddhists from outside of India who strove to transform a backwater without Buddhists or significant Buddhist buildings into a modern pilgrimage centre and flagship symbol for their form of Buddhism.

Other places have similarly been developed or 'rediscovered' as sacred realms, as can be seen from the example of Sedona, portrayed by Coats (2009) as a pilgrimage centre because of its spiritual magnetism. Sedona had long been an important place in Amerindian culture, but it was in essence reinvented and rose to prominence as a New Age pilgrimage site in the latter part of the twentieth century when New Agers began to flock there, convinced that its landscape signified and made manifest an 'other' and transcendent realm. This was not simply because of some spontaneous explosion of emotional enthusiasm; it was facilitated by powerful commercial interests instrumental in providing the publicity that brought Sedona to wider attention. Local agencies keen to develop the area as a tourist centre, especially for outdoor activities,[3] played a significant role in heightening awareness of Sedona's environment, while the area, because of its dramatic features, was used as a backdrop for large numbers of Hollywood movies and advertisements (Ivakhiv 2001: 160). Commercial interests thus served as an advertisement for the landscape, which captivated New Agers who thus came to the region looking for spiritual powers. As they did so, a number of such New Age adherents with consummate entrepreneurial skills engaged in a process of visually transforming the landscape so that it manifested the appropriate signs and structures to accord with their visions of what such a sacred landscape should contain. They identified its various features as 'vortexes' or 'power spots' that were then proclaimed as signs of Sedona's sacred power, and organised 'vortex tours' of this 'sacred' and 'magnetic' landscape. The publication of books about these now-identified vortexes, coupled with emerging stories about mysterious and/or miraculous events occurring around them, further enhanced the aura being created around Sedona (Ivakhiv 2001: 173). As Ivakhiv (2001) has also shown, a somewhat similar process also occurred at Glastonbury in England, with that town and area being transformed, in the modern day, into a New Age pilgrimage milieu aided by the entrepreneurial

MAGNETIC ASSUMPTIONS, PILGRIMAGE FLUCTUATIONS AND ECONOMIC INFLUENCES

The Shikoku pilgrimage is another example of a pilgrimage that appears to be popular in the present day because of its seemingly 'magnetic' qualities. Pilgrims who have told me how 'addictive' the pilgrimage is, and who enthuse about the special nature of Shikoku as 'another country' (*betsu no kuni*), as one Japanese woman termed it when trying to explain to me about how it felt different to her from the everyday world of Japan she lived in, clearly find it somehow special and provide it, for them, with feelings that draw them back time and again (Reader 2005: 255–266). As was noted earlier, miracle tales and associations with a prominent figure in Japanese Buddhism have played a part in developing Shikoku's image in this context; along with Shikoku's scenery and associations with a variety of religious practices and local customs, they have helped create what I have previously termed the pilgrimage's 'emotional landscape' (Reader 2005: 6). Yet one should not automatically assume that its popularity is attributable to some form of innate magnetism. The pilgrimage has not been consistently popular in historical terms, and in earlier eras—certainly until well into the twentieth century—had been infused with rather dark images which gave Shikoku the aura of a rather wild and dangerous place, with pilgrims deemed unruly and possibly larcenous miscreants, and as a place somewhat remote and cut off from the main centres of population in Japan (Reader 2005: 132–135). Those darker images were one reason why the Shikoku pilgrimage was, until recently, far less popular than many others—notably Saikoku—in Japan. As James Foard (1982) has shown, Saikoku was akin to a 'national pilgrimage' in the Tokugawa period and was encouraged as such by national political authorities. Through much of the twentieth century, too, it retained that position. Maeda Takashi's (1971) sociological study of Shikoku and Saikoku, for instance, demonstrates that throughout the Tokugawa period and during the nineteenth and much of the twentieth century, Saikoku was in some way more popular than Shikoku.

Shikoku, which until modern times was considered overall to be more marginal than was Saikoku, provides in its earlier history a clear example of how being remote from centres of population does not necessarily make places more magnetic but may even make them less immediately so. Its history, similar to that of many other pilgrimages in Japan, also suggests that whatever magnetism it might possess, may also be influenced by economic considerations and fluctuations. This is something that has been widely noted by Japanese scholars who have charted the ebbs and flows of pilgrimage and of pilgrim choices in Japan and who have produced some of the most compelling examinations of the links between economic change and pilgrimage participation. Shinjō's (1982) magisterial study of the subject covering around 1,000 years of history up to the mid-nineteenth century shows, for example, that the Tokugawa period overall was an age of pilgrimage growth, facilitated by improvements in the country's economic circumstances along with improved travel infrastructures, including better and safer highways and (in places such as Shikoku) the provision of ferries and bridges across rivers and inlets (Shinjō 1982; see also Blacker 1984, Vaporis 1994). Pilgrimage and the service industry supporting it were also significant in the development of the Tokugawa market economy (Shinjō 1982: 699–745, Thal 2005: 102). Yet this does not mean that the period was one of constant pilgrimage success and growth or that pilgrimage places remained constantly magnetic. Economic fluctuations changed pilgrim flows, with periods of growth or recession producing peaks and troughs of pilgrimage activity; the decade and a half at the end of the seventeenth and the start of eighteenth century and known in Japan as the Genroku period (1688–1703), for example, was an era of economic expansion that enabled infrastructure improvements and produced a growth in pilgrim numbers in places such as Shikoku (Shinjō 1982: 1020–1028, Kouamé 2001: 52). Yet the Tokugawa era was not one of consistent growth, as Shinjō's study illustrates and as has been further affirmed by Satō (2004: 74–85) and Maeda (1971: 86–89), both of whom show how economic peaks and troughs correlated with periods of pilgrim growth and decline in Tokugawa Japan. The periodic famines that afflicted Japan in the period, for example, had a negative impact on pilgrim numbers. Similarly, the period in the immediate aftermath of the Second World War, when Japan was economically devastated, was a period when pilgrims were scarce on just about every pilgrimage route in the country and in which serious concerns were raised about the potential of many of them to survive (Reader 2005: 150–151). As Satō (2004) indicates, such patterns have not changed radically thereafter, in that periods of economic growth and decline in the modern period have also influenced the rise and fall of pilgrim numbers. His study shows that economic growth in the mid-1960s was a factor in the growth of regional pilgrimages such as Chichibu whereas the more recent decline in pilgrimage fortunes across much of Japan, and notably Saikoku, from the 1990s on has been influenced by Japan's economic woes (Satō 2004: 142–151).

The modern age has in general produced conditions that have facilitated pilgrimage, including improved transportation and widespread and increasingly comfortable lodging facilities, along with moneyed economies that have provided growing numbers of people with the wherewithal to travel. The development of a pension system in the postwar era has enabled older Japanese people to retire, have free time and be able to afford to travel. This has been a causative factor in one of the most prominent sociological features of contemporary Japanese pilgrimage that is very much in evidence in Shikoku: the aging of the pilgrim population, in which people in their sixties and older now constitute by some way the largest age set in the Japanese pilgrimage market, and the shift in gender balances, with women now outnumbering men in the pilgrimage market (Osada, Sakata and Seki 2003: 226–227). Many of the pilgrims I have met have said that, having retired, they are now able to do pilgrimages as a result and that having pensions and savings that secure their futures is a factor in this. (Indeed, the newly invented Korean pilgrimage mentioned in Chapter 1 appears to be geared towards such a clientele.) Such factors certainly helped spur pilgrimage growth in the 1980s, a period when Japan was economically booming, more Japanese than ever before had money to travel, and more (especially those with pensions and retirement income) had leisure time to do, leading to a boom in travel within Japan and by package tour (Shimizutani 1986: 6–7, Kanzaki 1990: 178–179). It was an era in which overseas travel had not attained high levels of popularity compared to later eras and in which the popularity of travel within Japan was spurred by a widespread rhetoric of nostalgia and that linked travel to famous places, such as temples, to a rediscovery and reaffirmation of Japanese tradition and identity (Reader 1987b, Ivy 1995, Robertson 1991, Creighton 1997). It was in this era that many pilgrimages such as Saikoku reached their apex of popularity and that Shikoku began really to attract pilgrims in similar numbers to Shikoku (Satō 2004: 140, 162). Thereafter, and as Japan has faced numerous economic troubles since the early 1990s, the overall pilgrim growth widely reported for the 1980s has been replaced by uncertainty and, for many pilgrimages such as Shōdoshima and Saikoku, clear indications of declining pilgrim numbers.

The evidence from Japan is that, although economic growth periods can spur pilgrimages and, hence, enhance their magnetism, recessions can have the reverse effect. This point is reinforced by examples from elsewhere. Robert Bianchi (2004: 50, 58) shows that economic downturns can also affect the Muslim hajj pilgrimage, with participation rates from Middle Eastern Arab countries that are dependent on oil revenues rising and falling in accord with petroleum prices. The global recession caused by the banking crisis of 2008 has also had an impact, with Indian newspapers and economic journals reporting that the financial crisis was affecting pilgrimage sites in the country. One article commented that 'even the gods have been impacted by the global financial crisis' as it informed readers that previously pilgrims seeking to visit the southern Indian pilgrimage centres of Tirupati shrine in Andhra Pradesh and Ayyappa temple in Sabarimala, Kerala, by bus from Bangalore (the region's transport hub) had to reserve seats a week or more in advance and that transport firms did a 'roaring business'. However, by December 2008, with the recession biting, pilgrim numbers had fallen drastically, bus operators were reducing their services, and business was poor even at the annual peak pilgrimage period between November and January.[4]

THE ASCENDANCY OF SHIKOKU: A MODERN SUCCESS STORY IN AN AGE OF DECLINE

This does not mean that pilgrimages will always decline numerically in times of economic crisis. Shikoku's popularity, for example, thus far appears to be unaffected by the recent period of economic recession. Its emergence as contemporary Japan's most widely known pilgrimage has, however, come about as other pilgrimages have experienced problems, and in many respects, it offers an example of how a pilgrimage may become popular through adapting its image to new circumstances. It is also an indicator of the competitive nature of the pilgrimage market and of how the success and rise of one pilgrimage (in this case, Shikoku) may occur in conjunction with the decline of others in the same religious and cultural milieu.

As I stated earlier, Shikoku was, until quite recently, a less popular pilgrimage than Saikoku. In the postwar era, as Japan recovered after its war defeat and as it began to grow economically, pilgrim numbers began to rise on numerous routes throughout the country. Even so, until the late 1960s, Shikoku appeared far less magnetic than did Saikoku, which attracted twice as many pilgrims right until the end of the 1960s (Maeda 1971: 48–54). Through the 1970s and 1980s, however, Shikoku pilgrim numbers gradually caught up with, and by the 1990s, they had clearly overtaken, Saikoku. Two graphs in Satō's (2004) study of Japanese pilgrimage flows make the point clearly; in Shikoku from the late 1960s (when Satō's data starts from and when Shikoku pilgrimage numbers were just over 14,000 annually) to 2003 (his final data point, when numbers were greater than 82,000) numbers rise steadily almost year on year. By contrast, in Saikoku, numbers start higher at around 30,000 in the late 1960s, rising to around the 70,000 mark throughout the 1970s and 1980s. Thereafter, they show little further increase, hovering around the same level with minor fluctuations before declining gradually from the late 1990s onwards (Satō 2004: 137, 162). Shikoku has also outstripped regional routes that in earlier times had higher numbers because of their appeal to a local and regional clientele, such as the Chichibu Kannon route, which throughout the Tokugawa period and well into the present day regularly received more pilgrims than Shikoku. By the 1990s, however, Chichibu's numbers were in decline at the same period as those in Shikoku were rising (Satō 2004: 154–167). The new pilgrimage publicity campaigns outlined in Chapter 1 and launched by priests involved in Japanese pilgrimages such as Saikoku and Chichibu that have seen their numbers fall as Shikoku's have risen, can in part be seen as a product of this shift, resulting in the need of these other routes to find new strategies to enhance themselves and to try to counter the deleterious effects that economic recession is having on the Japanese pilgrimage market overall.[5]

Central to this transformation (or perhaps, one might say, central to Shikoku's recently enhanced magnetism) has been a potent recalibration of the Shikoku pilgrimage's public depiction and representation, one that has removed its earlier wild and dangerous image while presenting the pilgrimage as a symbol of 'traditional' Japan and a repository of Japanese cultural values. A number of interest groups for the most part working together have taken part in this recalibration, from the temples themselves, to regional transport companies that helped popularise the pilgrimage via bus package tours that developed from the 1950s onwards, to regional civic agencies and tourist offices that saw the pilgrimage as a means of bringing visitors to Shikoku in order to improve its economy, to mass media agencies, notably Japan's national broadcaster NHK, that saw the pilgrimage as a suitable focus for scenic television programmes aimed at emphasising issues of cultural identity and tradition (Mori 2005, Reader 2007a). The projection of the Shikoku pilgrimage as a highly 'traditional' enterprise associated with Japanese identity and cultural roots, and the emphasis placed on Shikoku's natural scenery and apparent adherence to traditional customs that have disappeared elsewhere in Japan, have been important factors in this process (Mori 2005: 174–177, 263). Such themes have accorded well with and tapped into one of the most striking elements of Japanese cultural discourse in the later decades of the twentieth century, in which discussions and images of cultural identity have been infused with a deep-seated nostalgia centred around rural images of innate harmony that are quintessentially Japanese but that have been lost in the modern urban and Westernised environment (Robertson 1991, Ivy 1995, Creighton 1997). As such they have been widely reproduced and utilised by a variety of agencies intent on promoting the pilgrimage and that have depicted it as epitomising the Japanese *kokoro no furusato* or 'spiritual homeland' (Reader 1987b). Mori (2005: 249) argues, indeed, that the pilgrimage's popularity in the recent period is not because it provides the hope of healing or for dealing with social unease, but because of the ways in which it has been projected in the media as a form of national commodity associated with such nostalgic themes. In such terms, Shikoku has effectively come to be seen as Japan's most 'traditional' pilgrimage, through which one could get into the heart of Japanese culture and invigorate one's sense of cultural identity. Through acquiring this imaged and orientation, it has effectively displaced Saikoku and has taken over its former 'national' status. Saikoku, in comparison, has lost out, and to a great extent, those pilgrims who, a couple of decades earlier, would have chosen to do Saikoku because of its position as a symbol of cultural heritage and tradition, are likely nowadays to choose Shikoku.[6]

However, despite Shikoku's seeming current success, this does not mean that those involved with the pilgrimage and its promotion are necessarily confident about its longer-term future. As will be seen in Chapter 7, they are aware that pilgrimages fluctuate in popularity and that other routes in the present day are struggling, and are worried that their pilgrimage might face similar difficulties before long. They recognise, too, that the pilgrimage's popularity may well be undermined because of Japan's continuing economic problems along with changing social attitudes, and are thus seeking new ways to publicise the pilgrimage and to rebrand it in ways that they hope will attract new clienteles.

I discuss these issues and look more closely at the roles of the previously mentioned agencies in subsequent chapters. Here, the point of emphasis is that the appeal of the Shikoku pilgrimage and its rise to prominence in the present day have not been so much about stories of miracle or seemingly innate sacred and magnetic qualities in its nature as they have been about images produced in the modern era by the interactions of a number of interest groups that include the temples and commercial and civic agencies. Similar to other Japanese pilgrimages (and pilgrimages in general), it has been subject to fluctuating economic conditions, as well as competition from other routes, all of which necessitate responses and strategies to maintain its standing. To understand why pilgrims go to Shikoku, then, and consequently why Shikoku has developed into the premier pilgrimage in Japan, requires far more than assuming that it has some form of special spiritual magnetism. It involves thinking about how the pilgrimage has been represented, shaped and reconfigured in contemporary contexts, and how its aura of 'packaged piety' (to use Ruth Harris's [1999: 11] term), has been shaped to make it highly attractive to potential pilgrims and to help it weather changing economic circumstances. In considering such issues, too, one needs to understand why certain places (for example, in the Japanese context, Shikoku) garner a large number of pilgrims at a particular juncture or period, whereas others (for example, Saikoku or Shōdoshima) do less well. This in turn informs us that whatever magnetism a pilgrimage site or route might have, in the eyes of potential pilgrims, may not be constant but may be highly contingent on how places are publicised, represented and imaged in the public domain and on how successfully other potentially competing pilgrimages may be projected and portrayed by the interest groups surrounding them.

MIRACLES, DEVELOPMENT AND SUSTENANCE

Both the Turners and Preston draw attention to miracles and apparitions as causative aspects of pilgrimages and as agents bestowing the spiritual magnetism that transforms a place into a pilgrimage site. Preston (1992: 37) cites Knock as an example of a site whose magnetism comes from apparitions and miracles. He recognises that it has not acquired any magnetism through its geographic setting, located as it is in the flat peatlands of central Ireland with few features to mark it out from the surrounding landscape. Yet, because of apparitions that occurred in 1879, when a group of local people saw a vision of Mary and other holy figures on the wall of the local church, and the miraculous repercussions and claims of healing that followed the apparitions, Knock was, he claims, imbued with an intense spiritual magnetism that enabled it to rival Lourdes (Preston 1992: 37). However, in making an explicit link between Knock's 1879 story of apparition and miracle and its prominence as a pilgrimage site, Preston appears not to consider that, after an initial burst of enthusiasm, Knock was little more than a local pilgrimage centre that, after being sustained for a quarter of a century by what Myra Shackley (2006: 95) has termed the 'momentum of the apparition', thereafter began to go into decline. This is not an uncommon pattern. As Robert Finucane (1977) has shown in his study of medieval England, miracle stories were commonplace in medieval Christian contexts, giving rise to hosts of local pilgrimage sites, many of which were unable to sustain clienteles for any length of time. William Swatos (2002), too, shows that interest in sites where Marian apparitions have been reported tends to wane rather quickly. Indeed, he argues that sites such as Lourdes that continue to attract pilgrims over a longer period are the exception to this pattern of transient interest (Swatos 2002: 184). At times, too, even in pilgrimages with long histories of miraculous stories, there may be times when those associated with a pilgrimage site appear keen to downplay such events, especially if they appear to conflict with the prevailing modes of representation and promotion of such pilgrimages. In Shikoku, for example, its recent period of national popularity has occurred in a context in which miraculous stories have been afforded very little space in the publicity materials produced by the temples and have even been downplayed—an issue I look at in Chapter 7.[7] Although miracle stories and apparitions may be a stimulating factor in the origins of (some) pilgrimages, they are not necessarily essential to their continuing success over the longer term. The 'momentum of the apparition' (or of miracles) may carry a pilgrimage site forward for a while, but to maintain or revive that momentum after the initial flurry, other more practical and worldly factors need to come into play.

Knock was, in effect, revived and acquired a status beyond the local some decades after its apparition-centred momentum had been lost. This was due the efforts of the Archbishop of Tuam, whose 1929 visit to Knock helped revive interest in the shrine. Thereafter, a number of prominent Irish Catholics and well-placed local activists, including the priest of Knock, gave support to the shrine, forming the Knock Shrine Society in 1935 and publicising the shrine throughout Ireland via various promotional events over the ensuing decades. Knock was thus made popular on a wider level not through the grassroots actions of ordinary pilgrims but from the interests of elite groups and senior ecclesiastical figures within Irish society in a rather top-down process. Their actions and publicity made the site well known throughout Ireland by the 1970s, when a national campaign in which posters promoting Knock were sent to schools through Ireland, further enhanced its public profile and standing, as did a campaign organised by those involved with the shrine to get Knock designated as Ireland's national shrine. This status was in effect affirmed in 1979 when Pope John Paul II (a ready and frequent visitor to and promoter of Marian shrines) visited Knock and said Mass there.

The extensive proselytising activities of a local entrepreneurial priest, Monseigneur James Horan, further enhanced Knock's profile. Horan, who became Knock's parish priest in 1967, raised funds to build a large church at the site that was capable of holding thousands of pilgrims at once for services. Crucially, too, Horan conducted a successful campaign to have an airport built—with funds granted by the Irish government—at Knock. It opened in 1986, thereby greatly expanding Knock's potential clientele and making it accessible as a daytrip destination from major cities in the

United Kingdom and beyond. Although claims of miracle might have initially brought local and regional attention to Knock in the nineteenth century, it was the concerted campaigns by prominent figures associated with the Catholic Church in the mid- to late twentieth century, along with infrastructure support including an airport that made the place readily accessible to people from beyond Ireland, that really put Knock on the national and international Catholic pilgrimage map.[8] Although these promotional activities were clearly based in the activists' own faith (all were members of the Catholic Church and had local connections), one can hardly claim that Knock's subsequent popularity can be attributed solely or directly to some spiritually magnetic qualities invested in the place by its claimed miracles and apparitions. The pragmatics of pilgrimage promotion and the mobilisation of support structures and infrastructure facilities at a national level that expanded knowledge about Knock and opened access to a wider clientele were as (if not more) significant in this regard, as they tend to be if pilgrimage sites are to maintain their momentum and grow over the longer term.

MAGNETISM AND (THE DIFFICULTY OF) ACCESS

In positing difficulty of access as a causal factor in the creation of spiritual magnetism, Preston is following a common pattern in studies of pilgrimage of associating pilgrimage with notions of distance, remoteness and hardship and as something exceptional and set apart from ordinary life. Such views are epitomised by Alan Morinis's (1992: 2) claim that pilgrimages are 'by definition, exceptional practices, irregular journeys outside habitual social realms'. However, closer examination suggests that ease of access, convenient modes of transport and proximity to population clusters are far more likely and important factors for creating viable pilgrimage sites and making them attractive than are remoteness and difficulty of access. Mary and Sidney Nolan's (1989) examination of Christian pilgrimage sites in Western Europe, for instance, shows that pilgrimage sites correlate to a great degree to population densities, transport routes and ease of access. Shrines and pilgrimage sites in the mountainous areas of Austria, for example, are located around the main transportation routes through the valleys. By contrast, areas that are virtually uninhabited are devoid of pilgrimage sites (Nolan and Nolan 1989: 336). Similarly, Juan Campo (1998: 42) points out that successful pilgrimage sites in North America are more likely to be highly accessible rather than remote; the presence of highways rather than their absence is significant.

An interesting example here is the Hindu cave site of Amarnath, located high in the Kashmir Himalayas, to which Hindu pilgrims flock each August, and which Preston (1992: 35–36) cites as an example of a site whose magnetism occurs due to its remoteness and difficulty of access. The cave is associated in Hindu mythology with the deity Shiva and it houses an ice stalagmite shaped like, and worshipped as, a Shiva lingam, which waxes through the summer months. The period when it reaches its apex is the peak pilgrimage season. Amarnath is certainly remote. There are no settlements around the cave, which is situated at an altitude of more than 3,800 metres and is snowbound for much of the year. It is two or more days' walk from the nearest town of Pahalgam,[9] there are no roads up to the cave, and although horses and porters can be hired (if one is wealthy enough), for most pilgrims walking is the only option.

Yet one would be hard pressed to show that its remoteness is the key factor—the source, as it were, of its magnetism—in drawing pilgrims there. Until comparatively recently, the pilgrimage was very much a minority event, and it was really only made possible for anyone other than those who were extremely austere, hardy and attuned to mountain hiking, because of a transient support structure of temporary tea shops and tents offering overnight shelter and food that sprang up during the pilgrimage period to enable pilgrims to endure the mountain conditions. In Chapter 4, I outline my experience of going to Amarnath in 1971 and discuss how this rudimentary support structure made the pilgrimage possible. Even so, the pilgrimage was hardly a major one in numerical terms. In the late 1980s, for example, only around 12,000 pilgrims a year visited Amarnath—hardly significant numbers in such a populous country as India where some pilgrimage sites can count their pilgrim numbers in the millions. Amarnath's remoteness and location in the high mountains may have given it a striking natural setting, but this did not translate into a magnetism that actually drew in pilgrims so much as a barrier that limited their flow.

In the past two or so decades, however, Amarnath's pilgrim numbers have escalated, rising from around 12,000 in 1989 to more than 400,000 in 2007 (Nanda 2011: 119). Political factors have played a part in this growth, for Amarnath is in the contested area of Kashmir, which has been the focus of an ongoing dispute between India and Pakistan. Hindu nationalist organisations have encouraged Hindus to participate in the Amarnath pilgrimage as a statement of Hindu pride and in order to reinforce Indian claims to the region and to demonstrate their opposition to Pakistan's counterclaims. Yet although political and nationalistic issues have been significant in Amarnath's expansion, what has been absolutely crucial to it have been the increased support structures that have been put in place to ensure that pilgrims can get there and back readily and safely. The Indian Army has been deployed in the pilgrimage season to provide logistical support, shelter and protection for pilgrims, whereas the regional Jammu and Kashmir government, keen to increase tourist revenues for the state, has established a shrine board to regulate the shrine and to manage the pilgrimage support infrastructure of accommodations and food provision. It now also provides free tent accommodation for pilgrims.[10] It has also recently opened a new and quicker route to the cave by building new roads to enable pilgrims to get to the town of Baital, just fourteen kilometres from the cave. As the state-supported Sri

Amarnath Shrine Board now informs potential pilgrims, one can now get to the cave and then back to one's hotel in Baital in one day, thereby obviating the need to stay even one night in a tent.[11] When I visited in 1971, the support industry was rudimentary and pilgrim numbers low. Now it has become highly developed, with organised package tours that are widely advertised in the media and on the Internet, that promise to make the trip easier and quicker for would-be pilgrims and that even describe the pilgrimage tours on offer as 'holidays'. Such tours offer train and/or road transport from cities in India to the nearest accessible town and then guided tours with porters, cooks and other assistance to the cave and back, with all meals provided, including dinner in the tents where pilgrims will be housed overnight.[12] Nowadays, one can even make use of helicopter services that make access quicker and easier still for the wealthy who are unwilling to go far on foot.[13]

Amarnath is not the only pilgrimage site in the Jammu and Kashmir region that has seen its popularity swell as it has become less remote. The shrine of Shri Mata Vaishno Devi, some 50 kilometres from Jammu at a height of 1,600 metres, is one of the Seven Sisters, which are shrines in the Siwālik region of Jammu dedicated to the deity Devi. At the time of Indian independence in 1947, it received around 30,000 pilgrims per year and was hardly a major pilgrimage centre. Even in the 1970s, it received roughly the same numbers of pilgrims as its six other Sisters. Yet in recent decades, it has emerged as the preeminent site in the region, with pilgrim numbers getting into the millions by the 1990s until by 2007 nearly eight million visitors per year were visiting the shrine (Foster and Stoddard 2010: 109–110). Crucial to this growth, according to Foster and Stoddard, was the Shri Mata Vaishno Devi Shrine Act of 1986, passed by the regional government because of its concerns about shrine mismanagement. The act gave control of the shrine to an administrative board charged with implementing reforms, improving access and providing better facilities for pilgrims. State support in the form of grants, better roads, improved accommodations and food provision, as well as banks, post offices and other services, coupled with widespread publicity via pamphlets, advertisements in the mass media and, now, on the internet, has helped expand awareness of the shrine throughout India, thereby transforming its clientele from a regional to a national one (Foster and Stoddard 2010: 116–117, Nanda 2011: 120). Such improved access has not just enabled pilgrims to get to and from the shrine more quickly but has also allowed the shrine and Jammu and Kashmir's tourist offices to publicise the shrine more widely and to promise would-be pilgrims of all ages that they can do the pilgrimage easily. Nowadays, as at Amarnath, helicopter services are available for better-off pilgrims. The shrine's website provides a link to such helicopter services while promising potential customers that not only will this make their journeys more comfortable but that they will be get 'priority darshan' at the shrine.[14] As Vaishno Devi has become increasingly accessible and less remote, it has become more widely marketed by the government. As a result, its clientele has grown, and it is no longer just one of the 'Seven Sisters'; it has surpassed the other six to become the preeminent shrine of the region (Foster and Stoddard 2010: 123).

There are plentiful other examples of how ease rather than remoteness and difficulty of access increases pilgrim numbers and the attractiveness (i.e., the magnetism) of a site. Both Ruth Harris (1999) and Suzanne Kaufman (2004) have shown that a key factor in Lourdes's rise to national prominence and acquisition of a vast pilgrim clientele, was the development of a railway system that linked it to France's major population centres. The exponential growth of pilgrims going on the Muslim hajj in the last three decades is intimately linked to the rise of air traffic and the provision of modern facilities to ease the pilgrim's discomfort and reduce the ardours of the pilgrimage (Bianchi 2004: 10, 49–50). James Lochtefeld (2010: 53–55) has described how the rise of a railway system in India brought previously remote pilgrimage sites within the remit of large numbers of Hindu pilgrims from the late nineteenth century onwards, increasing pilgrim numbers significantly and helping turn the once remote and marginal regional site of Hardwar into a national pilgrimage centre. Indeed, little more than a decade after the railway to Hardwar opened, it had become so intrinsic to the pilgrimage that when the government closed the line temporarily (to halt the spread of a cholera outbreak), pilgrim numbers virtually dried up (Lochtefeld 2010: 85). Making Hardwar more difficult to access did not increase its spiritual magnetism but the reverse. The example of Mansa Devi, a local temple near Hardwar, that has spectacularly increased its pilgrim numbers by such successful marketing ploys as building a cable car up to the temple in 1984, thereby enabling pilgrims to get there 'without the need for any exertion' (Lochetefeld 2010: 178–179) also indicates how magnetism appears to be increased by easy access.

I discuss these issues and the ways in which contributing agencies such as railway firms and other commercial interests have played a role in pilgrimage development in the enhancement of popularity of (some) pilgrimage centres further in Chapter 4. Here, the point to note is that for pilgrims who flock in greater numbers to places that are readily accessed, magnetism is not something determined by difficulty or remoteness so much as by the seeming intrusions of modernity and commercialism that facilitate access and by the crowds this produces. As Foster and Stoddard (2010: 122) indicate in their study of Shri Mata Vaishno Devi Shrine, the more pilgrims come to it, the more others are encouraged to come because of the crowds. Crowds, the bustle and the hubbub of the marketplace can prove highly attractive (a point to be discussed further in the following chapters).

By contrast, difficulty of access and the lack of crowds, are more likely to be negative influences that contribute to the decline of pilgrimage. In the previous chapter, I mentioned how the pilgrimage on the Japanese island of Shōdoshima was facing difficulties. During my recent visit there in 2010, the head of the island's pilgrimage temple association informed me that one of Shōdoshima's problems was its relative inaccessibility, compared to other pilgrimages in Japan. Shikoku was easily reached by air, train (one can reach the main population centres of the island such as Takamatsu, from Tokyo—more than 800 kilometres away—in four and a half hours), and road, with three new bridges spanning the Inland Sea and connecting it to Japan's main and most heavily populated island of Honshū. Its two partners in the airport exhibition are better connected, with both Sasaguri (whose hinterland includes the major city of Fukuoka and several other large towns in the industrial belt of northern Kyushu) and Chita Hantō (close to the major city of Nagoya), readily accessible by trains from major conurbations in less an hour. By contrast, the only way to get to Shōdoshima is by ferry, which is costly if bringing a car or microbus (the latter being the most common vehicle for pilgrims because the island's roads are too narrow for the larger buses and coaches that dominate the Shikoku pilgrim market). For those reliant on public transport, it is also time-consuming because the ferry ports themselves require complex journeys, often combining local train and bus services. Shikoku is a much longer pilgrimage and one reason for Shōdoshima flourishing in earlier times was that, as a smaller scale version of the Shikoku pilgrimage, it could be done in much less time than Shikoku (Oda 1996). However, as modern transport has made Shikoku more accessible than Shōdoshima, the time difference has been drastically reduced.[15] Everyone I talked to on the island (from priests to tourist office officials, to inn owners) in my most recent visit in 2010 cited Shōdoshima's relative difficulty of access as a factor in its decline. Decline can also be contagious. Priests whom I talked to at three temples on Shōdoshima each individually expressed the view that declining numbers were making the temples quieter, less atmospheric and less attractive to pilgrims. They all used the same term *sabishii* ('desolate, lonely, cheerless') to describe the feeling at the sites. Pilgrims, they said, were less likely to come now, because of the *lack* of pilgrims. A group of pilgrims I met in a local pilgrimage lodge confirmed the point; their village pilgrimage society had been visiting the island for decades, but now they were finding it harder to gather groups together. As numbers went down and the excitement and bustle of pilgrimage temples became replaced by a lonesome (*sabishii*) tranquillity, the pilgrimage was losing its attraction. Shikoku, not much farther away from their home area but now more easily accessed, was becoming more appealing.[16]

THE ORDINARINESS OF PILGRIMAGE IN THE MODERN WORLD

Rather than being exceptional, irregular and detached from habitual social realms, one could argue that pilgrimage sites and places are, especially in modern contexts, in many respects embedded in the realms of the ordinary. Philip Taylor (2004), for instance, is critical of the notion that pilgrimage is somehow 'out of the ordinary' and argues that such perspectives are diminishing as travel becomes more and more a normal part of the modern world. As he shows, pilgrim journeys to pray at the shrine of the Lady of the Realm have become normative and quotidian in Vietnam because of the processes of modernity, including economic developments, concepts of globalisation and Vietnamese responses to it and the development of modern, speedy transport systems, that have increasingly encouraged such travel and made it part of the modern Vietnamese experience (Taylor 2004: 135–138). Simon Coleman and John Eade (2004: 3–7) also follow suit in seeing pilgrimage as very much a feature and facet of the modern world, They argue that movement is a key criterion of pilgrimage and, as such, consider that, in the modern age in which travel, mobility and movement are commonplace, pilgrimage should therefore be viewed as a rather normal facet of the modern world rather than anything exceptional and set apart from regular life.

The 'everyday' nature of pilgrimage, and the problem of portraying it as concerned with the irregular and with ruptures from ordinary life, has also been shown by studies indicating that, for many pilgrims, the practice is deeply embedded in their quotidian lives. Anne Gold's (1998) seminal study of pilgrims in a Rajasthani village in north India—seminal because it is based in research grounded in the village where the pilgrims live and thus examines pilgrimage practices from the perspective of how they fit into the everyday lives of practitioners—illustrates how villagers carry out a variety of pilgrimages, from short trips to local shrines to pan-Indian bus pilgrimages associated with caring for the spirits and dealing with the ashes of their deceased. As Gold shows, although such travels (particularly the long distance bus journey pilgrimages) mean breaks in village routines, they and the processes of preparation required before setting out, along with the customs and obligations associated with these pilgrimages, are deeply rooted in the everyday lives of the villagers and their social structures, rather than being exceptional disruptions from them. Like pilgrims in numerous contexts, Gold's pilgrims take with them the values and views of their village (including food preferences) as they travel. One can see clear evidence of this preference for home and familiarity especially in food terms at major Indian pilgrimage sites such as Varanasi, where different ghats along the riverfront are associated with different regions of the country and have food stalls and the like catering to the tastes of these different regions.[17] In such respects, pilgrimage can be an extension of everyday life, as Taylor (2004: 164) observes at the end of a bus pilgrimage with a party of Vietnamese pilgrims:

> our provisional mobile community had not traveled so very far away from our everyday lives, our pilgrimage representing a microcosm of urban society, an expression of its tastes, preoccupations, and values and an episode in it.

Thus, pilgrimage serves as a way of emphasising the values of home and should be viewed less as an experience of transcendence than as a process in which the familiar is discovered, the routine reinvested, and the everyday sacralized in the guise of the extraordinary. (Taylor 2004: 162)

Similarly, many Japanese pilgrims I have interviewed have stressed how going on pilgrimages is an extension and reflection of their everyday lives as well as a reaffirmation of the values they hold close and wish to see expressed in Japanese society. The ways in which pilgrimage becomes part of one's normal life rather than somehow an exception to it is particularly evident among those who repeat pilgrimages frequently—something that is not at all uncommon. Pilgrims in Shikoku, for instance, may repeat the pilgrimage so often that it becomes an integral part of their lives rather than something that stands in stark juxtaposition to it (Reader 2005: 249–266). Moreover, the people of Shikoku themselves have been amongst the most numerous pilgrims historically and, as such, have been taking part in a pilgrimage that is part of their own regional and island culture and part of their local identities (Kaneko 1991). They may find that doing the pilgrimage enables them to be more attuned to and able to discover more about their cultural milieu while intensifying their understandings of their everyday environment and infusing it with a sense of wonder—a point made to me by a Shikoku resident who did the pilgrimage as a means of getting fit after an illness and who told me that through it, he came to realize what an extraordinary and valuable phenomenon the pilgrimage was to his island and its culture. This, in turn, led him to spend many years working voluntarily to ensure pilgrimage paths were properly marked and kept clear of undergrowth and to provide help and information for pilgrims on foot in the island. Although the pilgrimage was thus extraordinary, it was simultaneously part of his everyday environment and lifestyle.[18]

THE ORDINARINESS OF THE SACRED

The idea that the sacred is exceptional is also somewhat problematic. In the Japanese context, for example, the two historically dominant religious traditions of Shinto and Buddhism both indicate that anywhere and everywhere is potentially or implicitly the abode of supernatural or spiritual entities and places where they may be manifest. In Shinto cosmology, the landscape of Japan is synonymous with the domain of the *kami* (the deities of Shinto) who, in Shinto myths, give life to the land and natural environment and who thus permeate the landscape. Anywhere and everywhere are potentially the abode or place of *kami*, whereas every shrine has an origin story that shows how and why it is a place where the sacred, evidenced by the manifestations of *kami*, is present in this physical realm. Likewise, Buddhism perceives its sacred figures, the buddhas and bodhisattvas, as capable of manifesting anywhere, hence making their places of manifestation or apparition into realms of the holy. Temples are, in theory, places where such manifestations *have* happened; they are a recognition that the sacred is present in and part and parcel of the mundane world.

If any and everywhere is potentially and innately sacred, it follows that nowhere is inherently profane and that thus there is no clear or implicit distinction between the sacred and the profane (a category distinction that is highly problematic in Japanese terms[19]). In a sense, the sacred is an ordinary, mundane phenomenon. Not only are there myriad shrines and temples as testimony to this notion in Japan, but the country is also permeated by numerous pilgrimage routes that illustrate the potential ubiquity of the sacred. Kōbō Daishi is depicted in folk belief as forever wandering around Japan dispensing miracles, and stories about him are found throughout the country (Saitō 1988). Thus, although his spiritual presence is depicted as central to the Shikoku pilgrimage, it also features in numerous other smaller and regional pilgrimages throughout Japan that, such as Shikoku, claim him as their founder (Reader 1988). Similarly, Kannon, whose apparitions are central to the foundation stories of the Saikoku pilgrimage temples as well as to countless other similar routes in Japan, has a ubiquitous presence. Kannon's vow to manifest and intercede to save all in distress (see Chapter 1, note 1) means that she may appear anywhere. Drawing on this notion, countless temples throughout the country have Kannon-related legends that underpin their claims to be places where Kannon has manifest or can be encountered and that affirm their nature as Kannon-centred pilgrimage sites.

What is striking about pilgrimages in Japan is not so much that they are an extraordinary or exceptional phenomenon but that on some levels they are remarkably commonplace. Matsuzaki (1985: 122) notes that there were more than forty replicated versions of the Shikoku pilgrimage, each with eighty-eight sites and requiring more than a day to complete, in the Kantō area around Tokyo alone in the early twentieth century. A recent compendium of pilgrimage sites and routes in Japan has identified several hundred different multiple site pilgrimages in that country (Ozono 2000)[20]; strikingly, it did not mention vast numbers of shrines and temples that flourish or have flourished as single-site pilgrimage centres, such as Zenkōji, the Nagano temple whose famous hidden icon is the focus of a massive pilgrimage festival every seven years and that has given rise to numerous regional and localised replications of the temple as local pilgrimage sites (McCallum 1994); Konpira Shrine in Shikoku, whose pilgrimage tradition has been examined by Sarah Thal (2005); Ontake, Japan's second-highest mountain and a centre for mountain pilgrimages (Aoki 1984); or Ishizuchi-san, the highest mountain in Shikoku that is the centre of a mountain ascetic pilgrimage cult and has numerous replications throughout the Shikoku region (Nishigai 1984).

Because anywhere and everywhere is potentially a place where Kannon, Kōbō Daishi or some other figure in the Buddhist (or Shinto) pantheon is manifest, there is no barrier against any place, shrine or temple becoming incorporated into a pilgrimage route or proclaiming itself as a special place where one could encounter an entity from the spiritual realms. This contributes to a vibrantly inventive pilgrimage culture in which new pilgrimages have been created with some regularity over the ages. In the period between 1804 and 1810 alone, for example, some twenty-five new pilgrimage routes based on the eighty-eight-stage Shikoku model appeared in Japan, whereas the period between 1818 and 1830 saw the appearance of a further twenty-one pilgrimages of this type (Yoritomi and Shiragi 2001: 164). While the social and economic conditions of the time facilitated the spread and development of such pilgrimages, there was a clearly a sense in which the spreading and production of pilgrimages was contagious; as I have discussed in an earlier study of local pilgrimages in Japan, once one island in the Inland Sea or one rural area in Japan developed its Shikoku-style eighty-eight-stage pilgrimage centred on Kōbō Daishi, this encouraged neighboring islands or regions to develop their own in turn (Reader 1988). Kannon-centred pilgrimages using the thirty-three-stage Saikoku model, similarly spread in a contagious manner (Shinjō 1982: 1103–1144, Hayami 1983: 317–329).

In Chapter 3, I give further examples of new pilgrimages that have appeared in Japan and of how the appearance of one pilgrimage can spur the emergence of others. The point is that Japan is a place where pilgrimages are constantly being produced—a process of production that owes much to the general perception that pilgrimage is a popular pastime deeply embedded in the country's history of travel (Shinjō 1960, 1971) and where, as Hoshino (1987: 3–4) has shown, the roots of travel are very much based in pilgrimage, as well as to the general religious milieu in which any and everywhere is potentially sacred. There are so many pilgrimage routes and circuits, indeed, that the same temple may be included in several circuits simultaneously, so that one could, in theory, participate in half a dozen or so pilgrimages while visiting the same temple.[21]

Similarly, the Hindu landscape of India is replete with pilgrimage places. In Hindu terms, anywhere and everywhere are potentially an abode of a deity and the locus of divine manifestations in the ubiquitous legends that are found throughout the country. Numerous geographical features, from mountain sites (often associated with deities such as Shiva) to river crossings (the term for crossing, *tirtha*, being a normative Hindu term relating to pilgrimage) are marked out as potential sites of pilgrimage, while a vast number of local, regional and national sites of pilgrimage permeates the country (Bhardwaj 1973, Eck 2012). Indeed, Anne Feldhaus (2004) portrays the entire region of Maharashtra as a network of 'connected places' and as a landscape permeated by pilgrimage routes and places.

Catholicism, with its emphasis on saints and intercessionary figures such as Mary who are ever watching over and accessible to the faithful, also potentially views anywhere as the location of the sacred and hence as a potential place of pilgrimage. Marian apparitions can occur any and everywhere, and numerous sites around the world, from Japan and India, to Europe and the Americas, testify to this potential ubiquity. Catholic pilgrimages, similar to

Japanese ones, can also be contagious; as Finucane's (1977) study of medieval English miracle stories and pilgrimage sites indicates, miracle tales spread rapidly, leading to the continuing emergence of new saints' cults and new shrines to be visited. As the major pilgrimage routes to Santiago de Compostela developed in medieval Europe, a host of local churches and shrines close to the routes pilgrims took sought to benefit from the flows of pilgrims heading towards Santiago and promoted themselves as local places of pilgrimage (Webb 2002: 7). In the medieval period, numerous new pilgrimage sites were created in Europe as relics (often used by religious authorities as the magnet to attract pilgrims) were brought back from the Christian Holy Land and dispersed (often by theft) from place to place, with each translation of a relic marking its new abode out as a place of pilgrimage (Geary 1990: 58–63). As Diane Webb (2002: 33) notes, the sack of Constantinople in 1204 produced a huge new supply of relics for Western Christendom, thus spurring the emergence of new sites of pilgrimage as these relics were distributed across Europe. The rapid growth of potentially sacred objects via the relic trade thus contributed to a contagious culture of pilgrimage development and claims.

Western Europe, just like Japan and India, has numerous pilgrimage sites, as is shown by Mary and Sidney Nolan's (1999) study of the huge numbers of pilgrimage places that permeate the region. Of course, the mere existence of numerous pilgrimage sites does not mean that all would flourish, and the Nolans' study illustrates clearly that, although pilgrimage sites appeared and developed in large numbers across Europe, many also declined and disappeared. A close examination of any country or region in Europe will show similar patterns; for instance, a survey in the 1990s identified 660 pilgrimage sites, 250 of which were still active, in the Netherlands—not an especially large country and one where Catholicism, the tradition most closely associated with pilgrimage in European contexts, is a minority tradition (Margry 2008: 16). The multiplicity of choices that potential pilgrims have in any given region was brought home to me while visiting Coutances Cathedral in Normandy, France, in 2004. A poster there drew attention to diocesan pilgrimages being organised by the cathedral's Service Diocésan des Pèlerinages, and it listed twelve pilgrimages that it was organising for people in the diocese between March and November 2004; four were overseas, to Poland, to Italian shrines including Assisi, and to Christian shrines in Egypt and Morocco, but the other eight were in France, including some within the local Normandy region.

In numerous other geographical contexts, one can find similar examples of a spreading and pervasive map of pilgrimage locales in which the sacred is manifest in so many places that it is, in effect, a common, readily transferable and replicable commodity. This is especially so in areas which, like Japan, have highly developed traditions of replicated pilgrimages. I have already touched on this by mentioning how pilgrimages based on the Saikoku or Shikoku formats (i.e., either with thirty-three or eighty-eight stages, and centred on Kannon or Kōbō Daishi) have developed in Japan. The numerous pilgrimages that developed in the early nineteenth century (see the earlier

Of Swans, Lakes and Constructions of the Sacred 51

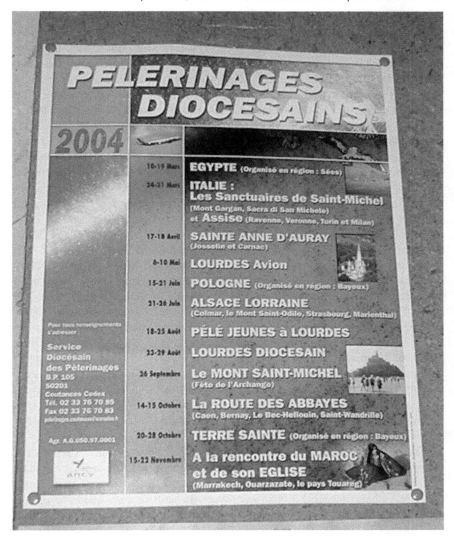

Figure 2.1 Poster at Coutances Cathedral, France listing the pilgrimages offered by the cathedral's office for 2004.

discussion) were regional or local replicas of the Shikoku model and were examples of a recurrent Japanese model in which this pilgrimage model, like that of Saikoku, has been regularly reproduced in small-scale and localised formats throughout the country (Reader 1988, Oda 1996, Shinno 1996).

Replication is also rife in India. Countless Maharasthran sites claim that they are replicas of significant north Indian holy places (Feldhaus 2003: 158–159) whereas both Diane Eck (1983: 40) and Christopher Fuller (1992:

208) discuss how shrines symbolising Kashi (the ancient city of Varanasi, often considered the most important of all Hindu places) are replicated throughout India. Varanasi/Kashi is 'everywhere', as Fuller says, meaning that it can be visited anywhere where there is a replica of it, and these can be found throughout the country. In one of southern India's most prominent temples, the Menakshi temple in Madurai, for instance, there are three replicas of the Vishwanatha temple, which is widely viewed as the most important of all Varanasi's temples (Fuller 1992: 208). Toni Huber (1999: 32–33) shows, too, that the prominent Tibetan pilgrimage centre of Pure Crystal Mountain is endlessly replicated throughout the areas where Tibetans live, with the physical terrain of Pure Crystal Mountain serving as the model template for such replicated constructions.

Replication is commonplace, too, in Christianity, whether in the initial development of the prominent English shrine at Walsingham, built in 1061 by a noblewoman, Lady Richeldis, after she had a vision in which Mary asked her to build a copy of Jesus's house in Nazareth (Coleman 2004: 47), the church complex of Lalibela in Ethiopia, built in the thirteenth century by King Lalibela after receiving visions from angels who instructed him to build replicas of Biblical sites such as the House of Golgotha and the Holy Sepulchre (Ousterhout 1990: 118–119) or in the copies or replications of Lourdes that can be found worldwide. I mentioned the Lourdes replica grotto in the Bronx in New York in Chapter 1; it is just one of a multiplicity of such copies, from Carfin in Scotland, to Cleator Moor in Cumbria in northwestern England, whose Lourdes grotto is the diocesan pilgrimage centre for the Catholic cathedral in Lancaster, where I live, to Lourdes grottoes in Japan (including one I visited at the Catholic Cathedral in Tokyo), to U.S. Catholic university campuses such as Notre Dame, which built its Lourdes grotto in 1896 (McDannell 1995: 155).

The replicative and reproductive nature of pilgrimage sites is also evident in the labyrinths that developed in medieval Europe as a means of replicating the concept of pilgrimage to Jerusalem and the Christian Holy Land in an era when overland pilgrimages were difficult or impossible to undertake. Known in medieval times as 'Jerusalems' because they were substitute versions for the real thing, labyrinths served as a form of metaphorical surrogate, a symbolic journey to enable pilgrims to perform the pilgrimage in spirit, and with convenience (Boss 2007: 135). Several prominent cathedrals were designated by the Catholic Church to perform this function, including Chartres Cathedral, whose labyrinth on the cathedral floor has become something of a focal point for recent moves to revive and promote labyrinths as a form of miniature yet spiritually symbolic metaphysical journey (Artress 1995, Ketley-Laporte 1997, Beaman 2006). One notes again how, when places become difficult to get to, this does not so much spur people to try to visit them but to find alternative ways of making them easier to access, and for ecclesiastical authorities to create replicas that enable people to easily do what had become inaccessible or difficult.

Figure 2.2 Replica Lourdes grotto at Cleator Moor, Cumbria, England.

The topic of replications has been accorded less attention in the context of pilgrimage that it merits, and it certainly deserves more than can be afforded here. It has been encountered already, in the context of the exhibitions and replicas cited in the previous chapter as elements in campaigns to heighten public awareness of pilgrimages in Japan, and it will appear again in later chapters. Here I draw attention to the phenomenon in order to further demonstrate the everywhereness of pilgrimage and to emphasise further the problem of viewing pilgrimage and pilgrimage places as exceptional, remote or set apart from the ordinary world.

WHY GO THERE? COMPETITION AND CHOICE IN THE PILGRIMAGE MARKET

The hopes, intentions, presence and activities of pilgrims are clearly central and crucial elements in pilgrimage site development. Pilgrim motivations have been widely discussed in the literature, and attention has been drawn to the multiplicity of reasons that might lead them to make their journeys, from a wish to get away from everyday routines and see new places, to hopes of encountering something special and beyond ordinary human realms; to worries about illness, hopes of healing and aspirations to acquire worldly benefits; to wishes to embark on individual spiritual journeys; and to aims of acquiring and bringing back items and souvenirs associated with a special place, deity or shrine. Yet critical to all of these desires and motivations has been the simple fact that there have been appropriate places for them to go to and that provide them with the stimulus to set out on a journey. Pilgrim motivations are a crucial factor in understanding pilgrimage, and it is the presence of pilgrims that turns somewhere from being simply a site where some miracle has been rumoured, some figure is said to have appeared, or some interest group has tried to invent a pilgrimage, into being an active pilgrimage site. In that sense, the notion that pilgrims 'create' pilgrimages is feasible—but behind that notion lie important questions that are perhaps less widely asked in the literature than it ought to be. Why are people going to *that* place or doing that *particular* pilgrimage? What is it about *that* route or place that attracts them, and how and in what contexts has that place or pilgrimage acquired such alluring dimensions? Why does a pilgrimage route or site assume a special resonance in the minds of pilgrims at a particular time or era, perhaps drawing custom away from others, and why do certain pilgrimages appear to be especially popular at different eras?

As I have noted previously, pilgrims in just about any area or religious tradition have a multiplicity of possible pilgrimage sites that they could choose to visit. In Japan, for example, the range of pilgrimage choices is immense, and although some may be influenced by devotion to a particular figure of worship (e.g., Kannon) that makes it more likely that he or she will do a Kannon rather than, say, a Kōbō Daishi pilgrimage, there are still plentiful Kannon pilgrimage choices—Saikoku, Chichibu, Bandō and others—that could be made. Even when one considers what pilgrims want from their travels, there may be relatively little difference between what is offered at the sites available. The most commonly cited motives of Shikoku pilgrims, for example, include commemorating the spirits of their dead kin, gaining merit that would benefit them in the afterlife, seeking favours and worldly benefits, making themselves better, and/or engaging with their cultural roots as Japanese people (Osada, Sakata and Seki 2003: 329–332). Yet having such motivations does not automatically mean that pilgrims will be drawn to Shikoku, for other Japanese pilgrimages also offer scope for the same things; Satō's (2004) study, indeed, indicates that pilgrim motivations are remarkably similar whether in Saikoku, Chichibu or Shikoku. In the present day, people are more likely to visit Shikoku than Saikoku and these other sites—a choice aided, as I have already suggested, by the ways in which the skilful marketing and publicity by the temples and related media agencies have made it especially attractive to contemporary Japanese people. Such images have made it more likely that, if a Japanese person decides to do a pilgrimage for the benefit of the spirit of a deceased family member, he or she would nowadays choose Shikoku rather than other, rival pilgrimages.

Bax's (1995) study of Medjugorje and Kaufman's (2004) of Lourdes also offer some insights into this issue. Bax, for example, shows that in the region of what was then Yugoslavia, Marian apparitions were not singular to Medjugorje; people in the nearby village of Bijakovići also saw such visions. Both villages sought to capitalise on the visions, and as a result, they became rivals competing for potential pilgrims. Those involved with each location kept an eye on the other, with every manoeuvre instituted by one village to attract pilgrims being replicated or countered by the other. Yet it was Medjugorje, due to a number of intersecting factors that included support from local religious authorities who threw their weight behind the Marian apparitions there while downplaying the claims of Bijakovići, and the activities of local and national Yugoslavian tourist agencies that capitalised on the Medjugorje visions to gain control of the transportation of pilgrims to the region, that won out and became dominant in the regional pilgrimage map (Bax 1995: 76–78). It was not that Medjugorje was implicitly more sacred or unique as the only site in that area and period with Marian apparitions. Its rise to prominence required more than the simple reporting of its apparitions and related claims of miracle. It also required a variety of seemingly worldly factors connected to politics as well as religion, along with overcoming the claims of a rival competitor nearby in ways that enabled Medjugorje to emerge as 'the' pilgrimage site of the region.

Kaufman (2004), too, shows that Lourdes was not the only place in France, nor indeed, in that region of France, where visions of Mary were seen by young women in the mid-nineteenth century. Yet, as she indicates, a variety of factors helped make it the most appropriate place of choice for the Catholic Church as it sought to revitalise Catholicism and develop new ways of promoting faith in an age of increased secularism being propelled by the modern French nation-state. Church officials considered that Bernadette was the most credible or publicly demonstrable young girl of those who claimed such visions. Moreover, the message offered at Lourdes served to make it a more amenable one for garnering widespread popular devotion than some other potential rivals for national attention and support from the church. For example, in 1847, young children in the Alpine hamlet of La Salette had a vision of Mary, who spoke in terrifying terms of humanity's sinfulness and who predicted disaster and suffering unless people repented—a contrast to the more soothing messages of the Lourdes apparition, which offered hope and comfort for the sick and suffering (Kaufman 2004: 86). Ruth Harris (1999) also indicates that shortly after Bernadette's visions, a flurry of similar claims by young people and children occurred in other parts of the region, but ecclesiastical officials and an Episcopal Commission of Inquiry set up to investigate these visions skilfully marginalised them. Such ecclesiastical control and care ensured that Lourdes and Bernadette presented an air of respectability, whereas other Marian visions at places such as Morzine in the Alps (which had many similarities to Lourdes geographically and economically) descended quickly into a spate of hysteria and claims of demonic possession of a sort unwelcome to the church and to civic authorities. As a result, the

Morzine visions were marginalised, whereas those at Lourdes were treated with respect and support (R. Harris 1999: 107–109). As Kaufman (2004) further indicates, Lourdes's emergence was also aided by the political and commercial engagement of local civic officials and merchants seeking new ways of developing local economies amidst the changing patterns of an emergent modern economy, and by the developing transport network, and especially a railway line being constructed by the recently formed French Railways, that conveniently went through Lourdes. French Railways—on the lookout for way to stimulate use of this new mode of transport—was thus disposed to help promote Lourdes as a destination, to run pilgrimage tour trains there and to benefit from the creation of a mass pilgrimage market centred on the town and its apparitions. Lourdes, in short, emerged and flourished as a pilgrimage centre not because it was the one and only site in the era or region where Marian apparitions and miraculous events had occurred, but because it was the site that most aptly suited the needs of relevant interest groups at the time.

Such examples not only reaffirm the point I made earlier about needing to think beyond simplistic explanations (e.g., miracles, magnetism and the sacred) of why places emerge and gain reputations a pilgrimage sites; they also draw attention to the competitive dimensions of the pilgrimage market. Although anywhere and everywhere may potentially be a place for pilgrimage, one has also to recognise that, as pilgrimage temple priests in Japan have remarked to me on numerous occasions, the potential number of pilgrims in the market is always going to be limited. Even in a modern monetary economy with a mass travel industry and a growing world population with increasing access to travel and the leisure time useful for going on pilgrimages, there will only be so many people who are likely to become pilgrims, especially now that there are alternative modes of travel such as leisure tourism that were not available in earlier, especially feudal, ages, when for most people the only ways they could get away from their daily routines and obligations was via pilgrimage. This naturally is going to mean that sites are in competition with each other for a share of a relatively finite market, with obvious results.

Competition, along with proliferation, one should note, does not necessarily mean that there will be pilgrimage growth across the board; it is just as likely that there will be a redistribution of pilgrim numbers and/or the decline of some pilgrimages in the face of the success of others. The success of Medjugorje and Lourdes did not mean that Bijakovići, Morzine and others would also become major pilgrimage centres but the reverse. As I have noted earlier, one should contextualise Shikoku's recent successful growth by remembering that Saikoku and other pilgrimages have been less successful in the same timeframe. Indeed, the development of new pilgrimages may make others less popular, and the more pilgrimages there are competing in the market, the more potential there is for one to emerge as a dominant force and for others to lose out. Nakamura's (1980) study of pilgrimage on Awaji

Island in Japan's Inland Sea illustrates this point aptly. There are five pilgrimage routes on the island, and Nakamura shows that each has been popular at different periods, with successively emerging routes displacing an earlier pilgrimage from its position as the most widely performed on the island. In 1980, for example, two quite new routes—a *shichifukujinmeguri* or pilgrimage to the Seven Gods of Good Fortune, a popular and eclectic group of Shinto, Buddhist and Taoist deities that have been the focus of pilgrimages since the Tokugawa period (Reader and Tanabe 1998: 156–173) formed in 1973 and a *Jūsan butsu mairi* or pilgrimage to the thirteen Buddhist figures associated in Japanese lore with the passage of the spirit from this realm to the next at death—have become the island's main pilgrimages. As they have done so, the other routes on the island, notably its thirty-three-stage Kannon pilgrimage, have seen their pilgrim numbers dwindle and have almost disappeared (Nakamura 1980). Miyake Hitoshi (2002: 117) underlines this point by commenting on the shifting patterns of pilgrimage popularity in medieval Japan; the Kumano pilgrimage, the most prominent of all early Japanese pilgrimages associated with the imperial court in the Heian period, became marginalised as another major pilgrimage location with connections to the imperial lineage, the Ise shrines, became a dominant force in the competitive Japanese pilgrimage world.

The shifting patterns of pilgrimage markets have been remarked on also by Jonathan Sumption (1975: 150) when he talks of how Canterbury, after receiving a massive boost after the martyrdom of Saint Thomas à Becket, later went out of fashion and by Finucane (1977: 193–196) who outlines how pilgrim loyalties changed, causing some shrines and saints in medieval England to lose support as other, newer, pilgrimage cults rose to displace them. In particular, there was a rise in Marian devotionalism from the fifteenth century that drew pilgrims to shrines such as Walsingham and away from places such as Canterbury, whose income from pilgrims in 1535 was a mere 3 or 4 per cent of what it had been in 1220, that were centred on saints' relics and tombs (Finucane 1977: 193). Duffy (1992: 195) also emphasises how medieval Christian shrines in England engaged in competition to try to get people to shift their allegiances and transfer their pilgrimage custom.

Pilgrimages exist in a network of interrelationships, in which competition and the potential of rival sites to draw away custom are important themes, a point widely recognised by just about every priest officiating at pilgrimage sites in Japan whom I have interviewed. Repeatedly they have commented on the competitive nature of the pilgrimage market and spoken of the need to ensure that *their* pilgrimage manages to function and succeed in that context, even if it means competing with others and taking their custom away. In December 1990, I was a guest at an end-of-year dinner in Fukuoka, the largest city in Japan's third-largest island, Kyushu, attended by the head priests of eight regional pilgrimage routes in the northern half of the island, along with the head of a major regional bus company that was actively involved in promoting the pilgrimages concerned. The atmosphere—suitably enhanced by saké and beer—was convivial, and much discussion centred on how each pilgrimage was doing while several of the priests sought tips from their fellows on how to boost pilgrim numbers. At one point, I remarked that everyone seemed very cooperative. Everyone nodded, and then one priest leant forward and said that although they did indeed cooperate where appropriate, in reality they were also rivals and in competition with each other. If someone visited the pilgrimage route that the priest sitting to my right oversaw, for example, it was a pilgrim who potentially might not visit the route *his* temple was on; although he was happy that the other route got custom he was always going to be concerned that it did not get all the pilgrims available. His comments caused every head to nod in agreement. Aware that although they might well cooperate (at the time all were working with a publishing agency to produce a now-defunct monthly magazine intended to spread information about their various routes, and all worked with the bus company mentioned here), the priests also were keen to ensure that potential pilgrims visited their (not his) route or site first, and they were forever on the lookout for tips and means whereby they could gain an advantage to this end.

Similarly, when I met the head priest of one prominent pilgrimage temple in Japan early one morning in December 1988, he told me that he had returned late the previous evening from another pilgrimage site several hundred kilometres away. I asked if he had been visiting as a pilgrim and to pay homage to that pilgrimage's figure of worship and he said no; he had been there to check out what that pilgrimage was doing and what innovations and new forms of publicity material they might be using. Later, I mentioned this conversation to a priest I knew well on the pilgrimage route that had been 'spied' on. He simply laughed and said he did the same thing with other routes and had, indeed, visited the aforementioned priest's temple to pick up marketing hints not so long back. In the intervening years, I have heard similar stories from other priests and have interviewed the same priests mentioned here on several occasions and learned of their latest exploits in checking up on other sites. I have even been plied for inside information and hints on what might be working in the pilgrimage market at present by priests who know that I often visit other pilgrimage sites in Japan and elsewhere. In other words, in Japan, those overseeing pilgrimages are aware that they exist in a competitive market in which their particular sacred place does not stand alone, but is part of a wider field of possible pilgrimage destinations, and that they need to remain vigilant and alert to ensure that they do not let other sites steal a march on them in any way.

SWANS, LAKES AND PILGRIMAGES

In understanding why certain places acquire recognition as pilgrimage sites, why and how they attract pilgrims, and why pilgrims choose certain places out of a plethora of potential choices, we need to move beyond limited concepts and notions associated with the sacred and spiritual magnetism or with simple notions of miracles producing mass enthusiasm that spontaneously create pilgrimages. Many places famed as pilgrimage centres clearly appear, to visitors and religious devotees, to be endowed with an aura that makes them feel in the realms of something holy. Yet such auras and sanctity are not innate or necessarily bestowed by miraculous events; they are constructed by a complex interweaving of factors, of which remoteness, miracle and such phenomena may not be as important as the availability of access, competition and the choices made by authorities who determine which claimant to sanctity should be supported and which not, as well as by circumstance and skilful promotion. Even so, this may not guarantee a constant clientele, for sites will always face competition, whether from other sites that can reinvigorate themselves in ways that capture the market or from new ones that arise to draw custom away from existing routes. The people associated with the upkeep of pilgrimage places thus face a continuing need to be vigilant about such challenges and to be on the lookout for ways to continue ensuring that they are visited. Moreover, the popularity of particular pilgrimages can fluctuate over the ages, thus creating the necessity for new attempts at promotion and, perhaps, at reshaping particular pilgrimages in accord with changing circumstances. The point made in Chapter 1, that certain shrines and sites have become so powerful that one might speak of the 'Wal-Mart' effect of Guadalupe on pilgrimage in Mexico or of 'Shikoku-isation' in Japan, is relevant here; competition is a reality of the pilgrimage market, with shrines aware that they need to remain inventive if they are to succeed or survive. The example of Shri Mata Vaishno Devi, which has in a relatively short space of time emerged as the dominant shrine of its region and outstripped its 'sisters', similarly exemplifies this process.

Here I draw attention to the title of this chapter, which alludes to Rick Fields's (1992 [1981]) account of Buddhism's development in the United States titled *How the Swans Came to the Lake*. Fields takes his title from the quotation cited at the start of this chapter, made by the Sixteenth Karmapa (the senior figure in the Tibetan Buddhist Kargyupa lineage) who, when asked why he visited America in 1976, said 'If there is a lake, the swans would go there.' For the Karmapa, this metaphorical lake referred to the interest of many Americans in Tibetan Buddhist thought and practice, yet of course it also indicated a physical reality, the land of America, in which the 'swans' were the lamas who flew to the United States to spread their teaching. One can draw an analogy here with pilgrimage and pilgrims; as I commented previously, a crucial reason why pilgrims go to pilgrimage sites is because they are there and hence offer the (potential) pilgrim the opportunity of somewhere conducive to go. Although pilgrims have flocked to pilgrimage sites for numerous reasons, critical to all of these desires and motivations has been the fact that (to use the Tibetan analogy) there has been a lake to go to, something to draw them and something that provided the stimulus to set out on a journey perhaps—as with Tibetan lamas heading for the United States and pilgrims heading for distant sites—of a great distance, or perhaps somewhere more local. In order to further discussion of this process and of how the lakes are constructed, endure and are made attractive to their potential 'swans', I now turn, in the next chapter, to a crucial element in such proceedings, namely, the religious authorities who oversee pilgrimage sites and institutions and the activities they engage in to this end.

3 Religious Authorities and the Promotion of Pilgrimages

INTRODUCTION: INVENTING MIRACLES AND PROMOTING A PILGRIMAGE

Buddhist temples in Japan had, until the end of the Heian period, been primarily reliant on aristocratic patronage for their support. Changing political, economic and social circumstances in the late Heian and early Kamakura (1185–1333) periods, however, presented temples with new challenges as the economic standing of their patrons was undermined by the rise to power of a new military class. With the waning of aristocratic patronage, Buddhist temples needed to broaden their appeal to find new means of support. Hokkeji, a Buddhist convent in the Nara region, was one of the institutions affected by such changes and, as Lori Meeks (2010: 28, 33–58) has shown, a key element in its strategy to attract new visitors was promoting itself as a pilgrimage site. During the early Kamakura period, nuns at Hokkeji promoted miracle tales and foundation stories (*engi*) centred on the temple's eighth-century female founder Kōmyō and effectively reinvented Hokkeji as a pilgrimage site where one could encounter the miraculous powers of its founder. The resulting flow of pilgrims brought new donations and offerings and helped secure Hokkeji's future.

Hokkeji was by no means the only Buddhist temple in that era to turn to pilgrimage as a means of increasing its clientele and strengthening its economic base; temples in outlying regions similarly used such strategies to attract pilgrims from the populated regions around the capital (Meeks 2010: 34–35). Examples such as this are found time and again in Japan, with clerics across the centuries displaying entrepreneurial talents to create, publicise and promote legends and narratives asserting the importance of their temples as pilgrimage centres. This tradition of pilgrimage creation and promotion is not limited to Buddhist temples alone. Richard Bowring (2005: 272) outlines how, in the twelfth and thirteenth centuries, priests at the Shinto shrines of Ise sought to popularise pilgrimages there as they searched for new sources of revenue to weather the changing economic and social patterns of the era after the income the Ise shrines derived from their estates dried up. The Ise shrines were widely considered the most important

Shinto places of worship in Japan, and shrine priests and town inhabitants alike proved adept at drumming up custom for their holy sites, sending out *oshi* (pilgrim guides)[1] across Japan to encourage people from distant places to make pilgrimages to the shrines while organising their itineraries in ways that made their journeys as convenient as possible and allowing them to engage in ritual services at the shrines (Breen and Teeuwen 2010: 44).

Such creative acts of pilgrimage invention and promotion are certainly common in the Buddhist tradition. Indeed, James B. Pruess (2002) has identified pilgrimage as a common Buddhist expansion strategy in which new Buddhist sites are created, often through the use of Buddha relics or of copies of the Buddha's footprints reputedly emanating from India. Pruess shows how this process works in Thailand, where a common pattern is for the discovery, creation or transmission (usually from India) of such sacred objects, followed by their enshrinement and the invention of myths sanctifying the place where they are enshrined. This strategy of creating new sacred centres readily accessible to local populations has been an important factor in enabling Buddhism to attract new converts as it spread across Asia (Pruess 2002: 214–225). It has been used skilfully also in Japan, as the Hokkeji example and many others that appear in this book amply illustrate.

THE INVENTIVENESS OF PRIESTS: THE SAIKOKU AND SHIKOKU PILGRIMAGES

Such inventive modes of proselytisation reaffirm the argument made in Chapter 2 about the sacred as a created rather than as an innate category. They also further illustrate the problems inherent in the notion that pilgrimage is generated spontaneously out of populist upsurges and as an antistructural process that challenges the authority of priests and religious hierarchies. As this chapter illustrates, pilgrimages are very often produced via the activities of religious specialists in order to advance the cause of their institutions and traditions and to develop faith in the objects of worship enshrined within them. The examples of the Saikoku and Shikoku pilgrimages are apposite here. Although historically verifiable data about the formation of both are sparse, there is enough evidence to indicate that the origins of both can be traced back to the travels of religious specialists associated with prominent religious centres who created the frameworks and routes that later pilgrims followed.

In Shikoku, for example, the first material evidence in textual terms of a pilgrimage route centred on the figure of Kōbō Daishi with eighty-eight identifiable temples on it, is found in the mid- to late seventeenth century. However, its beginnings can be traced back several centuries earlier, to the travels of mendicant monks and ascetics associated with Kōyasan (Mount Kōya), the Shingon Buddhist religious centre founded by the monk Kūkai (774–835) in the mountains of west-central Japan. Kūkai is one of the most famed figures in Japanese Buddhism. Born on the island of Shikoku, he first practiced austerities there before becoming a monk and travelling to China, where he encountered the Shingon Buddhist tradition and brought its teachings back to Japan, establishing Kōyasan as its headquarters. Widely respected and with powerful political connections he made Shingon and Kōyasan prominent features of the Japanese religious landscape. He died, according to his followers, while sitting in meditation at Kōyasan in 835. In 921, Kūkai was granted the posthumous title Kōbō Daishi ('the great teacher who spread the law of Buddhism') by the Japanese emperor, and Shingon authorities quickly seized on this to revive the fortunes of their sect and of Kōyasan, which had gone into decline in the century after Kūkai's death. They spread the legend that when they placed the Imperial decree awarding the title of Kōbō Daishi in Kūkai's mausoleum at Kōyasan, they found his body was still warm—proof, they claimed, that he had transcended death and remained alive in eternal meditation in the mausoleum, awaiting the coming of Maitreya the future Buddha. The story of a sacred figure still alive and in eternal meditation was spread far and wide, and was used to encourage people to come on pilgrimage to Kōyasan to 'meet' this living holy figure and acquire spiritual benefits from him. Monks from Kōyasan also began to travel around Japan preaching miracle stories about Kōbō Daishi, who transcended, in their stories, his sedentary position at Kōyasan and metamorphosed into a wandering holy figure. Stories of him travelling in the guise of a pilgrim around Japan dispensing miracles, healing the sick, rewarding the virtuous and punishing the greedy, became common throughout Japan, including the island of Kūkai's birth, Shikoku (Saitō 1988).

Shikoku also became a focus for the travels of mendicants from Kōyasan, who sought to retrace the footsteps of their sect founder and to visit places associated with his life. As they did so, they helped create a set of legends—augmented by later pilgrims—that sacralised the land of Shikoku and inscribed onto its landscape a pilgrimage route that developed over a number of centuries. Its eventual form, of eighty-eight temples to be visited in a circuit of the island, coalesced in the seventeenth century. Legends attributing the creation of the pilgrimage to Kūkai/Kōbō Daishi became part of the pilgrimage's growing corpus of stories and helped affirm a Shingon Buddhist dimension to the pilgrimage. The origins of the pilgrimage were thus in the activities of priests and ascetics associated with one of Japan's most prominent religious institutions and one of its major Buddhist sectarian organisations, in whose footsteps subsequent pilgrims travelled. Towards the end of the seventeenth century, the first pilgrimage guidebooks and collections of pilgrimage miracle stories were produced. These, too, were produced by ascetics and priests with connections to Shingon and Kōyasan, notably Yūben Shinnen (1638?–1691) who walked the pilgrimage some twenty times, compiled the first guidebooks and put together the first collection of pilgrimage miracle tales, in which pilgrims were offered hopes of miraculous cures and worldly benefits and were assured that they would meet Kōbō Daishi on the route. Shinnen also

Figure 3.1 Statue of Kōbō Daishi as a mendicant wandering monk.

solicited alms from donors to establish a pilgrims' lodge and to put up markers for pilgrimage. It was primarily from Shinnen's era and because of his activities that the pilgrimage began to develop as a mass activity.[2]

Similarly, the Saikoku pilgrimage owes its origins to the actions of Buddhist monks and ascetics from prominent temples deeply embedded in the hierarchic structures of Japanese Buddhism and close to the centres of Japanese religious, cultural and political power. From the tenth century onwards, Kannon pilgrimages had become a prominent element in Japanese Buddhism, spurred by beliefs in her intercessionary powers to provide miraculous healing, save people from suffering in this life and grant salvation in the next world. Kannon pilgrimage cults were promoted vigorously by charismatic Buddhist ascetics known as *hijiri* and *yugyōsha* who established hermitages in mountainous areas relatively close to population centres, where they devoted themselves to the veneration of Kannon. Such hermitages became the focus of pilgrimages by lay people hoping to access the charismatic power both of Kannon and of the ascetics themselves; several developed into prominent temples that were later incorporated into the Saikoku route.[3]

Eventually a pilgrimage circuit linking such sites developed and what scant documentary evidence there is from the period indicates that the organising force behind this process came from Miidera (also known as Onjōji), one of the main power centres of the Tendai Buddhist sect that was one of Japan's dominant religious forces in the period (eleventh and twelfth centuries) at hand, and that had close links to imperial and aristocratic power and patronage (Swanson 1981: 57, MacWilliams 2004: 42–43). The first mention of the pilgrimage is found in the records of Miidera, initially with an account of a pilgrimage made in 1093–1094 by Gyōson, a Miidera priest. However, although Gyōson did visit a number of temples now on the route, this could not have been a full Saikoku pilgrimage, because not all thirty-three temples in the route existed at the time (Hayami 1983: 270–271, Shimizutani 1986: 206). Gyōson's journey did, however, set the foundations for later priestly travels to circuits of Kannon temples, and in 1161, according to Miidera records, another priest, Kakuchū, made the pilgrimage, this time visiting thirty-three Kannon temples that had close links with Miidera. The account of Kakuchū's journey is considered by Japanese scholars such as Hayami Tasuku (1983: 277–285) to be the first historically accurate record of the Saikoku pilgrimage. Kakuchū's journey took him to thirty-three temples enshrining Kannon (thirty-three because of Kannon's vow in the Lotus Sutra to assume thrity-three forms to save humanity). It started at what is still listed as the first temple on the route—Seigantoji, popularly known as Nachi-san in the Kii peninsula—and ended at what is now Temple Ten but which initially was the last site on the route: Mimurotoji in Uji, just south of Miidera. Seigantoji and Mimurotoji were branch temples of Miidera, and Kakuchū had close links there, indicating that the pilgrimage itself was built around Miidera's sphere of influence (Hayami 1983: 286). Kakuchū's pilgrimage included the newly constructed temple Ima Kumano ('Now' or New Kumano) established in southern Kyoto in 1160 by Emperor Go-Shirakawa and placed under Miidera's control. Ima Kumano is important historically because it was built as a symbolic replication and representation, within the capital, of Kumano, the mountainous region in the Kii peninsula south of the then capital, which was closely connected with Japanese foundation legends as well as being visualised in early

Buddhism as the earthly gateway to Kannon's Pure Land (Hayami 1983: 272, Moerman 2005). By building the new temple close to court, the emperor was able to worship the deities of Kumano (closely associated with Imperial legendary origins) and 'visit' Kannon's Pure Land without needing to distance himself far from the centre of political power at court.

In the centuries after Kakuchū's journey, religious specialists from Miidera and its branch temples popularised the pilgrimage by proselytising miracle tales associated with it, including the legends of Tokudō and Kazan that became established as 'the' founding stories of Saikoku. They also served as pilgrimage guides and encouraged group pilgrimages to the temples. Ascetics based at Seigantoji—the Miidera branch temple at Nachi that was the first temple in Kakuchū's 1161 journey—were especially prominent in this context. Thanks to their proselytising, which involved created narratives praising the potency of its talismans and linking it with figures such as Kazan and Tokudō, Seigantoji was subsequently designated as the first temple on the route (MacWilliams 2004: 44–45).

Such inventive proselytising strategies were central to the formation and development of pilgrimages throughout Japan, such as the numerous regional replications of Saikoku and Shikoku that developed in the Tokugawa period. In such cases, the ubiquitous apparitional and miracle-working images of Kannon and Kōbō Daishi provided a ready tool for priests and other activists to appropriate at local and regional levels, as did the formats of Saikoku and Shikoku. New pilgrimages based on the Saikoku or Shikoku model developed throughout Japan, claiming equal significance to the originals and asserting that they, too, were empowered by the spiritual presence of Kannon and/or Kōbō Daishi. In 1830, for example, Buddhist priests on the Inland Sea island of Koshima, drawing on an island legend in which a local nun who had walked the Shikoku pilgrimage, claimed to have later visualised Kōbō Daishi in a dream at her hermitage in Koshima, proclaimed the island to be a special place sanctified by Kōbō Daishi and established a smaller scale copy of the Shikoku pilgrimage there (Itō 1981: 10, Shudō 1984: 141). It was one of many such that appeared in the Inland Sea region, with many of its islands, at the inspiration of local priests, creating their own localised versions of the Shikoku pilgrimage. Some (including the Shōdoshima pilgrimage) even appropriated miracle stories from Shikoku, as its priests and temples capitalised on the popularity of pilgrimage and on regional and local wishes to have their own versions of these nationally prominent routes (Reader 1988, Okawa 2009). Similarly, Saikoku-style regional and local pilgrimages with thirty-three stages developed throughout the country.

Such activities are early Japanese examples of the invention of pilgrimages, and of the ways in which they may be created initially by religious specialists and proselytised—often via post-invention miracle tales or by other strategies of promotion such as the recent emphasis in Shikoku on images of tradition—to the wider public. They also further indicate the ubiquity of pilgrimages, of how anywhere can be designated or be claimed as sacred, and of how the sacred is a readily appropriated and replicated commodity that can be utilised anywhere that claimants wish to do so.

CREATING PILGRIMAGES IN TWENTIETH-CENTURY JAPAN

This pattern of continued pilgrimage invention, reproduction and development guided by religious officials has continued into the present day in Japan. In the 1980s, for instance, priests around the country were keen to capitalise on what appeared to be a general period of pilgrimage growth in which pilgrim numbers were rising in Saikoku and Shikoku, and when there was widespread talk of a 'pilgrimage boom' (Reader 1996). Several new routes developed as a result, as well as a number that had been extant in the Tokugawa period and later gone into abeyance.

In northern Kyushu, for example, a new thirty-three-stage Kannon pilgrimage developed in 1987 as a result of the efforts of priests in Fukuoka prefecture. The pilgrimage centred on a manifestation of Kannon that became popular in the 1980s—the *boke fūji* (prevention of senility) Kannon. This was a response to the worries of Japan's ageing population about the rise in cases of senility and to a general sense among older people that they wanted to die with dignity and spare themselves and their families the painful ravages of senility. There is a long-standing Japanese tradition of praying for a painless death—a category within which seeking to avoid senility falls—and of temples offering such benefits to worshippers (Young and Ikeuchi 1995), and in the 1980s, as worries about senility became a major issue in Japan, many elderly people turned to Kannon for reassurance in this context. New statues of Kannon, in the guise of the prevention of senility Kannon, began to appear at temples and to offer support and succour to the worried elderly. This new Kannon form and statue was actually the product of interactions between commercial interests, particularly a company that made Buddhist statues, and Buddhist priests worried about the senility problem and aware of the concerns of elderly people in this respect. The company's head, Gotō Masaharu, was instrumental in this process, by proposing this particular form of Kannon, getting *boke fūji* statues made and persuading a number of priests to install them at their temples (Reader 1995).

Gotō's idea was quickly taken up by Buddhist priests, who set up several pilgrimages in the 1980s and early 1990s to respond to this growing concern. The first such was a thirty-three-temple pilgrimage route covering much of western Japan and the islands of Shikoku and Kyushu in 1984 and then more regionally focused ones in Kyushu in 1987 and Shikoku in 1991 (Reader 1995). Two priests whose temples were part of the initial 1984 western Japan *boke fūji* pilgrimage felt that this route was too geographically dispersed and without a coherent enough regional focus to attract many people and that a more focused route in their own region would be more efficacious. As a result, they embarked on a long process

68 Pilgrimage in the Marketplace

Figure 3.2 Statue of the *boke fūji* Kannon at Ima Kumano Temple, Kyoto.

of contacting other priests they knew and whose temples were in interesting and accessible locations (good scenery and the proximity of hot spring resorts, where the pilgrims would be able to relax at the end of a hard day's pilgrimaging, being major items of consideration), until they had persuaded thirty-one other temples to join with them. Each temple enshrined a statue of the *boke fūji* Kannon, and the temples together established a pilgrimage association and commissioned the production of scrolls and pilgrims' books that could be stamped at each temple, as well as a guidebook and other pilgrimage accoutrements and amulets that could be sold to pilgrims. The pilgrimage was formally inaugurated with a ritual ceremony in 1987.

To support their new pilgrimage, the priests liaised with regional interest groups, including tourist offices and travel firms, notably the Ukawa Bus Company, a regional transport firm specialising in pilgrimage tours and whose President, Ishii Takeshi, was a friend of the priests behind the pilgrimage. Ishii helped publicise the pilgrimage and gave press interviews about his wishes to build a pilgrimage tradition for the region that in due course could rival that of Shikoku while his company began organising and advertising pilgrimage tours of the newly formed pilgrimage. The priests were also very much concerned about issues of regional identity and support; in December 1990, they took me and Mr. Ishii to a meeting of other priests in the region in which the main focus of discussion was how they could help develop and reinforce a sense of regional identity through their pilgrimages while using these to support local temples and get people interested in Buddhism.[4]

It was just one of many pilgrimages that developed at the time. Another was an eighty-eight-stage Kōbō Daishi pilgrimage on the Inland Sea island of Suō Oshima in Yamaguchi prefecture, that had been in abeyance for many decades but was revived in 1988 by priests running one of the island's temples. Its reopening was marked by a large Buddhist ceremony attended by priests from much of western Japan, and by representatives of the pilgrimage temple associations of several other routes.[5] I interviewed the priests involved in this enterprise shortly after the opening ceremony, and they informed me that their wish to revive the route was grounded in their concerns for the welfare of their island and its declining and ageing local population. The economy was almost wholly dependent on fishing and farming and, as such, was fragile, leading to population flight as young people left to seek work in the cities. This was eroding community spirit and threatening the well-being of the remaining population and the support structures of the local Buddhist temples, including their own.

The revived pilgrimage, they hoped, would provide a new focus for the islanders, reaffirming their sense of pride in their home environment. It would also, they hoped, help resuscitate the local economy by attracting pilgrims from outside the island, who would require lodgings, spend money and, thus, help stimulate the economy. They said they had been inspired to do this because of the popularity of pilgrimage at the time (they specifically used the term *junrei būmu*, 'pilgrimage boom') and because they were aware of other routes similarly being developed elsewhere in Japan that were doing well. They also had support from the local town hall and tourist office, which helped with publicity and leaflets emphasising the island's beauty, local produce and rural charms and the sense of Japanese tradition and identity that could be discovered there.[6]

In both cases, the pilgrimage had been invented or revived not because of any miraculous event or apparition or because people had claimed to have achieved spiritual experiences there. Rather, two sets of priests in different places, both concerned about issues of regional welfare and identity, both wanting to engage with social problems (senility in one case, rural depopulation in the other). They were keen also to shore up their own temples in an era in which rural decline was causing some rural religious institutions to close due to lack of support while capitalising on a general view at the time that pilgrimage was a popular and effective way to deal with such issues. Both sets of priests manifested a sense of business acumen in being aware of the prevailing interest in pilgrimage at the time. For both pilgrimages, the presence of good environments such as hot spring resorts and tranquil rural scenery, coupled with the support of civil organisations such as tourist offices and local commercial concerns that helped publicise the pilgrimages as a means of generating regional identity and attracting visitors, were crucial. As the priests emphasised, too, creating and promoting these pilgrimages was a means of getting people interested in visiting temples—a necessity for their economic survival just as it had been for Hokkeji centuries earlier. The example of one temple on the Kyushu route that had been facing closure because of a declining local population, but that had been saved by joining the pilgrimage and thereby receiving new visitors, seemed to underline their argument (Reader 1996). Such new and revived pilgrimages are examples of how Japanese Buddhist priests have in the modern era regularly created and promoted pilgrimages as a means of enhancing the standing and fortunes of their temples, their religious tradition and their communities. They are further evidence of a recurrent theme in pilgrimage development indicated by the Korean pilgrimage example cited in Chapter 1—of how pilgrimage may often be a process inaugurated by priestly innovation coupled with the help of commercial and civil authorities.

PILGRIMAGE GUIDES AND PROMOTERS

In order to ensure that the newly created *boke fūji* pilgrimage in Kyushu became established and attracted pilgrims, the interest groups concerned did not just embark on the standard round of publicity via various leaflets and guidebooks. They also established an association of pilgrimage temples (*Reijōkai*) and instigated a system of pilgrimage guides (*sendatsu*). Both these have been important institutional elements in the successful promotion of pilgrimages in Japan. One of the first such associations of pilgrimage temples in Japan was the *Shōdoshima Reijōkai*, which was formed in 1913 to coordinate temple services for the pilgrims, and it paved the way for many others, perhaps the most successful of which has been the *Shikoku Reijōkai*, which was set up in 1956, shortly after the development of mass-transport-organised tours made enhanced coordination among pilgrims, tour companies and temples essential. Previously, the temples had not been organised in a coordinated way, partly due to lack of appropriate technologies to allow them to communicate rapidly with each other and work together as an entity. As technologies developed and as bus companies running tours wanted to coordinate their travel and publicity activities with the temples, the need for better organisation became evident. Thus, the Shikoku Reijōkai was established. Its subsequent success in helping spur the postwar revival of the pilgrimage and its rapid growth from the mid-1950s onwards (Reader 2005: 167–169) has set an example for other pilgrimages. In the modern period, it has become standard for multiple-site pilgrimage routes to have such organising bodies to coordinate their activities, which now include running websites about their pilgrimages. The Kyushu temples followed this practice, for the priests concerned were in no doubt that an active and committed *Reijōkai* would be crucial to the new pilgrimage's success.

One of the first steps the newly established Kyushu *Reijōkai* took was to set up a *sendatsu* ('pilgrimage guide') system and induct a number of lay people as *sendatsu*. This term has a long history in Japan. Historical accounts of pilgrimages in the Yoshino-Kumano region and later in Shikoku inform us of groups of pilgrims led by *sendatsu* who knew the route, could guide the pilgrims, show them how to perform devotions, and help arrange accommodation and special rituals for them (Shinjō 1982: 200–220, Reader 1993, 2005: 171–172). *Sendatsu* served also as proselytising figures travelling around the country spreading word about such pilgrimages. A similar related role is that of *oshi,* the pilgrimage promoters and guides mentioned earlier, who were linked to, and travelled round the country promoting and organising pilgrimages to prominent shrines, temples and pilgrimage routes such as Ise (Shinjō 1982: 151–220, Nishigaki 1983: 107–119).[7] Earlier in this chapter, I mentioned the *oshi* of Ise, who played a significant role in organising and promoting pilgrimages there; Barbara Ambros (2008: 4–7, 160–161) also shows how *oshi* were important in the promotion of the regional Ōyama pilgrimage cult that flourished in Tokugawa Japan, as well in numerous other pilgrimages of the era. Such figures are not unique to Japanese pilgrimage but can found in various guises in multiple contexts elsewhere, as with the *pandas* (pilgrimage guides) who are associated with Hindu pilgrimage sites (van der Veer 1988).

The importance and value of *sendatsu* to pilgrimage development can be seen in Shikoku. One of the early acts of the *Shikoku Reijōkai* after its inauguration in the 1950s was to set up a formal, institutionally ordained and hierarchic *sendatsu* system. This involved conferring a rank of *sendatsu* (coupled with various insignia to be worn) on those who had done the pilgrimage four or more times, establishing a hierarchy in which higher ranks were granted dependent on how many times the pilgrimage was performed (but also dependent on the relationship such people had with the

72 *Pilgrimage in the Marketplace*

temples) and holding annual meetings for *sendatsu* to instruct them in issues of Buddhist teaching and to encourage them to publicise and promote the pilgrimage. A pilgrimage newsletter, *Henro*, was founded and financed by the Iyo Tetsu bus company, the initiator (in 1953) and the main conveyor of package tour pilgrimages in Shikoku, and produced in conjunction with the *Reijōkai*, as a means of keeping *sendatsu* up to date with current pilgrimage news. It is sent each month to every *sendatsu*.

The system has been successful in getting regular pilgrims to become recruiting agents for the pilgrimage, with *sendatsu* taking part in regular publicity events to bring the pilgrimage to wider public attention, organising pilgrimage tours and persuading people the agents come into contact with to do the pilgrimage. Some have become professional pilgrim guide leaders as a result and are simultaneously commercial organisers of pilgrimage tours who make their living from the pilgrimage and religious agents narrating miracle tales and encouraging pilgrims to perform rituals.[8] They form a sizeable group of people (around 18,000 in 2008[9]) who perform the pilgrimage on a regular basis, with many doing it again and again to acquire a higher rank in the *sendatsu* system (Reader 2005: 167–172, 220–222). Many of those I have interviewed in Shikoku—from temple priests to officials of bus companies that use the services of *sendatsu* to lead their tours and help drum up support for them—consider that the *sendatsu* system has been an important factor in Shikoku's contemporary popularity.

Other pilgrimages in Japan have recognised this by establishing their own *sendatsu* systems. Some of the newly formed routes of the 1980s have, indeed, established such a system at the time of formation by conferring the rank on a number of interested people even before they had had chance to do the pilgrimage several times (Reader 1993: 40). The Kyushu route is a case in point; the priests felt it was essential, if their new pilgrimage were to be successful, to develop a coterie of *sendatsu* who could act as agents and proselytisers helping to build a pilgrimage clientele. As such, they contacted people they felt might be keen to take on such a role, and organised bus parties to take would-be *sendatsu* around the route to teach them about, and heighten their enthusiasm for, it. By December 1990, they had recruited 110 *sendatsu* for their promotional campaigns and encouraged them also to form local pilgrimage societies (*kō, junpaidan*) that could further spread the word about the pilgrimage. The bus guides from Ishii Takeshi's Ukawa Bus Company were also awarded the rank of *sendatsu*, thereby cementing the commercial links between the temples and the company further.

BUILDING LANDSCAPES AND PUTTING ON SHOWS:
SACRED STATUES AND PROSTITUTES

Just setting up a pilgrimage and engaging in the sorts of organisational and promotional mechanisms is not necessarily going to satisfy the wishes and aspirations of pilgrims who (as is discussed further in Chapters 5 and 6) come with all manner of expectations about what they might see and about what sorts of facilities, entertainments and diversions they may want while they are visiting sites and taking part in pilgrimages. Pilgrims want to see things that tell them that they are coming to a special place; they 'are more likely to visit an attractive, nicely appointed temple', as James Lochtefeld (2010: 101) puts it when discussing how Hardwar's growth as a pilgrimage centre has been accompanied by extensive building activities that have expanded the religious sites of the city. The pilgrims I have travelled with in Shikoku displayed similar views. They wanted and expected the temples they visited to be striking and grand and were especially impressed by Zentsūji, Kūkai's birthplace and the largest temple complex on the Shikoku route, yet they felt disappointment at seeing smaller temples on the route that lacked such grandeur, even appearing to question whether they merited the status of pilgrimage temples (Reader 2005: 15–16). Georgia Frank (2000: 100) makes this point well when, commenting on the desires of early pilgrims to the Christian Holy land who wanted to see striking shrines and churches that would confirm to them the importance of the places they were visiting, she states that pilgrimage is a 'visual practice', a point reaffirmed also by Robert Maniura (2004: 178–179). For Christian Holy Land and Shikoku pilgrims alike, visual splendour plays an important role. Simplicity does not create an aura and magnetism in the way that grand buildings do.

In this area, religious authorities play a significant role, as is richly illustrated by Sarah Thal's (2005) study of the pilgrimage shrine complex of Konpira on Mount Zōzu in Shikoku, in which she describes how successive generations of shrine priests built a sacred landscape there from the late sixteenth century onwards.[10] Although the shrine straddles a mountain that rises dramatically out of one of the few flat regions of Shikoku, its priests never relied simply on its striking physical landscape and natural environment and on the various legends and miraculous stories that developed there (often spurred by their own proselytising efforts) to attract and inspire pilgrims. They also assiduously created a built environment that enhanced the visual dimensions of Konpira, creating new halls of worship and introducing new figures of worship and rituals that fitted with the changing modes of successive eras. Its priests continually sought new ways to enhance the allure of the mountain shrine. Thus, for example, Yūten, the head priest of the complex in the mid-seventeenth century, transformed the mountain landscape via an extensive complex of new buildings and by adding twists and turns to the path up the mountain to enhance the sense of mystery pilgrims might feel as they wound up through the forests. He also established a new path so that there was one way up and one down, thereby expanding the available space to create new altars and sites of worship on the ways up and down and increasing the number of places where pilgrims might pray and make offerings (Thal 2005: 62–63). Such building activities were also fuelled by pilgrim donations and were driven both by the wishes of shrine authorities to increase the grandeur of their sites and of pilgrims who wanted to see continuing evidence of the significance of the places they were visiting. Similar patterns have ensued in Shikoku in recent times, where the growth in pilgrim numbers over the last two to three decades has led to increased wealth for the temples and to extensive building work, including new statues, halls of worship and other facilities intended to enhance the sites concerned. Priests in Shikoku have commented to me about how pilgrim wishes are a factor in this process, with pilgrims wanting to see new statues and the like and priests feeling the need to respond to such wishes.

Buildings alone, however dramatic, are rarely enough on their own to sustain pilgrim interests, a factor understood by generations of Konpira priests. This was certainly so in Tokugawa Japan, a period in which general economic growth, a developing transport infrastructure (including shipping lanes across the archipelago) and a system of control in which the only way anyone outside the elite could gain permission to temporarily leave the feudal domains they were indentured to, was to go on pilgrimage, helped foment a vibrant pilgrimage market (Shinjō 1982: 699–752, Vaporis 1994: 204–215, Thal 2004: 72–73). Even so, there were so many pilgrimage routes and sites competing for the custom of potential pilgrims that shrines such as Konpira could not simply rely on their existing reputations, scenery and/or potential of their gods to offer benefits and rewards to pilgrims. The market was competitive, not just when, as was noted in Chapter 2, economic downturns reduced pilgrim numbers, but even in times when social and economic conditions were favorable to pilgrimage. Konpira's priests, aware they had to continually compete with other places in order to attract pilgrims, had to constantly find ways to make their site more attractive than other sites, and they had no qualms about engaging in seemingly worldly activities to this end. They hosted markets and put on Sumo wrestling tournaments, theatrical performances and other entertainment events to attract would-be pilgrims, and although they did try to rein in some of the excesses that developed (e.g., they banned gambling and later also tried, unsuccessfully, to ban prostitution), overall the intertwining of entertainment and religious practices became the shrine's mainstay. As Thal (2005: 74) comments, Mount Zōzu and its gods grew

> amid a bustling pilgrimage economy of entertainments and commerce: performances, prostitution, and gambling proved as integral to the growth of the site as amulets and worship.

Konpira's priests did not see such entertainment as antithetical to the nature of the gods enshrined there, nor did they envisage their shrine as swathed in an aura of austere sanctity detached from the profane world. Rather, they recognised that the worldly and the sacred were inextricably bound together and that the gods themselves were comfortable with this. Yūzan, the head priest at the complex from 1691 to 1736, for example, considered that 'the hustle and bustle of the town were as important to the well-being of the god and the domain as were the quiet precincts on the mountain' (Thal 2005: 74).

Like the priests in modern-day Japan, mentioned in Chapter 2, who checked on what their competitors were up to, Konpira's priests also kept an eye on their potential rivals. They, too, travelled around the country visiting other popular religious sites and copying ideas if they could help Konpira attract more pilgrims. If new figures of worship were proving popular in the pilgrimage pantheon of the era, they would be adopted and enshrined at Konpira. Thus, for example, Kannon, probably the most popular figure of all in Tokugawa pilgrimage contexts, was enshrined at Konpira by Yūzan in 1699 (Thal 2005: 74–76). As Konpira's popularity increased, its income grew, enabling its priests to further develop its built landscape and to travel further afield to promote their shrine and check out new ideas. All this helped turn it, by the nineteenth century, into one of Japan's most prominent pilgrimage centres. Although pilgrims were deeply interested in miracles and avidly lapped up the collections of miracle stories produced at the shrine, they were also enthused by the spectacle and entertainment on offer, to the extent that prostitution and miracles proved to be Konpira's key attractions well into the early years of the twentieth century (Thal 2005: 297).

The Konpira example shows how active and engaged priests can develop and consistently reshape a site, making it into a major centre of pilgrimage that both reflects and responds to the changing vicissitudes and patterns of the era, in which priests can incorporate new deities and legends and reshape existing practices while offering various modes of diversionary entertainment to keep potential pilgrims amused and to ensure that shrines remain continually attuned to the trends of the time and to the shifting inclinations of their (potential) clientele. In so doing, priests did not make boundary differentiations between the sacred and profane or regard the commercial and entertaining as inappropriate or beyond their scope and remit as shrine priests guarding over a sacred arena. If Sumo tournaments, market events and theatrical performances helped draw in pilgrims, then they were put on by the priests, who (as evidenced by Yūzan's perception that the hustle and bustle of the town was as important to Konpira's deity as was the tranquillity of its mountains) saw them as contributing to, rather than detracting from, the allure and the sanctity of the place.

INVENTING AND PROMOTING PILGRIMAGES IN THE EUROPEAN CATHOLIC CONTEXT

Such inventive activities are not something limited to Japanese Buddhist priests but can be found across the religious spectrum, a point illustrated by looking at Catholic pilgrimage contexts. I have already mentioned, in Chapter 2, how ecclesiastical interests helped in the emergence of Lourdes and Medjugorje as pilgrimage centres, for example, by favouring them over other places with similar claims, and how the campaigns of Catholic clerics helped build Knock into a major pilgrimage site. Studies of the Santiago de Compostela pilgrimage, too, widely recognise the dynamic role of senior ecclesiastical figures in promoting the cult of St. James, in affirming the significance of Santiago as his holy site, and in spreading the word about it far and wide. Sharon Roseman (2004: 76) for example cites the 'energetic Bishop Diego Gelmirez' as a forceful protagonist in making Santiago into a 'renowned destination for pious Christians' and talks of how he travelled widely in twelfth-century France and Italy promoting pilgrimages to his cathedral. Roseman (2004: 76) also here cites Marilyn Stokstad's (1978: 16–17) statement that St. James's tomb and church would have been 'very humble indeed if it were not for the talents of the medieval propagandists. The large number of pilgrims to Spain did not arise out of spontaneous piety alone'.

Ruben Lois Gonzalez (2012) also emphasises the role of ecclesiastical figures in the construction of the pilgrimage, from the ninth-century bishop Teodomiro, who first affirmed the story of the appearance of St. James's relics in Santiago and ordered that a church be constructed there (see also Frey 1998: 9), to the way in which Bishop Gelmirez revisited this legendary discovery in the twelfth century and used it to enhance Santiago's status as an ecclesiastical centre, thereby enriching its church and facilitating the subsequent construction of the cathedral. David Sox (1985: 24) further emphasises how Santiago's status as a major pilgrimage centre was enhanced through the work of the Cluniac Benedictine order, which helped develop the route, organised pilgrimages to Santiago and made it widely known throughout Europe.

The importance of the clergy in developing and disseminating pilgrimage cults in medieval times is emphasised also by Robert Finucane (1977) in his discussion of how the geographical extent of a saint's pilgrimage cult depended on how far the priests and monks involved with it could travel, with some remaining merely local and others extending across regions. When higher-ranked clerics such as bishops threw their weight behind a saint and its pilgrimage cult, the saint's geographical spread and levels of popularity were greater, as with St Thomas à Becket and Canterbury or the pilgrimage to the tomb of Thomas Cantilupe in Hereford Cathedral, which especially benefitted from the assiduous promotional activities of the cathedral's bishops (Finucane 1977: 157–187). Finucane (1977: 29) also draws attention to the association between pilgrim numbers and impressive buildings, with his remark that there was 'a noticeable correlation between the acquisition (or translation) of saints' bones and new building projects financed by pilgrims' offerings'.

Such building projects of course added to the spectacular dimensions of sites and made them better able to attract future pilgrims. Evgenia Mesaritou's (2012) study of the shrine of Padre Pio at San Giovanni reaffirms this point by showing how Catholic Church officials along with the friars of the Capuchin order to which Padre Pio belonged have reclaimed control over the figure and cult of the deceased saint, who, in his lifetime, was a figure of controversy for the church.[11] Since his death, the Capuchin friars and the Catholic Church have skilfully managed Padre Pio's charisma in order to promote a pilgrimage cult around him, but one that they can manage and control. A central strand in their strategy has been the building of a new church, designed by the famed architect Renzo Piano, which has expanded the capacity of the shrine, allowed it to hold large-scale masses and enhanced San Giovanni's potential drawing power. The monks in Padre Pio's Capuchin order were keen to recruit Piano to build the new church because of his prominence as a famed international architect (a factor that would potentially enhance the shrine's profile beyond the ranks of the faithful) and kept up a campaign until he agreed to their request.[12] Although the new church affords centrality to Jesus (thereby assuaging the earlier concerns of Catholic authorities that the cult of Padre Pio was marginalising him), Padre Pio remains prominent, with his figure and visage strategically inserted into various biblical narratives. For example, in one sculpture showing Mary Magdalene and Nicodemus holding Jesus's body after the crucifixion, the face of Padre Pio is imposed onto Nicodemus (Mesaritou 2012). The new church has helped expand pilgrim numbers and has helped give the saint's cult a more international dimension in which some visitors appear to visit the shrine primarily because of their interest in architecture. The monumental nature of the new church does not appeal to all pilgrims, some of whom feel it is too large and impersonal and directs the focus away from the saint to whose place they have come (Mesaritou 2012). Its style and size certainly contradict both the tenets of the Capuchin order, which decree that churches should be small and unadorned, and the ideals of poverty and sobriety emphasised by earlier promoters of the Padre Pio cult (Luzzatto 2007: 291–292). However, its stature has, along with the fame of its architect, been important in increasing the numbers of visitors to the site. It is a Catholic example of the point made earlier, about how the development of dramatic built landscapes can be a potent drawing force in pilgrimage, and an example of how skilful manipulation and marketing by religious officials can boost pilgrim numbers to shrines.

RELICS AND THE PROMOTION OF PILGRIMAGE

As was mentioned above, a key element in the emergence of Santiago de Compostela as a pilgrimage centre was the discovery (or perhaps it would be better to say the legendary discovery) of the relics of Saint James that were claimed to have appeared in this then-remote Galician place in the ninth century. Relics have played a significant role in the formation and construction of pilgrimage sites in numerous traditions from the Buddhist, as was noted earlier by Pruess (1992; see also Faure 1991: 132–147, Trainor 1992, 2007,

Germano and Trainor 2004), to the Catholic Christian. Diane Webb (2002: 7), indeed, argues that relics and their supply were crucial to the development of Christian pilgrimage, whereas numerous studies have shown how deeply involved ecclesiastical authorities were in their production, ratification, distribution and use in the creation and promotion of pilgrimage cults. Thus, Patrick Geary (1994: 167–168) has discussed how Christian proselytisers and hierarchies in early and medieval times used the relics of holy figures to create new centres of worship and to develop places of pilgrimage, sacred geographies and networks in medieval Europe, whereas David Sox (1985: 7) talks about how, in the early days of Christian pilgrimage, Syrian monks would stimulate the practice by creating relics to give to pilgrims.

Relics were also used in exhibitions to attract pilgrims and stimulate popular devotionalism in medieval Europe. In 1238, for example, an exhibition at Aachen included Jesus's loincloth and Mary's shift (Webb 2002: 33). Such exhibitions continued well beyond the medieval era. Trier Cathedral in Germany, for instance, continued to hold exhibitions through the nineteenth and into the twentieth centuries at which the purported Holy Tunic of Jesus was displayed in order to encourage pilgrimages there (Sox 1985: 88–89). Such activities, of course, quite strikingly resemble the displays of normally hidden icons (*kaichō*) that I have discussed as mechanisms used to boost pilgrimages in Japan.

Relics were not just disseminated or created; they also were often, as Patrick Geary (1990) has so vividly described, stolen (or liberated, according to those who purloined them) to transfer the power and presence of the holy figure embodied in the relic, from one shrine to another. This 'translation' (as it was so termed) was theologically justified in medieval eyes. If a relic would allow itself to be removed in this way from its place of residence, it meant that it was not being appropriately cared for where it was and that it wished to be taken to its new abode, thereby strengthening the potency of the new place while demeaning the location from which it had been removed. Among the most famous of such relic thefts was the removal of a relic of St. Foy from Agen by the monk Arinisidus of Conques, probably in 865 or 866; the relic was spirited away to the monastery of Conques and was used to enhance Conques's reputation as a pilgrimage location. It also demonstrated how different institutions competed with each other in the pilgrimage market; a key reason for the theft was to boost the appeal of Conques over and against the rival monastery of Figeac (Geary 1990: 58–63, 86). The practice clearly worked, as Conques was thereafter able to attract large numbers of pilgrims, including pilgrims going to Santiago who stopped at Conques because of its relic (Sox 1985: 44).

Relic theft is thus a further means whereby inventive and competitive religious authorities have sought to steal a march on their rivals while boosting the pilgrimage potential of their own shrines. This practice is not unique to medieval Christianity but was rife also in Buddhism in earlier eras, as Trainor (1992) demonstrates. Nor is it limited to the medieval era, as Sox

(1985: 41) notes by citing examples of twentieth-century relic thefts in the United States and Rome. Nor is the use of relics to foment pilgrimage cults necessarily just a thing of the past either. Sox (1985: 7) provides an interesting insight into how such inventive practices continue to be used within the Catholic Church as a means of empowering churches in more modern times, by divulging how he was shown a roomful of relics at Vatican, waiting to be shipped out to new churches. In 1990, the administrator of St. Mary's Cathedral in Edinburgh, Monsignor Patrick Grady, spoke of his plans to use the relics of Saint Andrew, which were kept at the cathedral, to attract pilgrims to the cathedral and through them to eventually establish a national (Catholic) shrine and Saint Andrew pilgrimage site in Edinburgh.[13]

OF INDULGENCES AND PAPAL IMPRIMATURS

Just as Japanese Buddhist and Shinto priests displayed skilful entrepreneurial skills in publicising their sites, so too did the priestly authorities of Christianity. As Horton and Marie-Hélène Davis (1982: 20) have said, a key element in popularising pilgrimages in medieval Christendom was 'good advertising from officialdom'. Jonathan Sumption (1975: 153) reiterates the point by speaking about how 'attractive packaging was an essential element in a saint's appeal' and how this was emphasised with striking decorations and tombs at their shrines and by votives and stories written up by priests to advertise the miraculous powers of their shrines. Intrinsic to such official advertising and packaging were inducements such as indulgences that promised pilgrims special graces and the remission of sins, along with proclamations of Holy Years in which making pilgrimages to specific shrines was decreed to bring enhanced merit to participants. These were an important motivating factor for medieval pilgrims (Finucane 1977: 44–45). The granting of indulgences promising a remission of sins or a reduction of time spent in purgatory, for instance, played an important role in popularising Walsingham as a pilgrimage centre in medieval England; through the use of indulgences and promises by the local bishop of Ely that pilgrims would gain remission of sins, Walsingham became part of 'the international indulgences industry' (Waller 2011: 33). The emergence of new technologies was also important in this respect, with the development of the printing press instrumental in enabling medieval shrines to produce more indulgences on a mass scale and hence to promote themselves more widely than before (Waller 2011: 33). The papacy, unsurprisingly, was adept in such contexts, assiduously promoting pilgrimages to Rome throughout the medieval period via the papal declarations of Holy Years and special indulgences (Webb 2002: 27).

Such techniques remain in use in more modern times, with Pope John Paul II proving especially adroit at using his charismatic status to promote various Catholic pilgrimage sites during his lifetime. His many visits to Catholic sites such as Lourdes, Knock and Fatima, appeared, indeed, to be a 'boon to the pilgrimage travel industry' and served to give such sites a 'papal stamp of approval' and boost pilgrim numbers (Sox 1985: 6–7, 195). The tradition of issuing papal indulgences and declaring Holy Years for specific pilgrimages has also been a potent marketing and recruiting tool in modern times. Santiago de Compostela, for example, benefitted from John Paul II's declaration of 1993 as a Holy Year, leading to millions of pilgrims visiting Santiago in that year, including over 100,000 walkers (Frey 1998: 251). Similarly, the number of pilgrims to the shrine of Padre Pio at San Giovanni del Rotondo went up by a third in 2003 when John Paul II announced that pilgrims going there in that year qualified for a total remission of sins.[14] Indulgences and holy years, in other words, function in similar ways to Japanese *kaichō* events in offering increased graces to pilgrims and increasing their numbers.[15]

Pilgrims, as I commented in the previous chapter, are attracted to sites because they are full of people, and this point has been well understood by religious authorities over the centuries, from popes and bishops, to Japanese shrine and temple priests alike. Proclamations of Holy Years and the use of spectacular entertainment events, exhibitions and relic displays, serve as magnetic mechanisms enticing pilgrims to embark on pilgrimages. They have accordingly been strategies widely used by priests who know full well how readily pilgrim numbers can be enhanced by the creation and sustenance of a fervent marketplace around pilgrimage sites and who realise that success brings crowds of pilgrims that in turn add to a site's attraction. Ensuring that quiet, tranquil and remote locations remain so, by contrast, is far less efficacious.

PRIESTS AND THE COMMODIFICATION OF RELIGION?

In his study of religion and commercialisation, Laurence Moore (1994: 11) refers to the Amish community centred in the area of Lancaster, Pennsylvania, in the United States, as follows:

> the Amish have struggled to show what religion might look like if left untouched by the processes of commodification. Yet anyone who has travelled east from Lancaster on Route 30 and viewed the manufactured Amish attractions that draw tourists by the thousands to the area will recognize the futility of attempted isolation. If you do not commodify your religion yourself, someone will do it for you.

This point has been well understood by religious authorities such as the priests of Konpira who, in striving to make their places of worship into thriving pilgrimage sites, have not shied away from commodifying and publicising their sites through inventing pilgrimage narratives, erecting new chapels and statues, hosting markets and putting on entertainment shows.

I would indeed suggest that such an awareness is virtually universal among religious authorities, to that extent the Amish are very much an exception and a minority in religious terms in seeking to eschew contact with the commercial and commodified world. As the examples cited in this chapter indicate, it is far more prevalent (and, indeed, one might say, realistic) for religious authorities to be prepared and ready to interweave commercial considerations into their activities in order to sustain the places they oversee and to increase their clienteles. They, in effect, commodify their religion not because to do otherwise would be simply to invite others to do it for them, but because, as with the priests of Konpira or those putting on exhibitions in airport malls, they have pragmatic understandings of, rather than artificially idealised visions about, the sacred, which they recognise cannot be set apart from the everyday human world. They are aware of the integral relationship of commerce and religion and know that the maintenance of their icons, figures of worship, sacred places and priestly communities, and the support of their teachings and spreading of the word that lies behind them, depend on practical support.

As this chapter has shown, the keepers and priests of sacred places view the sanctuaries they oversee not as some form of idealised realm that must be kept clear tranquil, remote and free of any hint of marketing, commerce and money but rather as a form of commodity to be publicised, promoted and 'sold' so that it attracts a wider clientele, and hence increases the support levels of the institution and enhances what they perceive as the special nature and significance of the place. This should not be seen as a simple materialistic ploy by mercenary priests or as a cynical attempt to cash in on popular beliefs. As the various examples cited in this book thus far show, such marketing and promotion have a grounding in the concerns of religious officials to ensure the sites they oversee, and the sacred figures their shrines and temples enshrine, are supported, maintained and brought to the attention of (and hence can provide benefit to) wider audiences. For the nuns at Hokkeji, the continuing viability of their institution and what it stood for, was of immense importance—just as was the case with the priests of the Chita, Sasaguri and Shōdoshima pilgrimages cited in Chapter 1, for whom the possibility of declining pilgrim numbers required action, or the priests in Kyushu seeking to help people worried about the onset of senility while simultaneously sustaining the viability of their temples. None of them was operating simply in a cynical business fashion, with their eyes fixed solely on moneymaking and on viewing pilgrims (and the wider public) as potential customers to be fleeced so that they could become rich. For a priestly devotee of Kannon or Kōbō Daishi looking after a temple enshrining one of these figures, getting more pilgrims—and hence enhancing the status of their object of devotion rather than restricting numbers or decreeing that only the austerely devotional can enter—serves as the most viable way of carrying out their priestly duties and increasing the potential levels of devotion to their figures of worship. Much the same can be said of Catholic authorities who over the centuries have stolen or produced relics, promised indulgences, created Holy Years and built new and striking monuments and churches to entice pilgrims while, at times, trying to upstage their rivals.

This does not mean that there are no tensions between marketing activities and messages about the spiritually regenerative, enlightening or healing powers of pilgrimage and faith. The priests running the airport event cited in Chapter 1 made it clear that they were aware that there was a potential for incongruity in the setting of the event. Yet they also recognised that if they were to revive the pilgrimages that they had spent their lives supporting, and if they were to carry on spreading popular Buddhist teachings to those who visited their temples—if indeed they were to just keep their temples afloat—they needed to take such steps. Indeed, from a Japanese Buddhist perspective the notion of 'entering into the marketplace' has a long historical and reputable tradition. The story of the fifteenth-century Zen monk Ikkyū, who lived among and drank with beggars, drunks and thieves in the squalor of the marketplace in Kyoto and, in so doing, showed that the world of enlightenment is embedded in the realities of the mundane world, remains popular (Stevens 1993). The lotus flower itself is an important Buddhist symbol that features widely in Japanese Buddhism, both in one of its most important texts, the Lotus Sutra, but also in Buddhist iconography. The lotus flower is a symbol of enlightenment—one that grows out of the mud. As such, in Buddhist terms, it is an emblem of how one cannot separate the highest realms of Buddhist thought (i.e., enlightenment) from the earthy and mundane realm of mud. These images of the mud and of the marketplace as innately connected to the world of enlightenment occur frequently in the Japanese Buddhist context, and they speak of the inseparability of the mundane and the sacred. Modern priests promoting their sites through a commercial lens and at an airport mall are expressing a similar ethic. They may be commoditising their pilgrimages, but they also are recognising that in so doing, the sacred and the worldly are not discrete entities and that the latter is vital if the former is to be sustained and enhanced.

4 Merchants, Transport, Guidebooks and the Democratisation of Pilgrimage

INTRODUCTION: THE TEMPORARY TEA SHOPS OF AMARNATH

The first pilgrimage I went on was in 1971. I was in India, a footloose graduate more intent on wandering than working when I heard about a pilgrimage place in the mountains of Kashmir called Amarnath, the cave temple with a stalagmite that is venerated as a Shiva lingam. Having spent some months walking in the Himalayan foothills, I thought it would be interesting to walk to Amarnath and see what a pilgrimage was like at firsthand, and so, in early August 1971, I set out along the pilgrimage trail from Pahalgam, the Kashmiri town that is the main access point for Amarnath. I did so early in the pilgrimage season, well before pilgrim numbers were expected to reach their apex (along with the waxing of the ice lingam), to not be too bothered by crowds. Even so, I had plenty of people to talk to along the pilgrimage path—even for a day and a half walking with a group of Indian sadhus, communicating in a mixture of my poor and since forgotten Hindi and their rudimentary English. Apart from a very few better-off pilgrims who were travelling on horse- or pony-back and who were led by guides who cooked for them overnight, the pilgrims were all on foot.

Alongside the growing tide of pilgrims, another group caught my attention: a moving array of merchants, accompanied by pack animals laden with tents and other equipment, who were also were making their way along the Amarnath trail not as pilgrims but in order to provide services for the pilgrims. In the valleys and flat areas alongside streams, the merchants pitched their tents and laid out wooden boards to set up temporary tea shops where pilgrims could eat, drink tea and sleep overnight—all for a fee, of course. Some of these merchants were also selling warm clothes, blankets and foodstuffs to the passing pilgrim trade. As such, small clusters of temporary inns and shops—in effect, transient villages and marketplaces—sprang up along the way to cater to the pilgrims, who made full use of them.

At the time, I recall having somewhat idealistic and self-righteous thoughts about how outrageous it was for these people to be making money from earnest pilgrims, who were engaged in the arduous trek and some of whom seemed ill-clad for the potentially cold nights and changeable weather of the Himalayan foothills. Although I realised the merchants had brought their goods and tents up by pack animal from the nearest road or railheads, had incurred high overheads as a result, and thus needed to charge prices higher than down in the plains and towns below, I was nonetheless annoyed at what they charged for a cup of tea and felt it was especially unreasonable given that the merchants had a captive market. The fee for sleeping in their tents, too, although hardly costly, appeared excessive for just using a piece of tent floor space. The pilgrims, too, at times muttered about being taken advantage of—yet I also remember that they, like me, were pleased that food and tea were available and that they had shelter in an area where, even in August, the nights could be freezing cold and the weather potentially dangerous to anyone sleeping outdoors. I also conversed with some of the merchants, one of whom asked me what I thought the pilgrims would do if there were no support services. And although I initially resented the prices being charged for a glass of hot tea, I was glad to imbibe the warm, sweet liquid to refresh me after several hours of walking in the high terrain and to have a space to sleep in the relative warmth of the tent rather than having to hazard the night air. The pilgrims seemed of similar mind.

Nearly forty years later, that image of the merchants and their services still remains with me. The cave at Amarnath is a pilgrimage site because of its ice pillar and stories associating it with Shiva while its dramatic scenic setting helps enhance feelings that the place is somehow special (even if, in an area of breathtaking scenery, the 'ordinary' is itself quite special and dramatic). Yet even if Amarnath was thus marked out in the eyes of devout Hindus as a special place, another critical factor ensured that it became a viable place of pilgrimage for all but the hardiest and most ascetic: the merchants whose services made the pilgrimage feasible for the pilgrims. Perhaps if the merchants had not been there and pilgrims had been fewer, that might have enhanced the sacred nature of the site in the eyes of those who wish pilgrimage places to be remote and tranquil and want any hint of the mundane and commercial to be eradicated from them. Yet, without the merchants, who readily admitted that their purpose was to make money; without the transient marketplaces they created; and without the pilgrims whose travels were made possible as a result, Amarnath would have been just be a remote cave with a striking natural phenomenon, seemingly charged with magnetism yet devoid of pilgrims.

The Amarnath pilgrimage in the early 1970s was, in effect, sustained by the people whose goal was to profit commercially rather than to worship deities and pursue spiritual goals. In 1971, even with such support, pilgrim numbers remained relatively low; as late as the end of the 1980s, as I mentioned in Chapter 2, only about 12,000 people made the pilgrimage each year. Since then, increased support and better services have enabled Amarnath to become more accessible and prosper, as tour companies have provided package tours and as the regional government (aided by the Indian Army that maintains a high profile in the politically contested region) has developed better support services for pilgrims, including new roads to make the trip quicker. One can now book Amarnath package tour pilgrimages online, such as the nine-day Amarnath pilgrimage tour offered by India Tours, in which the pilgrim is met at the nearest airport (Srinagar), taken to Pahalgam to stay overnight in a hotel before being guided to and from the holy cave, each night sleeping in tents and having dinner cooked, before ending with three nights in Srinagar staying on one of the famous 'deluxe houseboats' moored on Lake Dhal and enjoying two days' sightseeing and relaxation around the lake and Srinagar itself.[1] Some package tours, as I noted in Chapter 2, also now make use of helicopters to allow even easier access for those who are rich enough and who wish to avoid much hiking.

LIKE FLIES TO HONEY? ECONOMIC BENEFITS AND THE PILGRIMAGE BUSINESS

The process evident at Amarnath illustrates a common dynamic in which entrepreneurial interests (often aided by civil and by religious authorities) provide support structures that may, as at Amarnath, become increasingly sophisticated over the years. If making pilgrimages more accessible and comfortable clearly increases their potential clientele, it can equally also provoke criticisms and complaints, such as in the following comment by Monsignor Pavao Zanic, Bishop of Mostar in what was then the state of Yugoslavia, reflecting on the rapid growth in popularity of the pilgrimage to Medjugorje:

> Wherever somebody says that Our Lady appeared then people come as a fly to honey—you get the miracles first, the cars and the buses next. (Wylie 1991: 23)

Although Zanic's comment may be partially explained by his known hostility to the Marian apparitions at Medjugorje (Vukonic 1992: 83–84) it also aptly reflects the recurrent complaint that I cited in Chapter 1, of those who view the commercial as a distasteful intrusion into the sacred realm of pilgrimage. Zanic's comments are based in his observations of what happened after the apparitions were first reported in the former Yugoslavian village in 1981. People certainly flocked there, encouraged by advertisements and services proffered by commercial agencies eager to capitalise on the phenomenon. Italian tour operators, for example, began organising Medjugorje tours using new coaches and aircraft, and they published brochures and magazines and advertised the pilgrimage so widely that, by 1987, just six years after the first apparitions, Medjugorje was being visited by 400,000 Italian pilgrims per year (Vukonic 1992: 87). As was noted in Chapter 2, regional and national tourist agencies also promoted the site and provided infrastructure support, thereby helping develop it into a significant pilgrimage centre, in a process not dissimilar to what happened at Amarnath and many of the other places discussed in this book, while enabling it to outstrip its local rivals.

It is hardly surprising that nonreligious agencies and economic actors are interested in pilgrimages, which can provide business opportunities and immense potential economic benefits for those who can tap into them by providing services that pilgrims are willing to use. Such providers need not be consumed by religious faith, of course, as was the case with the merchants of Amarnath. Similarly, faith is not a prerequisite for those living around pilgrimage centres and making their living from providing services for pilgrims. As Lochtefeld perceptibly notes, most residents in Hardwar, whose economic livelihood relies on pilgrimage, are not particularly pious. They are simply ordinary people who happen to live in a religious economy (Lochtefled 2010: 108). They are unsurprisingly happy to benefit and to make their livings from that economy, as are residents and interest groups in other places where pilgrimage is a major economic resource, such as Saudi Arabia where, according to recent estimates, pilgrimage nowadays contributes around $30 billion to the national economy—around 7 per cent of the oil-rich country's gross domestic product (GDP).[2] It is little wonder that there is a saying in Mecca that 'we do not need any agriculture—God has given us the pilgrims as our annual crop' (Coleman and Elsner 1995: 57). It is a sentiment with which people running businesses in San Giovanni Rotondo, the town where Padre Pio's shrine is, might well concur. In 1919, the year after stories that Padre Pio was manifesting stigmata began to draw people to San Giovanni, a senior cleric from the Capuchin order reported to his superiors that the 'business acumen' of the townspeople was a powerful motivating factor in this process (Luzzato 2007: 41). Once an impoverished backwater, the town has been transformed into a thriving mercantile centre of shops, hotels and restaurants centred on the pilgrimage cult of Padre Pio that, by the early 2000s, was generating an estimated $55 million annually for the town[3] and had led to the development of about 150 hotels (a sixfold increase since the late 1970s) and 250 restaurants and cafes. The town, as Sergio Luzzato (2007: 292) wryly remarks, benefits from the 'flourishing business of sainthood'. Towns in India such as Hardwar, Pushkar and Varanasi have effectively grown because of their status as pilgrimage centres, and activities related to pilgrimage dominate their economies. The largest single occupational group at Pushkar, for instance, is that of *pandagiri* (pilgrimage priests) who help in rituals and guide pilgrims around temples and who constitute approximately half of the town's workforce (Gladstone 2005: 188). In Japan, too, there is plentiful evidence to show how well many of those involved in the pilgrimage business have done over the ages. Pilgrims visiting the shrines of Ise in the Tokugawa period, for example, have left records showing how struck they were by the opulence of the homes of the guides who ran the Ise pilgrimage trade and organised their visits there (Kanzaki 1990: 187). In Taiwan, too, as Chang Hsun (2012: 306) indicates, both the Zhen Lan Temple (which has experienced a significant growth in pilgrim numbers since 2000) and local businesses around it have received an economic boost from the increased flow of pilgrims.

The pilgrimage business has likewise been a boon to the town and region of Lourdes, which by the mid-nineteenth century was in economic crisis due to the collapse of its traditional production and milling of grain. This led to local impoverishment and a population exodus before Bernadette's visions revitalised the region, reversed its population decline and led to a significant expansion of the town (R. Harris 1999: 28–29, 172–175). In the face of economic depression, local and regional civil authorities, merchants and entrepreneurs were, unsurprisingly, keen to take the opportunity the visions offered and to provide both information and the means (in terms of cheap lodgings, information and other facilities) to encourage pilgrims from across the economic spectrum to visit the place (Kaufman 2004).

Pilgrimage has clearly become Lourdes's 'crop', just as it has for the populations and civil and religious authorities of many other pilgrimage centres. Its critical importance to the region's economy was demonstrated in 1903 when legislators, driven by the avid secularism of the French Republic, sought to close Lourdes down as a pilgrimage site on the grounds that it pandered to superstition. The move was opposed by local government officials and businessmen, who argued that this would not just have an impact on religious interests but would cause economic decline and affect banks, the railway system and investors in general (Kaufman 2004: 194). The economic benefits of pilgrimage and 'superstition' (as the legislators saw it) trumped arguments based in secular rationalism and a modernising ethos. Merchants, civic officials and businesspeople in numerous places have similarly supported pilgrimages for economic reasons. Sarah Thal (2005: 100) shows that Konpira's pilgrimage cult was 'spread and supported by the owners of affiliated businesses as they used the deity to recruit customers', whereas Nam-Lin Hur (2009: 64) reports on how the merchants in Nagano, Japan, faced with an economic crisis in 1829, petitioned the town's great pilgrimage temple, Zenkōji, to hold a *kaichō* in order to boost pilgrim numbers and hence help alleviate their economic woes.

Economic interest is certainly a factor in persuading local officials and businesses to support pilgrimages and do what they can to ensure they flourish; similar to the interest groups at Lourdes and Nagano, they are aware that if pilgrimages go into decline, they and their local communities will suffer. This is evident from the declining fortunes of the Shōdoshima pilgrimage discussed in Chapter 1. The downturn in pilgrim numbers is severely undermining the island's economy, with lodges, inns, souvenir shops and restaurants that made their living off the pilgrimage, being forced to close down. This has in turn threatened the island's long-term economic, social and cultural well-being and is a significant factor in the population exodus that is further damaging the island. The owner of one pilgrims' lodge there told me that only ten of the thirty lodges that had existed two decades ago remained as of 2010, and with pilgrim numbers continuing to decline, she worried about the future of the rest, hers included. Island civic officials and pilgrimage temple priests alike are similarly concerned about the economic problems that falling pilgrim numbers are bringing; fewer pilgrims meant not just fewer nights spent in inns but fewer meals eaten in local restaurants, and less spent on souvenirs and the like, thereby contributing to a continuing downward spiral.[4] Businesses in and around Sasaguri have been similarly concerned at the decline in pilgrim numbers there, and have as a result been keen to join with the pilgrimage temples in promotional campaigns. The Sasaguri Ryokan Kyōkai (the Sasaguri Association of Inns), for example, cosponsored a *degaichō* exhibition put on by the Sasaguri temples in the city of Kumamoto, in the southern half of Kyushu, in September 2007 in the hope of boosting pilgrim numbers and saving their businesses. I discuss a further example of such business, civic and temple cooperation in Chapter 7, where I examine recent developments in Shikoku.

INTERACTIONS, TENSIONS AND LEGITIMATIONS

It is thus unsurprising that various commercial agencies and civil interest groups have been keen over the ages to stimulate and encourage the practice of pilgrimage and to offer services that enable them to profit thereby. Despite the aforementioned reservations of Monsignor Zavic, religious groups and priests involved in running and developing pilgrimage sites have generally concurred with rather than repelled such commercial engagement.[5] A good example is provided by the Mahabodhi Society in its campaign to 'reinvent' and promote Buddhist pilgrimage sites in nineteenth-century India. The Mahabodhi Society saw rail travel as a powerful tool in this process, encouraging Buddhist pilgrims to use the railways and negotiating special concession fares for those who wanted to visit Buddhist sites. (This tactic of pilgrimage promotion had been used earlier by the Assumptionist Fathers in nineteenth-century France, when they called for Lourdes to be the focus of a national pilgrimage and negotiated with the rail company to get special reduced rail fares for pilgrims in conjunction with this campaign [Kaufman 2004: 26]). The Indian rail services cooperated by granting concessionary pilgrim fares in 1935 and in the same year running a 'pilgrimage special' from Darjeeling (where a significant number of Buddhists, mostly Tibetans, lived) to Sarnath, one of the tradition's main centres. The Mahabodhi Society in return praised rail companies for publicising Buddhist pilgrimage sites and advocated rail pilgrimage as 'safe, friendly and convenient'. Indian State Railways reciprocated by placing advertisements in the society's monthly magazine *The Maha Bodhi* in the late 1930s to advertise their services and to support pilgrimages to Buddhist sites (Huber 2008: 304–305).

The Shikoku temples, too, have worked with and benefitted significantly from the support and actions of a variety of agencies, from local commercial firms to civic authorities and regional tourist agencies (Reader 2005,

2007a, Mori 2005). Later in this chapter and in Chapter 7, I look further at this case. Yet even if such interactions have been mutually beneficial to temples and companies alike, this does not mean that these interest groups are necessarily operating within the same agendas and frameworks. Priests at the Shikoku temples, for example, while recognising that bus companies such as Iyo Tetsu—the Shikoku-based company that inaugurated the first bus package tours and that still is a key agent in ensuring that the pilgrimage remains successful—have helped the temples immeasurably, are also conscious that their primary concerns and interests are different in nature from those of the commercial agencies they interact with. Although the temples might emphasise that the promotion of religious agendas and faith are their main concerns, commercial enterprises have a primary aim of making and enhancing profits and developing their commercial portfolios and the interests of their shareholders.

The priests in Kyushu involved in setting up the Kannon pilgrimage discussed in Chapter 3 were clear in this point, as was the president of the bus company whose support was so useful to their endeavour. Both parties not only wanted the pilgrimage to succeed, but they also were open about their differing motivations for so doing. For the priests, faith and increased support for their temples and the Buddhist tradition they belonged to were the key issues they wished to talk about and to propagate. For the bus company president, however much he talked of wanting to help the region, to generate a sense of regional identity and pride and to promote faith in the Buddhist tradition he was a devotee of, he was clear that, as president of a commercial company, profits and the expansion of his company's clientele were his primary concerns. Without them, his company would fail. This did not mean that the company was only interested in profits or that he viewed the temples and pilgrimage purely instrumentally as something to be exploited for profit—or that the priests were wholly disinterested in the potential economic benefits that their engagement with commercial firms could bring. Both the company president and the priests alike recognised that their interests dovetailed and that economic benefits and enhanced faith and practice were inextricably linked. For the priests, economic survival (without which they would be unable to maintain their temples and continue to promote their faith or provide religious services for pilgrims and other supplicants) was an important element in their engagement with the bus company, even if the mutual rhetoric both shared centred far more on comments about enhancing faith, regional culture and identity, and thereby neatly avoided overt discussion of the economic dimensions of their enterprise.

Similarly, the bus company president sought to frame his interests within a rhetoric of piety that accorded profit making (a crucial raison d'être of his company) a noble status and that even implied that the real interest of his company was in supporting local culture and faith, with any profit merely an unexpected, unintended consequence.[6] This could be seen as a classic example of what C. Wright Mills (1940: 907) described as 'situated actions and vocabularies of motive'—of how people may speak in terms of moral motives when engaging in what are evidently activities of mercantile benefit to themselves. Mills uses the example of the businessman who joins the rotary club and proclaims its public-spirited nature as a reason for so doing. This, he says, is clearly an example of someone who feels that assigning an altruistic motive to what might appear to be a business and profit-centred activity is important (Mills 1940: 907).

Commercial firms that engage in pilgrimage business ventures are often keen to talk in this way. In numerous discussions with such organisations in Japan, I have rarely, if ever, heard anyone say that he or she is only in the pilgrimage business for monetary reasons. Commonly, people initially couch their commercial motivations with seemingly altruistic motivations. In April 1987, for instance, I had a conversation about such issues with an official from the Hankyū Railway Company, a private rail company based in Osaka that, at the time, was promoting a *Hankyū Shichifukujin Meguri* (the Hankyū Railway's Seven Gods of Good Fortune Pilgrimage). All seven sites (a mixture of Shinto shrines and Buddhist temples that reflected the Seven Gods' eclectic nature [Reader and Tanabe 1998: 156–163]) involved in the pilgrimage were close to Hankyū stations and hence could best be done using its trains, and Hankyū was offering special concession tickets to those who wanted to do the pilgrimage. The pilgrimage had been thought up by company officials, who had good relations with various shrines and temples along their lines and regularly used them in publicity campaigns, for example, when encouraging people to use the Hankyū line and adjacent temples and shrines for the customary annual New Year shrine visit that marks the beginning of the year in Japan. Seven Gods of Good Fortune pilgrimages were very popular in Japan at the time, because they tended to be short and easily done in a day or so and because the gods, associated with good fortune and luck, have a very positive, cheerful image. In 1973, an enterprising Buddhist priest, Iwatsubo Shinkō, had established such a pilgrimage on Awaji, an island in the Inland Sea that is easily accessible from major population centres in the Osaka-Kobe region. He persuaded the local tourist office and regional transport companies to support the pilgrimage, which proved to be so popular that it became a key tourist resource for the island as well as generating a surge in Seven Gods pilgrimages throughout Japan (Reader and Tanabe 1998: 199, Ōishi 1989: 189–191). Several railway companies in different parts of the country established their own Seven Gods of Good Fortune pilgrimages to capitalise on this popularity, and Hankyū was thus joining in a wider trend. When I talked to the official, however, his initial explanation of why Hankyū was doing this was to talk about the company's sense of responsibility towards the region where it plied its business, towards the upholding of Japanese cultural traditions and towards local shrines and temples that were part of the region's cultural heritage. The new pilgrimage was, as such, the company's attempt to link such things together for the greater good of the region, a position that certainly sounded, similar to Mills's rotary club members, altruistic and noble. When probed further, he did then admit that, yes, the company did hope to increase custom as a result and that there was an ulterior and mercantile motive to it all.

Likewise, when in 2008 the Saikoku temples were trying to reverse the downward trend in pilgrim numbers, as well as the *kaichō* campaign mentioned in Chapter 1, it also engaged in a publicity campaign with Japan Rail West, which serves the region where the Saikoku temples are located. The campaign offered concession rail tickets that also provided entry to the temples and special gift items for pilgrims, and it was widely supported with posters at Japan Rail stations and on its website and elsewhere, advertising the pilgrimage and emphasising the beauty of its temples and their settings. When I talked to rail officials involved in the campaign, they were keen to tell me that Japan Rail was doing this for the public good, as a way of enhancing knowledge of an important Japanese historical tradition and cultural institution, thereby contributing to public understandings of Japanese culture. Similar to the Hankyū official mentioned earlier, they also agreed, in response to further questioning, that ultimately the key issue for Japan Rail was a commercial one related to increasing customer numbers.[7]

In my various discussions over two decades with officials of Iyo Tetsu and other bus companies in Shikoku, similar juxtapositions of talk about the public good and support for island cultural traditions, alongside recognition of ultimate profit motives, have occurred repeatedly. Iyo Tetsu entered the pilgrimage business in the 1950s by running bus tours of Shikoku, thereafter becoming the main provider of such services, for commercial reasons related to its long-term survival. Pilgrimage offered it a potential lifeline and an economic opportunity in an era when the prognosis of rising car ownership and rural population decline meant that many of its bus services (which were dependent on rural populations) were unlikely to be profitably sustainable in the longer term. Hence, some means of diversification was necessary. At the time, Japanese law changed to allow bus companies to run organised tours (previously they had been restricted to timetabled passenger routes), and with the Shikoku pilgrimage being the island's most significant attraction, company officials decided that running pilgrimage tours would be a viable strategy to sustain and enhance the business. It has worked well, with bus package tours expanding exponentially from the 1950s through to the mid-1990s (Seki 1999), at which point the dominance of the bus tour started to be challenged by the turn towards car pilgrimages.

To advance its commercial agenda and to secure favourable support for its tours, the company has developed very close ties with the Shikoku temples. Company officials I have interviewed have spoken on several occasions about this relationship, as have temple priests. On various occasions when I have been visiting priests at different temples, bus company officials (not just from Iyo Tetsu, as other major Shikoku companies such as the Kotosan company of Takamatsu also operate similarly) have called by to discuss future plans or to pay courtesy calls. The atmosphere between the companies and

Figure 4.1 Poster advertising the Japan Rail/Saikoku pilgrimage campaign.

temples appears overall to be close and based around shared interests. Iyo Tetsu has cooperated with the temples to sponsor publicity campaigns and exhibitions, and, as was noted in the previous chapter, it also has been a key sponsor of the *sendatsu* system that has helped spread awareness of the pilgrimage in modern times (Mori 2005, Reader 2005: 163–167).

The Shikoku Reijōkai has recognised the company's contribution in such terms by awarding Iyo Tetsu honorary *sendatsu* status—an honour marked by a red pilgrim's staff presented by the temple association to the company and displayed in a glass case at its headquarters in Matsuyama. Iyo Tetsu—similar to many other bus companies—engages *sendatsu* to assist with its tours and its bus guides are often keen to talk in devotional terms about the pilgrimage, the temples and miraculous events to the parties they guide. I have interviewed Iyo Tetsu bus guides who have expressed highly devotional attitudes, and have heard various stories of their bus guides criticising pilgrims for being too intent on enjoying themselves and not being sufficiently devout at the temples. This does not mean that all company employees are devout, as I have also talked to some for whom taking pilgrims around the route is just a job.[8]

The pilgrimage is of immense economic importance to the company, whose officials recognise that it became involved in developing package tours for strategic business reasons. They also have tended to phrase their discussions of the pilgrimage along the lines of the officials cited earlier at Hankyū and other companies—as acts of service helping uphold a significant local tradition vital to Shikoku's identity—while emphasising that piety and care for pilgrims is intrinsic to their activities. This does not mean that they are simply cynical and engaging in artifices when they talk about their support for the pilgrimage. Rather, there is a recognition that providing a good service in ways that make pilgrims keen to use them again and in ways that ensure that religious authorities continue to endorse them is a vital business strategy, along with an awareness that, as a Shikoku-based company, the pilgrimage is a powerful element in their local identity.[9] At the same time, the ways in which companies such as those discussed earlier feel the need to couch their economic motives within a rhetoric of accounts and piety serves as a further indication of the unease that is manifest when religion and economics are discussed, even though, as has been emphasised throughout this book, the two are inextricably entwined.

PACKAGE TOURS, CONVENIENCE AND SAFETY: DEMOCRATISING PILGRIMAGE AND UNIVERSALISING ACCESS

Economic motivations are evidently and understandably high on the agenda of commercial firms and of civil agencies that benefit from large influxes of pilgrims into their towns and regions, even if they sometimes like to couch their actions in altruistic terms. Their involvement and the services they provide, whether economically driven or not, have a powerful impact on the ways in which pilgrimages develop and are performed and in widening participation in them. The infrastructures that are developed through their actions—frequently nowadays involving hotels rather than tents, and aeroplanes, high-speed trains, cars and buses rather than horses and ponies—have made pilgrimages into a viable mass phenomenon accessible to increasing numbers of people and into an increasingly safe activity removed from worries about being lost, not knowing what to do in strange lands and so on.

Such activities have deep-seated historical origins. In medieval Europe the merchants of Venice provided what Sumption (1975: 188) describes as the 'earliest all-inclusive package tours' that enabled pilgrims to avoid the dangers of the overland route to Jerusalem and assuaged their worries by providing them with accommodation, food, information and guides so they would be cared for when visiting the Christian holy places. The rise of Venice as an entrepôt for medieval Holy Land package tours was accompanied by the development of a tourist office established by the city authorities to assist pilgrims and to guard against complaints that might have an impact on their trade, put future pilgrims off and hence threaten the economic interests of the city (Chareyrou 2000: 41). In a similar era, Japanese pilgrimage guides were organising package tours to places such as Kumano and Ise, helping their customers to avoid the worries of travelling into the unknown by organising their itineraries, showing them the correct paths to follow, providing them with accommodation and guiding them through rituals and getting them access to priests and the sanctums of shrines and temples (Kanzaki 1990).

These services have been central to the eradication of danger and fear, concerns that have been a serious impediment to many potential pilgrims over the ages. In premodern times, pilgrimage could certainly be a dangerous enterprise, as is amply illustrated by historical accounts of the pilgrimage to Mecca in earlier eras, which provide numerous examples of diseases, attacks, starvation and other horrors that beset pilgrims and endangered or cost them their lives, such as the pestilence that killed about one-sixth of all pilgrims there in 1893 (Peters 1995: 309). The Santiago pilgrimage was also highly precarious in premodern times; as Rachel Bard (1989: 190) says, it was 'fraught with uncertainty and sometimes real danger'. Japanese pilgrims, too, faced uncertainties and perils along the way, with pilgrim deaths being a regular occurrence on the Shikoku route and danger an accompanying reality for pilgrims there (Maeda 1971: 99–103, Reader 2005: 132–133).

Similar patterns of danger, unease and death can be found throughout the premodern pilgrimage world, and they served as a serious limiting factor to who could realistically become pilgrims, as did the other factors—finances, social attitudes and legal structures—that made travel difficult until comparatively recently. Long-distance pilgrimages were effectively, as a result, restricted for the most part to the hardy and those who were willing to put their lives at risk,[10] rather than being feasible for women (especially on their own), the elderly, the very young and the infirm. People such as the female Shikoku pilgrim in her late sixties who was taking part in a pilgrimage package tour I went on in 1991 and who had difficulties climbing the steps to one of the Shikoku temples because of her heart problems (Reader 2005: 232–233) would hardly have been able to consider going on the pilgrimage in the pre–bus tour era without risking her life. She belonged to a gender and an age group that until the advent of bus tours and their accompanying infrastructures, such as good lodgings, was a real minority in Japanese pilgrimage terms. Although women accounted for almost one-third of Shikoku pilgrims at some periods in the Tokugawa era, this was a far higher percentage than any other Japanese pilgrimage of the era (Satō 2004: 118). The figure is also misleading in that they were mainly young women from within the island taking part in group pilgrimages around some regional sections of the route that served as an adult initiation ritual on the island (Maeda 1971: 182–183). There were few women coming to the island from outside or making the trek around the whole route; pilgrims were by and large male and generally young. Even these male pilgrims tended to a great degree to be quite local. In the Tokugawa period and through the nineteenth century, the vast majority of Shikoku pilgrims came from the island itself and from proximate areas across the Inland Sea, with almost none from the more distant (e.g., northern Japan) parts of the country, for whom the time needed just to get there and back on foot made it next to impossible (Maeda 1971: 159).

The development of a national rail system from the late nineteenth century onwards, along with boat (and later air) services and road networks enabling people to get more quickly to and from Shikoku, and train services and bus package tours within the island, has not just made the pilgrimage safer; they have made Shikoku easier to reach and quicker to do as a pilgrimage. As a result, its pilgrimage clientele now comes from all over the Japanese archipelago, including the northern prefecture of Hokkaidō, geographically quite distant from Shikoku but now a prime source of pilgrims, as well as from Japanese emigrant communities in Hawaii, Latin America and the United States mainland (Osada, Sakata and Seki 2003: 226–228). The gender structure, too, has changed significantly with the rise of bus tours and greater modes of convenience and safety, as has the general age profile of the pilgrims. By the turn of the current century, women were in the majority (57 per cent according to Satō [2004: 218]) whereas those older than sixty have become the largest age group in Shikoku, counting for around two-thirds of all pilgrims there (Osada, Sakata and Seki 2003: 226).

The development of organised tours and infrastructures, along with, in the modern era, increasingly comfortable means of travel, has not wholly eradicated danger from all routes, as is evident from news reports indicating that the high altitude and rapidly changing Himalayan weather can still claim the lives of Amarnath pilgrims, and occasional reports of pilgrims dying in stampedes and crushes during the hajj.[11] However, overall they have progressively made pilgrimage far safer and more accessible, thereby, as the Shikoku example indicates, breaking down gender boundaries and making it more readily open to higher (and, indeed, lower) age groups as well. Pilgrimage tour operators in Shikoku, for example, regularly advertise their services with the assurance that they allow pilgrims to travel with a sense of peace of mind, safety and comfort (Reader 1987a). By so doing and by thereby opening up pilgrimage to segments of society that had not previously been well represented in the pilgrim community, they have effectively democratised the practice in Japan and made it safely reassuring. They have done so elsewhere too, as David Gladstone (2005: 189) illustrates in his discussion of how pilgrimage in India has become more democratic and more of a mass phenomenon in modern times due to cheap mass transport, the elimination of the hazards of travel and the development of increasing amounts of affordable pilgrim lodgings. Similar democratisation aided the growth of Lourdes as a mass pilgrimage site in the second half of the nineteenth century, when convenient travel infrastructures enabled people to come from all over France (and farther afield) and affordable places to stay made it accessible to those of modest means across the social spectrum and across gender boundaries. Such developments were especially valuable to female pilgrims, who were offered the opportunity to get away from traditional conservative village backgrounds and encounter the modern urban life and shops that were emerging around Lourdes (Kaufman 2004: 35–43).

The exponential growth of hajj pilgrim numbers to Mecca in modern times is another example of how the development of mass transport systems coupled with improved organisational structures, facilities and safety measures have increased access to once-distant pilgrimage places. For centuries geography, distance and poverty had been major obstacles for those seeking to do the hajj, but during the nineteenth century, this began to change as the development of steamships and railroads made travel safer and faster (Bianchi 2004: 49). Even so, pilgrims still faced the likelihood of disease and insanitary conditions which, as was noted previously, at times caused widespread death among Muslims travellers. From the twentieth century onwards, the development of better hygiene facilities and immunisation reduced such risks and made the pilgrimage less precarious. Yet even so, most pilgrims (about three-quarters in all) still travelled by sea and land as late as the 1960s. In ensuing decades, however, the development of mass air transport, supplemented by a growing package tour and hotel industry that has offered increasingly comfortable (and even sumptuous) accommodation (an issue I look at further in Chapter 7), has made the Arabian peninsula considerably closer in temporal terms and more comfortable for Muslims throughout the world. It has enabled people from far-distant countries such as Indonesia (which has the world's largest Muslim population) to make the journey in hours rather than months or years—and more safely and with less risk of disease.

Figure 4.2 Pilgrim accommodation in Knock.

These developments have occurred in tandem with several significant economic and social changes. The rising tide of independence since World War Two removed barriers to travel that had formerly been imposed on Muslims in numerous countries in Asia and Africa, who had been who discouraged or prevented by the colonial governments of the time from going on the hajj for fear it might instil a sense of independence into them. Independence also brought economic growth for some of these countries, whereas many parts of the Muslim world have benefitted from oil revenues—all of which meant increasing numbers of Muslims were able to afford to go on pilgrimage (Bianchi 2004: 49–70).

These factors have increased the numbers of pilgrims significantly. In the 1930s, pilgrim numbers for the hajj were estimated to have been around 30,000 in all (about one in 10,000 of the world's Muslim population at the time), whereas in the 1950s, pilgrim numbers rarely reached 100,000. Subsequently air transport has meant that the numbers are annually well into the millions (Bianchi 2004: 49), and each year nowadays around one in 500 of the world's Muslims does the hajj. Although other factors have also spurred this rise (including a rising tide of Muslim international consciousness that cannot be wholly separated from reactions to perceived threats to Islam from policies such as the so-called war on terror, as well as a growing Muslim population worldwide) a crucial element in this process

98 *Pilgrimage in the Marketplace*

has been the mass transport business aligned to the increasing safety and viability of the journey.

Although there may be those who think that hardship and danger might increase the allure of pilgrimage places,[12] eradication of these elements (or, at least, their marginalisation, in which pilgrims can now choose ways of avoiding them) has been intrinsic to the expansion of pilgrimage. The result has been, certainly, an enhanced commercial presence in pilgrimage contexts, but the corollary of this has been the growing democratisation of pilgrimage, in which gender and age boundaries have been eroded and distant sites have come within the ambit of people who formerly would have had little or no chance to visit places important to their religious traditions, such as Shikoku and Mecca. These are issues that those bemoaning the commercial dimensions of pilgrimage and the erosion of the formerly remote and dangerous nature of some sites might do well to consider.

IMPACT: DEMOCRATISATION, TRANSPORT AND THE PROMOTION OF CULTURAL IDENTITY

The democratising process has also helped make pilgrimage fit in with the processes of modernisation and has shown that, far from being tied to or a product of the premodern world, pilgrimage accords with and is stimulated by modernity. As Ruth Harris (1999: 247) has commented about Lourdes,

> National pilgrimage was made possible by mass circulation press, train links and the managerial techniques of the hospital administration; it cannot, therefore, be dismissed as the final appearance of anachronistic superstition.

India provides another good example not only of how pilgrimage clienteles are increased through the development of quicker and more widespread transport networks, but also of how such processes may be aligned to other aspects of the modern world in helping create new cultural frameworks within which pilgrimages can flourish and through which they may also assume new orientations. In the early twentieth century, few Indian villagers were able to go on pilgrimages. Poverty, poor transport and lack of the means to get away for extended periods, tied them largely to their own localities. Modern developments—including mass education and mass media that have helped develop a more extensive national consciousness and made people more widely aware of Hindu holy places, a mechanised transport system that have made such places readily accessible, and improved health facilities that made travel safer[13]—have changed this (Fuller 1992: 205). The railways played a significant role in developing pilgrimages while simultaneously helping shape a modern national cultural consciousness that accorded with the contours and orientations of the modern nation state. As

Ian J. Kerr (2001a: 48) has commented, rail travel helped strengthen the notion of a sacred national Indian geography. The railways enabled people to travel beyond the confines of their local regions and to develop a sense of awareness to match; from being inhabitants of villages with little communication or connection to more distant places, they became parts of a wider, interconnected nation, and this effectively helped instil in them an understanding of India as a national and cultural phenomenon. As such, as railways spread from the second half of the nineteenth century onwards, they increased the potential clientele of pilgrimage centres throughout the subcontinent and were a significant factor in the growth of pilgrim numbers in India, whether at regional Muslim pilgrimage sites such as Ajmer (Kerr 2001a: 56), or at Hindu sites such as Hardwar (Lochtefeld 2010: 50). In making pilgrimages more feasible for greater numbers of people, they also helped boost female pilgrim numbers (Kerr 2001b: 312), another example of how modernity and mass transport have helped break down gender barriers and widen access.

The more people were able to travel beyond the ambit of their home regions—and at all times of year—the greater potential pilgrimage places had to transcend their local orientations and become national in scope (Bhardwaj 1973: 5, Kerr 2001b: 316). Places such as Hardwar that were initially little more than local or regional in context were transformed into national pilgrimage sites that could feature on national itineraries and could become potential pilgrimage goals for people from distant parts of the subcontinent. Those running the railways were certainly quick to grasp the potential of pilgrimage and to realise that it could serve as a very useful way to persuade customers to use their newly built lines. Thus, they embarked on marketing campaigns that promoted the 'desirability of pilgrimage' (Kerr 2001b: 324). The Indian Railway Board (an umbrella organisation overseeing the railway system) produced publications extolling the value of travelling by rail, such as its 1911 book *The Travellers Companion Containing a Brief Description of Places of Pilgrimage and Important Towns in India*, which encouraged people to visit pilgrimage sites. The sections on pilgrimage were later published separately in Hindi and Urdu translations, whereas railway magazines further drew attention to pilgrimage places in order to promote rail travel (Kerr 2001b: 324).

Indian Railways were thus operating in a manner similar to French National Railways which, as we saw in Chapter 2, promoted rail travel to Lourdes in the second half of the nineteenth century in order to boost custom on its newly built line in the region and to help develop its own stature as a national service. Japan's Railway Ministry similarly used pilgrimage sites as a mechanism to promote rail travel and to encourage people to use the developing national rail network. In 1922, it produced a book titled *Omairi* that encouraged visits to shrines and temples using rail services, and portrayed such visits as ways of imbibing Japanese culture and experiencing its history (Tetsudōshō 1922). One of the aims of the ministry was to promote a national sense of identity and pride in Japan's cultural heritage, and

100 *Pilgrimage in the Marketplace*

it established a national agency, the Japan Travel Bureau (JTB), to aid in this. From the 1920s onwards, the ministry and the JTB began to produce various guidebooks that included prominent pilgrimage sites accessible by train, and that showed how pilgrimages such as Shikoku could be done quickly, conveniently and comfortably by train and other modes of transport (Mori 2005: 45–47). This linking together of rail travel, pilgrimage and a sense of national culture and identity was, of course, intended to make pilgrimage more attractive to a wider number of people. Pilgrimage as promoted by such national rail agencies was thus portrayed as a form of travel connected particularly with the enhancement of a modern national cultural identity—a theme that has continued to permeate much contemporary pilgrimage publicity in Japan (Reader 1987a and b, 2007a).

This process has continued in more recent times. Mori (2005: 174–177) shows, for example, how the national rail operator (Japan Rail) promoted themes of nostalgia and identity in its 'Discover Japan' campaigns designed to get people to explore their own country (and patronise rural and underused rail routes) and how it tied the Shikoku pilgrimage into this process from the 1970s on. This drew also on the widespread themes of nostalgia and interest in images of 'traditional' Japan that were a major part of Japanese travel and of travel and religious publicity in the 1970s and 1980s that I commented on in Chapter 2 and that has persisted into the present day. Regional government agencies have become interested in the pilgrimage as a means of boosting local identity and the economy, especially by attracting tourists from other parts of Japan to the island. Thus, they, too, sought to promote the pilgrimage as a cultural property and as a regional tourist asset, often linking such activities to national campaigns aimed at persuading more Japanese to visit rural areas and providing infrastructure support to make the pilgrimage route more accessible (Mori 2005: 200–205, 225–227; see also Chapter 7).

RESHAPING PILGRIM UNDERSTANDINGS AND PRACTICES

Railways were not just a means to get to pilgrimage sites or an element in the development of modern national consciousness and of identity formation. They affected how pilgrims viewed and understood their journeys, and became very much part of the experience of pilgrimage. The example of Tibetan Buddhists using the train pilgrimage services to Indian Buddhist sites that were promoted by the Mahabodhi Society and Indian Railways from the 1930s is a case in point. Few Tibetan pilgrims had been on trains before, and the experience proved transformative; many saw the train journey as the highlight of their pilgrimage and began to wish that their homeland had railways. Pilgrimage thus became a means of introducing people in the Tibetan community to the mechanical 'wonders' of the modern age, and they liked them enough to rapidly abandon older pilgrimage practices and to use rail wherever they could rather than walking. They began also to talk of rail travel as strenuous and a form of hardship ritual in its own right (Huber 2008: 309–310). Rail travel, in other words, began to displace ascetic foot travel in their visions of pilgrimage. It is a clear example of how readily pilgrims may adopt new modes of convenience and how little they might view ascetic practice as intrinsic to pilgrimage, an issue I discuss further in Chapter 5.

Buddhist and Hindu organisations alike embraced the railways while accepting that this new mode of transport would radically alter how people did pilgrimages. The Mahabodhi Society's aforementioned readiness to encourage railway pilgrimages was reflected also in the activities of Hindu organisations. Hindu organisations, too, declared that it was legitimate to travel by rail without losing the merits of pilgrimage, and such declarations also helped shift the emphasis in Hindu pilgrimage away from asceticism and foot travel (Huber 2008: 304). This greatly expanded the potential of Hindu sites to extend their clientele beyond the local and become national sites capable of attracting pilgrims from far and wide. As has been seen in earlier chapters, this embracing by Indian religious organisations of new means of travel now extends to helicopters and other means of conveyance. Such affirmations of the legitimacy of using modern means of transport can be found across the pilgrimage spectrum. As the Indian examples cited here indicate, religious authorities, faced with the choice between ascetic purity and the possibility of encouraging mass participation, appear more than ready to choose the latter and affirm the importance of universal accessibility and nonexclusiveness. As will be seen in the next chapter, so, too, have pilgrims readily embraced these means of travel, which have not only made pilgrimage more accessible for more people, and the convenience and comforts they have brought with them.

DEMOCRATISATION AND THE TOURIST IMPULSE

The progressive improvement of conditions and services, and the speeding up of pilgrimage, have been intrinsic to the enhanced attractiveness of pilgrimage in the modern day. They have equally strengthened the potential for ludic and tourist activities, which have historically, as has been emphasised in earlier chapters, been part of the attraction of pilgrimage sites and which have been enhanced as the pilgrimage service industry has been able to provide more comfort and support for pilgrims. Sumption has discussed how the rise of package tour pilgrimages to the Christian Holy Land brought about by the commercial acumen of Venetian merchants in medieval Europe made pilgrimage easier and safer and, in so doing, how this increased the scope and potential for ludic behaviour among pilgrims. As a result, he argues, by the fifteenth-century tourism was replacing spirituality as a leading motive for pilgrims (Sumption 1975: 257). Similarly, in Japan, where the interweaving of pilgrimage and tourism has been evident in the ways in which sites such as Konpira based their attractiveness for visitors around religious practices and narratives related to the gods along with the entertainment and sightseeing opportunities a visit to the shrine offered. From early on, too, *kaichō* and *degaichō* exhibitions of sacred icons were packaged as entertainment and tourist events (Ishimori 1995).

This linkage with tourism is one that has been a recurrent theme in the study of pilgrimage. Although, as evidenced by my comments in Chapter 1, there has been a sense of unease in some quarters about associating pilgrimage with entertainment, there have also been many who have queried the viability of making clear differentiations between tourism and pilgrimage. Victor and Edith Turner's (1978: 20) famous statement that a 'tourist is half a pilgrim, if a pilgrim is half a tourist' was an early marker of this perspective, whereas Susan Naquin and Chün-Fang Yü (1992: 22) extended this point further by arguing convincingly that it is methodologically unhelpful to make differentiations between the two in the context of pilgrimage sites. Ellen Badone and Sharon R. Roseman's (2004) edited study of pilgrimage, and Badone (2004: 184–187), further emphasise that it is highly problematic to think of pilgrimage and tourism in dichotomous terms. In Japanese contexts, Hayami (1983) has shown how central tourist themes were for the development and popularity of pilgrimages such as the Chichibu Kannon pilgrimage in the Tokugawa period. He indicates that, for residents of Edo (present-day Tokyo), Chichibu's beautiful scenery and attractions (close enough to home to be accessible but distant enough to escape their home environments) offered the opportunity for pleasant visits coupled with prayer and supplications; they could thus be pilgrims and tourists at the same time (Hayami 1983: 329). Pilgrimage sites, from Rome to Jersualem to Ise and Saikoku, have often been tourist attractions because of their historical associations and because they manifest such things as fine architecture, statues and other art, as well as opportunities to shop, buy souvenirs and enjoy the services provided for pilgrims. The same is so in India, where pilgrimage sites such as Pushkar and Varanasi are simultaneously tourist destinations. The phenomena that attract pilgrims there—the temples, architecture, festivals, and so on—are what also attract tourists. Pilgrims and tourists share the same infrastructure and act in similar ways, whereas many travel agencies specialise in pilgrimages *and* in leisure travel (Gladstone 2005: 177–178). To that extent, the tourist dimensions of such sites appear to be becoming more potent in modern times. Visitors to Hindu pilgrimage places are often not just keen to go sightseeing and to express a combination of pilgrimage and tourist motives in their travels, but may even emphasise that they are tourists rather than pilgrims (Bhardwaj 1985: 247, Gladstone 2005: 173). As Lochtefeld (2010: 101) comments, Hardwar, which developed as a pilgrimage site, has become 'a tourist destination in its own right'.

The democratising process, spurred by the engagement of commercial firms, has made the inherent linkages of pilgrimage and tourism more marked

Figure 4.3 Roadside advertisement by a travel firm in Shōdoshima offering pilgrimage and tourist bus tours.

still. The Japanese example of Enoshima—a popular pilgrimage site with a well-known shrine not far from Tokyo—is indicative here. By the early twentieth century, it had become linked to the capital by rail and this increased the number of people who were able to visit the shrine. Because it was within easy access of the sea, Enoshima also became known as a place for summer bathing with the result that people could combine pilgrimage visits to its shrine with such activities, so that it 'took on more of the flavor of a resort than a place of pilgrimage' (Ishimori 1995: 19).

In Chapter 5, I look more closely at how pilgrim desires for comfort have further deepened the associations between pilgrimage and tourism, and in Chapter 7, I look at how recent pilgrimage developments have intensified this process still more. Here, the point to note is that the links and potential convergence between pilgrimage and tourism have been systematically enhanced by the expansion of opportunities offered through the development of package tours and mass transportation. These have also added another factor into the pilgrimage dynamic: the importance of schedules and timetables. This is a product in many ways both of the package tour business, which requires people to be in place and hotel A on night B and so on, and of the plane and train schedules that pilgrims use. Pilgrims who make long-distance pilgrimages by aeroplane (for example, to Mecca) have return flights that they need to catch and, hence, need to ensure that they can fit in all the necessary rituals and visits to different sites within the wider pilgrimage, within the time allotted before they have to be back at the airport (and, indeed, perhaps their workplaces). Pilgrimage tours, such as those run by companies such as Iyo Tetsu and the tour I have described elsewhere (Reader 2005: 217–248), are based on ensuring the buses reach particular lunchtime restaurants and evening lodging venues at convenient times, are able to deposit their passengers back at their destinations at the right time to catch planes or trains back to their homes, and so on.

Scheduling becomes an important part of mass pilgrimages in other respects too; as hajj numbers have grown, authorities in Saudi Arabia have sought to ensure that the mass activity runs smoothly by arranging schedules to ensure that all pilgrims pass through the various parts of the ritual process as efficiently as possible. That, of course, means that pilgrims may not be free to linger when they wish or take extended time at certain points in the process. They are obliged to fit in with the general flow. The Shri Mata Vaishno Devi Shrine in Jammu requires pilgrims to register for their visits and to keep to a fixed schedule, adhering to prearranged times of attendance, including the time at which they make the ascent up the mountain to the shrine. The physical means of access to the cave temple is limited, and in order to fit the maximum number of pilgrims in, strict scheduling is required, as is the need for pilgrims to maintain a 'continuously moving queue'.[14] It is in such contexts that the helicopter tours offered by Pawan Hans Helicopter Limited and other firms and advertised by the shrine's website (see Chapter 2) come into their own. Not only do they make access easier, but they also assure pilgrims that, without worry, they can keep to the appropriate schedule and be at the shrine in their prescribed slot.[15] Planning is emphasised in numerous guidebooks and publicity materials relating to Shikoku as well. In 2006, for example, NHK produced a guidebook to the pilgrimage which instructed pilgrims of the importance of constructing a 'pilgrimage plan' (*junrei puranu*) that they should keep to and that would involve arranging every night's lodging, working out which trains and buses to take (if one were using public transport) and how far to walk each day if going on foot (NHK 2006: 128–129).

GUIDEBOOKS, POSTERS AND PUBLICITY MATERIALS

A key element in the development of the pilgrimage business, its increasing democratisation and its schedules and concepts of planning has been the mass development of various modes of information to aid pilgrims. Along with transport developments, the advent of printing presses and cheap and readily accessible literature providing information for pilgrims on where to go, where to stay, what could be seen and so on has been a central and crucial feature of mass pilgrimage development. Guidebooks and publicity pamphlets were part and parcel of Lourdes's potent mix of attractions—along with rumoured miracles, hopes of healing and other intercessionary graces, mass transportation, cheap accommodation and readily available pilgrimage souvenirs and goods—that brought in pilgrims and made it into a mass pilgrimage site in nineteenth-century France. Inexpensive and readily available guidebooks (many of them produced by Lourdes religious authorities) enabled potential pilgrims to find out that they could travel cheaply to and find economic lodgings at Lourdes and to realise that the pilgrimage could be affordable even for those of modest means (Kaufman 2004: 18, 35). Guidebooks, pamphlets and other marketing materials helped represent the shrine as a modern phenomenon, extolling not just its miracles but also the modern facilities, such as the railway, the newly developed electricity that illuminated the town and shrine and the mechanically reproduced religious goods that were available there. Through such an emphasis, they encouraged rural inhabitants to go to Lourdes to experience the wonders of modern life. Along with mass produced newsletters produced by Catholic authorities, such materials helped shape pilgrim behaviour and activities. They encouraged pilgrims to enjoy all aspects of the town and behave like tourists, providing them with lists of places to see and advising them how best to use their time, including suggesting renting bicycles to get around to the sights more easily and drawing attention to shopping and other facilities that could be combined with devotional shrine visits (Kaufman 2004: 17–46).

Printed materials were an important factor in the growth of interest in pilgrimages in Japan as well, where one could in essence produce a history of pilgrimage sites through the lens of guidebooks, which serve as a means of tracing how pilgrim needs, attitudes and opportunities may develop over the ages. James Foard (1982) has done this with regard to the Saikoku pilgrimage, showing that guidebooks are not just items providing information on how to do a pilgrimage or about a site; they are important also in creating pilgrim expectations about what they will see and experience and about what they should do as pilgrims. The Tokugawa era was a period of rising literacy in which the development of a mass publishing industry and of libraries where woodblock prints and such materials could be consulted, enabling increasing numbers of people to access materials emphasising the virtues of pilgrimage, drawing attention to miracle stories and providing information on sites that could be visited and the facilities available there (MacWilliams 2004: 46, Thal 2005: 100–102). Such materials contributed significantly to the growth of pilgrimage culture. As more people travelled, the demand for guidebooks grew, and this, in turn, helped encourage a more individualised approach to pilgrimage in which pilgrims could work out their own itineraries and know where to stay and what to buy on route.

The Saikoku pilgrimage was in the vanguard of such developments, taking on an increasingly market-oriented dimension during the Tokugawa and on into the Meiji era and beyond. As Foard (1982) indicates, there was a progressive development in the nature and construction of guidebooks in these eras. Early guidebooks tended just to outline the temples and routes, along with the miracle tales associated with them, but over the ages, and in conjunction with the growing material wealth of the pilgrims themselves who came to benefit from Japan's general economic advances, they began to focus increasingly on diversions, comforts and the opportunities that were available for pilgrims to enjoy themselves in worldly ways. Such developments in Saikoku guidebooks, Foard shows, reflected the wishes of pilgrims to enjoy sights and attractions near the temples and to eat well as they did so, and new facilities developed along the route to encourage them in this regard. Thus, by the latter part of the nineteenth century, guidebooks were drawing attention to interesting diversions and sightseeing places near the temples, good restaurants and hot spring resorts, and the culinary attractions of each place and region visited. Naturally, places within ready reach of the pilgrimage route were quick to open restaurants, inns, hot spring resorts and the like and to advertise their attractions, food and other luxuries, to benefit from the flow of pilgrims passing through their areas. Guidebooks, too, emphasised the historical dimensions of the temples and their cultural and artistic splendours, so that from the seventeenth through to the nineteenth century and beyond, the pilgrimage itself took on more and more the air of a cultural tour with various entertainments that could be enjoyed along the way (Foard 1982).

SHIKOKU AND THE PUBLICITY INDUSTRY

There is an extensive publishing industry in Japan based around pilgrimage guidebooks; in a visit to one bookstore alone in Osaka in 2008, I counted more than fifty pilgrimage guidebooks (several on Shikoku and Saikoku each, along with guides to several other regional pilgrimages) on the shelves.[16] There are also a number of publishers, such as Toki Shobō, based in Osaka, that specialise in pilgrimage guidebooks. Toki Shobō has published more than fifty such titles in recent years, although company officials also have indicated that, although their guidebooks to Shikoku continue to sell well, those that focus regional pilgrimages are suffering falling sales in line with the general decline of those pilgrimages. Moreover, the development of new online guides and phone apps were also posing a threat to their market while offering pilgrims new modes of accessing information.[17] Hoshino and Asakawa (2011: 42) have recently drawn attention to the proliferation of Shikoku guidebooks—usually, as they note, richly illustrated with colour photographs of rural scenes that eliminate signs of the modern world. The national tourist agency JTB alone published three separate guidebooks to the Shikoku pilgrimage between 2006 and 2008.

Such guidebooks are the most recent manifestations of a publishing tradition that is closely linked to the development and historical growth in popularity of the pilgrimage itself. In Shikoku, there is evidence that simple guides began to appear soon after the pilgrimage itself began to coalesce. The Buddhist priest Chōzen, whose account of his 1653 pilgrimage is the first to indicate the existence of an eighty-eight-stage pilgrimage in Shikoku, wrote that, while on his journey, he purchased and used a text that appears to have been some form of information source about the pilgrimage, and that some scholars believe to have been the first Shikoku guidebook (Yoritomi and Shiragi 2001: 89). The production of guidebook materials developed further from the late seventeenth century onwards, although it was not until the twentieth century that one sees much evidence of the patterns that emerged in Saikoku guidebooks in the Tokugawa period, of an increasing focus on diversions, side trips and culinary opportunities, manifesting themselves in Shikoku guidebooks.

By the 1920s, however, the progressive emphasis found in Saikoku pilgrimage guidebooks on entertainment, sights and attractions began also to be evident in Shikoku. So did discussions of how the pilgrimage and island manifested idealised images of 'traditional' Japan.[18] As Japan's transport infrastructures along with its economic development and improved lodging facilities enabled people to travel more readily, it was not just rail companies that began to promote pilgrimages in order to encourage people to use their services. The newly emergent Japanese tourist industry did likewise. By the 1920s pilgrimages such as Shikoku, Chichibu and Saikoku were featured in travel magazines such as *Tabi* ('Travel') that were produced by the Japanese tourist industry, which focused on domestic tourist travel at a time when overseas travel and international tourism were rare. It was an era when increasingly powerful nationalist sentiments dominated the public sphere in Japan, and these helped emphasise idealised notions that accorded almost mystical significance to Japan's cultural traditions and to its landscape.[19] As was mentioned earlier, JTB also began to publish pilgrimage guides that by the mid-1930s were emphasising the idea of doing pilgrimage the 'modern' way—which meant using transport such as trains, cars and buses rather than walking (Mori 2005: 54–55).

Travel to pilgrimage locations such as Shikoku was thus promoted as a way of affirming national identity and cultural belonging, as well as a form of tourism and as a practice in accord with a modernising society. Many of those involved in publicising the pilgrimage also steered attention away from religious faith and austerities in order to make the pilgrimage fit more readily into a modern tourist and nationalist ethos. The travel industry in particular sought to attract a potential new clientele by telling people that they need not be put off doing pilgrimages by anything as mundane as a lack of faith or religious commitment. The travel writer Iijima Makoto, for instance, published a guidebook to the Shikoku pilgrimage in 1930 based on articles he had written for *Tabi* and other travel magazines, in which he proclaimed that he was an atheist[20] with an agenda to open up the pilgrimage—hitherto limited, he claimed, to people with religious faith—to a wider, non-faith-oriented tourist audience. Iijima thus portrayed the pilgrimage in the guise of tourism rather than as faith-centred travel, and his guidebook focused on scenic and local attractions along with speedy and convenient ways to travel (Iijima 1930, Mori 2005: 47). Other guidebooks of the era similarly drew attention to convenient ways to do the pilgrimage, along with local attractions to be found in Shikoku. Such was the ethos of the times that even Buddhist priests such as the Zen monk Ōzeki Gyōō, who did the pilgrimage in the 1936, wrote about how they used cars and other convenient modes of transport to get around and about taking time out to enjoy sightseeing and to go swimming (Ōzeki 1936).

The travel industry, as such, seized on the Shikoku pilgrimage, among others, to boost its trade and even if the descent of Japan into war, first in China and later globally from the 1930s on, brought a temporary halt to such developments, it created a pattern that has continued in the postwar era. In the postwar era, one of the first enterprises to develop this theme further was the Shikoku Rail company, which was reported in the regional newspaper *Shikoku Shinbun* in June 1954 as seeking to revive pilgrimage numbers (which had been badly affected by the war and Japan's defeat and economic troubles after 1945) by producing and distributing some 2,000 copies of a guidebook that presented the pilgrimage as a journey of religion and tourism together (*shūkyō to kankō*) and that was aimed at attracting 'tourists' (*kankōkyaku*) to the island (Mori 2005: 155).

Later guidebooks, including those produced by the Shikoku temples themselves, have developed these themes further and generally place more emphasis on the touristic and photogenic aspects of pilgrimage and on images depicting seemingly unspoilt rural splendour, in which white-clad pilgrims (whose clothing is usually so spotless that it is obvious they could not have really been walking the route) are portrayed on mountain paths lined with moss-covered Buddhist images or in the courtyards of ancient temples. Such guidebooks also have tended to provide information not just on the temples and the route, but also on convenient and comfortable places to stay, while providing contact addresses and numbers for tourist offices and local travel companies as well as information about restaurants and other attractions (notably hot springs) along the route or readily accessible from it.[21] In very recent times, many such guidebooks have become available online (Reader 2011b) or accessible as apps for mobile phones and iPads.[22] Shikoku guidebooks, in other words, have not just reproduced the patterns of development described by Foard for Saikoku, but have also replicated the processes of modernisation in publishing in general, thereby ensuring that the pilgrimage itself remains firmly tied to modern patterns of technological development.

The combination of practical information and nostalgic imagery evident in such publicity materials as guidebooks[23] has been influential in heightening the pilgrimage's appeal and popularity in contemporary Japan. Such carefully constructed images suggesting authenticity of a particularly rural type are tied to notions that in Shikoku one can discover the essence of 'traditional Japan', a theme that has been manifest in various publicity campaigns (Mori 2005: 177). Coupled with the conveniences of modernity evident in bus tours and other modes of convenient transport and infrastructure, they have made the pilgrimage more attractive and more accessible especially to urban Japanese.

The national broadcaster NHK has been a major actor in this process. Publicly funded and with a remit to promote national culture, NHK has often highlighted Japanese temples, shrines and pilgrimages as exemplars of Japanese historical and cultural heritage. The Shikoku pilgrimage, because of its long history, photogenic nature and scenery, has been a popular subject for the broadcaster as a result, even as it has been constrained by Japan's constitutional laws that prevent the use of public money for promoting religious institutions and organisations. As such, when NHK has focused on pilgrimages such as Shikoku, it has done so through emphasising it as a cultural phenomenon while downplaying or eliminating any focus on its religious connotations.[24] Working in cooperation with the Shikoku temples and other regional agencies, NHK has produced a series of travelogues and documentaries on the pilgrimage, often involving well-known personalities and television presenters to introduce the temples, the route and the surrounding scenery, as, indeed, have other Japanese television and media broadcasters (Reader 2007a, Hoshino and Asakawa 2011: 147–148). Such programmes have been influential in increasing the awareness, especially of better-off, urban, middle-class Japanese to the pilgrimage, while simultaneously 'selling' it to them as a manifestation of Japanese cultural heritage rather than as a religious and faith-based practice (Reader 2007a). The pilgrimage has also been the setting for a number of TV dramas and films focused on people who engage in the pilgrimage to deal with various personal issues and human-life dramas, and has featured in a number of popular Japanese manga (cartoon) stories (Hoshino and Asakawa 2011: 147–149). These, along with the NHK programmes mentioned above, have, in the words of Hoshino and Asakawa (2011: 43–46), effectively 'mythologised' (*shinwa wo tsukuridasu*) the pilgrimage and produced an image of it (and of Shikoku itself) as a special space set apart from the everyday life of Japan, yet redolent of its cultural spirit, rich in nature and full of warmhearted people, and where human communication is paramount. As such, it is projected as the antithesis of the large cities from which most pilgrims come.

As I have discussed elsewhere (Reader 2007a), the temples have worked with NHK and various regional and media groups to put on exhibitions highlighting the pilgrimage, its art and the temples that have taken place at department stores and museums through Japan. Along with the aforementioned television programmes and such literature as the guidebooks that have been produced by NHK and the temples, these have further increased public knowledge of and interest in the pilgrimage, while making it ever more into a media-ised commodity. In such ways, the publicity materials— initially simple and then more complex, tourist-oriented guidebooks but now more visual materials such as television programmes—have served both to publicise the pilgrimage and to portray it as a highly photogenic and scenic commodity that appeals to people seeking to 'discover traditional Japan' while enjoying numerous diversions such as hot spring resorts along the route.

In such terms Shikoku image construction and publicity presents an interesting contrast—yet a striking similarity—to how Lourdes was depicted and represented in the nineteenth-century literature Kaufman (2004) describes and that I mentioned earlier. The guidebooks, postcards and other printed media that developed to publicise Lourdes encouraged people from rural setting, villages and small towns to discover the wonders of modern life that were developing at Lourdes (Kaufman 2004: 35). They were, as such, selling an image of the modern to a largely village and rural clientele. The Shikoku imagery appears to be doing almost the reverse, projecting and selling an image of the rural, rustic and traditional to a modern urbanised population. Yet both are, in effect, doing much the same in creating ideal images of the 'other' that exoticise and romanticise the places to be visited, thereby selling a culture that does not truly exist in reality, in much the same way that tourist literature does (Bruner 2005: 191–192). By attracting in this way clienteles who are encouraged, whether at Lourdes or in Shikoku, to enjoy the surroundings, see the sights and so on, they are further deepening the intersections with tourism that have been a recurrent feature of pilgrimage from its early days.

COMMERCE AND THE SHAPING OF PILGRIMAGE

I return to these themes in Chapter 7, where I examine some more recent developments that, I suggest, are further intensifying the tourist dimensions of pilgrimage. These are, as this chapter has indicated, a significant aspect of the engagement of commercial concerns and other interest groups in the promotion, support and development of pilgrimage. Whether in making available convenient and affordable lodgings and food, in the provision of guidebooks and informational materials or in the development of increasingly accessible and comfortable means of travel, such concerns have shaped pilgrimage and contributed significantly to its evolution as a mass-consumer item accessible to ever-wider segments of society. In so doing, these items have almost inevitably helped encourage and strengthen the ludic dimensions of pilgrimage and have created many of the opportunities that pilgrims have had for such things. Those who engage in the pilgrimage marketplace in such contexts- for example by putting on pilgrimage tours, building railway lines or producing guidebooks or, like the merchants of Amarnath, providing tea, food and shelter—are not primarily driven by the desire to promote devotionalism to a particular deity or holy figure, or to enhance the standing of a religious institution for reasons of faith. As various examples cited in this chapter have indicated, they are normally motivated primarily by commercial impulses, even if these may be tempered also by factors such as a commitment to local culture and communities and the like. Such commercial agencies, however, should not be seen as nothing more than economic parasites capitalising on the devotional orientations of pilgrims or be pilloried as agencies intent on transforming or reducing pilgrimage into a consumerist endeavour. Rather, they are important enabling institutions and mechanisms that have been instrumental in the shaping of the pilgrimage market and that are formative elements within the structure of pilgrimage. They have opened pilgrimage to wider numbers of people—significantly, for example, breaking down the barriers that prevented many women and others from being pilgrims in earlier times—and have been a force for turning pilgrimage into a practice within the remit of most if not all. In so doing they have certainly also contributed to the ways in which some of the inherent dynamics of pilgrimage (such as its orientations towards tourism and entertainment) may be intensified. However, in this context, they have also been influenced (as have the priests and the religious entrepreneurs discussed in the previous chapter) by those whose custom they seek and whose interests and wishes have played a major part in this context and process. These are the people who take up (usually with enthusiasm and alacrity) the services that commercial interest groups provide and without whom pilgrimage centres and those in the pilgrimage service industry would cease to function—the pilgrims themselves, and it is to their engagement with the marketplace that I turn next.

5 Pilgrims in the Marketplace
Shaping, Producing and Consuming Pilgrimage

Isesangū daijingū e mo issun yori ('the pilgrim to Ise also drops by for a moment at the shrine')

—Tokugawa-era Japanese popular saying

INTRODUCTION: COMPLAINING, EXPECTING, INVENTING

Pilgrims have a long tradition of complaining about the ways they are treated, and even at times appearing to resent the expenditures on services necessary for their travels. The pilgrims discussed in the previous chapter who muttered complaints about how much they were being charged for the tea and foodstuffs they relied on to sustain their pilgrimages to Amarnath are indicative of a wider pattern found across pilgrimage cultures in this respect. Thus, for example, Kagita Chūsaburō, who walked the Shikoku pilgrimage in 1961, complained regularly in his subsequent published pilgrimage account, of the money-grubbing tendencies of innkeepers who charged him to stay overnight (e.g., Kagita 1962: 99–100). Similar complaints have been reiterated by other Shikoku pilgrims in the decades since. Thus, for example, as I have discussed elsewhere, a party of pilgrims I travelled with in Shikoku complained repeatedly about their pilgrimage tour organiser, feeling that he not only rushed them everywhere but that he also was something of a mercenary (Reader 2005: 231–239).

The Moroccan academic and hajj pilgrim Abdellah Hammoudi also complains of being exploited in his pilgrimage travels. In Morocco, he and his fellow pilgrims have to give bribes to officials to get included in their country's list of those who can get permits for the hajj. On arriving in Saudi Arabia, they are regulated at every step by Saudi authorities, for whom they are little more than 'commodities', and are harried by merchants eager to extract money from them (Hammoudi 2006: 32, 72–84). Peter van der Veer (1988: 188) similarly portrays pilgrims to Ayodhya in northern India as harassed and manipulated by *pandas* (pilgrimage guides) who corral them into using their services in a 'totally impersonal pilgrimage market'. David Gladstone (2005: 185) comments that although Indian pilgrims at Pushkar recognise that they need the services of temple priests to perform rituals that are indispensible elements in their pilgrimages, they nonetheless regard the priests as little more than thieves. Anne Gold (1988: 220, 275) similarly reports that the Rajasthani pilgrims she studied were wary of being exploited on their pilgrimages, and viewed *pandas* as venal and obtrusive—even if they also valued their knowledge of how to perform rituals at the sites.

Such complaints reverberate through history. Aimery Picaud, the probable clerical author of the fifth book in the twelfth-century *Liber Sancti Jacobi*, the first guide to the pilgrimage to Santiago, readily brands ethnic groups such as the Basques and Navaresse who inhabit the regions through which pilgrims passed, as thieves and worse out to rob and exploit pilgrims (Viellard 1984, Bard 1989). On pilgrimage to the Christian Holy Land in 1480, the Dominican German friar Felix Fabri complained about how his tour guides rushed him around (Kaelber 2002: 59–60, Howard 1980: 38–39). Medieval European pilgrims complained so frequently about the mercenary nature of the merchants whose services they relied on to make their Holy Land pilgrimages that Venice's civic authorities instituted not just a tourist office to assist pilgrims but also a complaints bureau to assuage their concerns and help preserve Venice's image and hence its command of the market (Chareyrou 2000: 54–55).

Such complaints—whether ancient or modern—reflect the reality that making profits out of others is a recurrent human characteristic, that the bottom line is a powerful motivating factor for those in the pilgrimage business and that, as Hammoudi (2006) evocatively demonstrates, pilgrims have often been exploited by (some of) those whose services they depend on. Yet such complaints may also be embedded in the self-perceptions of pilgrims who are not simply aware that they are central to the whole process of pilgrimage but who also often appear to regard themselves as 'special' and to think that their status as pilgrims entitles them to special treatment. Along with his complaints of exploitation Aimery Picaud, for example, felt that pilgrims to Santiago had a 'right'[1] to hospitality on their pilgrimages (Viellard 1984: 125). This elevated self-perception can still be found today, as is evident in how some Santiago foot pilgrims see themselves as 'authentic' and as existing in a different category from mere 'tourists' who do the pilgrimage by cars or bicycles (Frey 1998: 129–134)—a point underlined also by Hoinacki's critical comments, cited in Chapter 1, about people who do the Santiago pilgrimage on bicycles.

Similar themes are evident in Shikoku. Kagita, for example, considered that being a pilgrim afforded him an exalted status. Indeed, he reports proudly that he took a temporary Buddhist ordination and acquired the status of a 'great monk' (*daisōjō*) with the ability to heal others for the duration of his pilgrimage (Kagita 1962: 51). He criticised other pilgrims he met for being less elevated than himself and for arriving late at lodges and disturbing his rest, complained about poor accommodation (and its cost) and felt aggrieved when he could not stay overnight at some places because they were already full of those (including bus pilgrims) who, he felt, were less worthy than himself (Kagita 1962: 49–50, 53, 85). Buddhist temple priests were not spared either. Some were excoriated for not maintaining their temples properly and one in particular came under fire for running a dilapidated temple, with Kagita (1962: 52) opining that if he had three months to spare, he would be able to mobilise the community and rebuild it. Although few other foot pilgrims in Shikoku view themselves in quite such a grandiose way as did Kagita, the underlying sentiment he expresses—that his status as a foot pilgrim merits special treatment—is much in evidence in Shikoku and occur in numerous pilgrim diaries and accounts (e.g., Harada 1999: 128).

Pilgrims have also been adept at skilfully manipulating matters in order to get privileged treatment. Aimery Picaud underpins his claims of the 'right' of Santiago pilgrims to hospitality with stories of how people who refuse such help are punished by divine retribution, such as the woman who, while baking, rejected the request of a pilgrim for a crust. As a result her bread immediately turned to stone (Viellard 1984: 122–123). In Shikoku, the custom of *settai* (giving alms) has long helped support mendicant pilgrims, some of whom in past eras begged for and were given alms such as money, food, drinks and free lodging by local people. Asakawa (2008) outlines in detail what he calls Shikoku's 'culture of alms' (*settai bunka*), and other authors have also shown that such alms-giving has been a common occurrence historically (Maeda 1971: 223–248, Shinjō 1982: 1070–1102, Reader 2005: 202–206). The custom is grounded in the legend that Kōbō Daishi is constantly wandering the pilgrimage while begging in the traditional manner of a Buddhist monk to support his travels and that any pilgrim could in effect be him. Stories in which a mendicant begs for and is given alms (in which case the donor is then miraculously rewarded) or is refused (causing the refuser to be cursed and suffer thereafter) are among the earliest miracle tales in Shikoku, and they express the imperative for locals to assist pilgrims while elevating the pilgrim to a specially exalted sacred status. In a striking resemblance to Picaud's tale of the recalcitrant baker whose bread turns to stone, late-seventeenth-century pilgrimage tales in Shikoku relate how formerly abundant local foodstuffs such as peaches and shellfish turn to stone because villagers refuse to give any of them as alms to begging pilgrims who turn out to be Kōbō Daishi (Reader 1999). Such stories were clearly developed by pilgrims as a means of 'persuading' residents to give them special treatment. They led to a well-established and structured social pattern of almsgiving in Tokugawa times in which locals considered it a social duty to care for those passing through their regions and because they believed that merit would accrue from so doing (Maeda 1971: 222, Koaumé 2001, Reader 2005: 122–126). Even if few pilgrims solicit alms these days, the custom of *settai* is still followed by some Shikoku residents, who give help especially to walking pilgrims based in their sense that almsgiving is an important local cultural tradition that should be maintained. In origin,

Pilgrims in the Marketplace 115

however, the custom is very much a product of pilgrim actions and of the stories that pilgrims created in order to privilege themselves.

COMPETITION AND PRACTICAL VALUES

Although pilgrims may complain about being harrassed and exploited by various agencies trying to make money from them, they have, as was noted earlier, been adept at creating narratives that benefit themselves. They are also able to benefit from the often competitive nature of the pilgrimage service industry and its agents, whose very existence and success are highly dependent on their ability to attract such custom. As was seen in Chapter 4, the mass development of the pilgrimage market and the burgeoning array of agencies and the plethora of sites competing for custom all offer pilgrims immense choice about when, where and how they will travel and what they seek from the places they visit. As such, although pilgrims may be the economic 'crop' of pilgrimage places, they are a 'crop' with real market power to determine whether pilgrimage sites and routes develop, flourish or fall by the wayside. Changing patterns of pilgrimage consumption—such as the declining fortunes of regional pilgrimages such as Shōdoshima and the general shift in the Japanese pilgrimage market towards Shikoku discussed earlier in this book—may be spurred in some degree by skilful publicity and marketing, but they also depend on the choices of (potential) pilgrims. Pilgrims also benefit from the competition for their custom when they visit particular sites; although pilgrimage guides in India may be a source of annoyance and harassment, they can also help pilgrims to get the best possible deals at the places where they need to stay. At Pushkar, for instance, competition is so fierce that the pilgrimage guides who wait at the bus stands to persuade newly arrived pilgrims to use their services and hotels are constantly forced to offer them better and better deals to get their custom (Gladstone 2005: 189).

Such pragmatism and worldly nous are widely found among pilgrims. As Anne Gold (1988: 147) comments, there is a highly transactional orientation to the pilgrimages of Rajasthani pilgrims and to their relationships with their gods. Similar traits have been observed by myself and others in the context of Japanese pilgrims, for whom more immediate worldly benefits and the accumulation of merit that will assist them in their passage to the next realm after death, may feature far more highly than, for example, hopes of miracle (Reader and Tanabe 1998: 199–201, Osada, Sakata and Seki 2003: 329–331). Taylor (2004: 140–141) likewise emphasises the practical and instrumental nature of pilgrimages to the Vietnamese shrine of Bà Chúa Xú, in which worldly concerns are at the top of pilgrims' agendas along with matters of speed and comfort.

In such terms, pilgrims may undertake their journeys not so much as a spontaneous response to rumours of miracle but through a lens of pragmatism and with a keen eye as to which location is popular at any given time; to what processes of pilgrimage are the most feasible; to what benefits may be attainable; to what diversions, sights and entertainments may be on offer; and to what they wish to expend as well. Although Gold (1988: 220) shows that the Indian pilgrims she traveled with almost universally felt that expending money was one of the most desirable and appropriate aspects of pilgrimage, she notes that they were also wary of being exploited and spending over the odds. Pilgrims in Shikoku are often ready to spend readily and as will be seen in the next chapter, one of the prime stimuli they, along with pilgrims in general, have is shopping for souvenirs. They also may want increasingly comfortable accommodation and good food, but they also have a clear sense of what is appropriate or not, and as the complaints of Kagita (1962) and others cited previously about the costs of accommodation indicate, they are not generally willing to just dispense with money to further their aims. They retain a clear sense of economic values and an awareness of their power in the marketplace. If, as has often been suggested in studies of pilgrimage, they vote with their feet, they also do so with their wallets and with a sharp eye on convenience, practicality and what other benefits, pleasures and practical experiences can be acquired as a result.

SHAPING AND EVANGELISING: PILGRIMS AS (SELF-)PROMOTERS

Pilgrims have been skilled in advancing their own agendas and in increasing their status in other ways also. Far from being passive, they are often dynamic agents in the shaping of pilgrimages, seeking to do this in ways that benefit their own interests and enhance their own status. Pilgrims, as Barry Stephenson (2010: 190) says, 'do not simply or merely consume, they also produce'. They have agency in how pilgrimages are shaped and practiced, they act as promoters and evangelisers of pilgrimage, and in so doing, they often engage in self-promotion and status enhancement. They influence the development of pilgrimage sites through their expectations of what they want to see and of how sites should be structured. They perform multiple pilgrimages, create new markets through their travels, and shape the infrastructures and influence the types of entertainment, diversions and comforts available at pilgrimage sites. They also foment demand for particular types of goods to be consumed—an issue discussed in the following chapter.

The creativity of pilgrims in developing legends and tales of miracle—both as a means of self-enhancement and as a way to stimulate the hopes that can motivate pilgrims in their journeys—has been mentioned earlier. Some pilgrims draw on their perceived exalted status to enhance themselves in other ways as well, turning pilgrimage into a career occupation and/or becoming what John Shultz (2011a: 99) calls 'pilgrim-evangelists' who have played an active role in promoting and developing the Shikoku pilgrimage while simultaneously promoting their own cause. Such evangelists, who are often in effect 'professional pilgrims' who make something of a livelihood out of pilgrimage, are not restricted to Shikoku; one can find numerous other examples from the medieval palmers who performed multiple pilgrimages in Christian Europe and promoted pilgrimage cults accordingly, to the *oshi* and *sendatsu*, or pilgrimage guides, who have been discussed in earlier chapters, who were central to the development of numerous pilgrimage cults in Japan. Status enhancement has often been an aspect of such development, a point evident in the *sendatsu* systems of Japanese pilgrimages such as Shikoku, where (as was noted in Chapter 3) one attains different ranks with the *sendatsu* system, and hence acquires higher status within the pilgrimage community as a result, based on the numbers of times one has done the pilgrimage or, in the context of the Islamic world, where acquiring the status of hajji (someone who has done the hajj) provides heightened social status within the Muslim community. Those who acquire the position of *sendatsu* in Shikoku for example, can serve as pilgrimage guides and play a significant role in promoting the pilgrimage and expanding its clientele, as was noted in Chapter 3. In so doing, of course, they not only improve their status (including gaining higher ranks within the *sendatsu* system) but can also earn a living and/or develop public reputations that bring them personal, and often economic, benefits from their activities. Status enhancement, pilgrimage promotion and personal career development may thus go hand in hand.

Shultz provides some further interesting examples of Shikoku pilgrims both historically and in the present day who have drawn attention to themselves and enhanced their public profiles and status through their writings and related activities as pilgrim-evangelists. Although pilgrim diaries and accounts from the time of the seventeenth-century proselytiser of pilgrimage Shinnen (discussed in Chapter 3 and by Shultz [2011a: 104–105]) are important in the tradition of pilgrimage promotion, Shultz (2009, 2011a, 2011b) particularly looks at the rapid growth in pilgrim diaries, published accounts and online blogs and other electronic resources about Shikoku that have developed in the last decade and a half as the pilgrimage itself has increased in popularity and national status. This growth complements the recent surge in the numbers of guidebooks about Shikoku produced by various interest and commercial groups that I referred to in Chapter 4. It also provides an important source of information and encouragement for potential pilgrims. In particular, the expansion of internet resources has been important, here, with several activists establishing internet sites to provide information about the pilgrimage and encourage others to take part in it while sharing their experiences and practical information with other pilgrims. Prominent amongst such activists is Kushima Hiroshi, whose website the Kikusui henrokan was among the first and is perhaps the best known of such pilgrimage websites in Japan.[2] Kushima, who has done the pilgrimage a number of times, not only offers advice and encouragement for existing and would-be pilgrims but also provides a library of online pilgrim accounts of their walking experiences, plus information on the route and its developments, along with reviews of publications on the pilgrimage and numerous

118 *Pilgrimage in the Marketplace*

links to other pilgrimage-related sites (Shultz 2011b: 105–109). Kushima has, in such terms, become a figure of authority in the pilgrimage community through his website, enhancing his own status while promoting the pilgrimage, especially for walkers.

Some of those who have published diaries and established websites have promoted their own careers as much as, or perhaps more than, they have promoted the Shikoku pilgrimage. Shultz provides a number of interesting examples here, such as Akimoto Kaito, who managed to gain a great deal of corporate sponsorship for his foot pilgrimage around Shikoku in 2001, which he promoted as a 'peace walk'. Akimoto had had an international upbringing, living in Pakistan, the United States and Japan as a child, and he claimed that this multicultural background provided him with an understanding of Christian, Muslim and Buddhist cultures and thereby enabled him to undertake what he portrayed as a pilgrimage of peace around Shikoku. He was also an actor involved in moviemaking and Internet-streaming companies, and he intended to create a streamed online video of his pilgrimage. However, his technical abilities were not up to the task, and he was unable to realise his ambitions in this respect, but he nonetheless generated an immense amount of media publicity, ostensibly for the pilgrimage, but more significantly for himself, through his activities and journey. The vast amount of technical gear he took with him, from laptops and cameras to camping gear, proved a barrier and a burden, causing his backpack to weigh so much that it was a real struggle to carry it up hillsides—a drawback that Akimoto turned to his own benefit by portraying the uphill struggles that ensued in heroic terms, thus garnering further publicity for himself. Akimoto even, later, sent his fifteen-year-old son on the pilgrimage, in part, Shultz notes, to help the son confront the difficulties he was having at school but clearly also to draw attention to the boy (who also appeared interested in a media-oriented career) and to further Akimoto's own career. The son, who received a great amount of media attention during his pilgrimage in 2004, later published a book on his experiences, which clearly enhanced his and his father's media profiles (Shultz 2011b: 107–110).[3]

Shultz also draws attention to other recent pilgrims whose pilgrimages have been conducted in a glare of self-created publicity, through which participants have, usually after generating a media furore before setting out, established websites, published diaries of their journeys and even set themselves up as pilgrimage gurus dispensing advice to others. Notable among such figures has been the professional wrestler Shinzaki Jinsei, who comes from Shikoku. As is common with Japanese pro wrestlers, a gimmick is needed to make them stand out and attractive to fans, and for Shinzaki, it is his Shikoku connection. When he enters the ring, he is dressed in pilgrimage clothing, and he incorporates all manner of pilgrimage ritual actions into his wrestling performance. Shinzaki has been heavily promoted in this guise by the Buddhist priest Amano Kōyū, who insists his aim is to increase the profile of the pilgrimage via the persona of Shinzaki, with whom he went on a highly publicised pilgrimage tour to this end. Shinzaki's personal website[4] depicts him in prayer mode, dressed as a pilgrim, and offers advice on all manner of spiritual issues, gaining him followers who have themselves been inspired to do the pilgrimage as a result (Shultz 2011a: 107–108).

Other personalities who have acquired a public following through their pilgrimage activities include Fujita Yoshihiro, better known under the diminutive of Yokkun, and widely referred to in books and online as Yokkun-sensei ('Yokkun the Teacher'). Yokkun became a pilgrimage 'star' in Japan as a child because of his multiple pilgrimages around Shikoku, dressed in full pilgrimage regalia and accompanied by his grandmother. She originally took him on the pilgrimage when he was two years old, to memorialise his father, who had died suddenly. His grandmother continued taking him on pilgrimages, and in 2003, when he was just seven, she published a book detailing their first ten circuits together. This account portrays Yokkun as a special pilgrim who, at the age of three, was able to memorise Buddhist sutras and lead others in prayers and rituals. By the time Yokkun had reached the age of fifteen, he had completed twenty-five circuits, always by motorised transport, and these journeys, coupled with his grandmother's skilful depictions of them, have helped him achieve widespread recognition in Japan. He has subsequently featured on cable television programmes documenting his pilgrimages and has developed a website where he and his grandmother not only promote the pilgrimage and dispense advice to others but also sell a variety of pilgrimage goods such as Yokkun-centred calendars and videos.[5] Yokkun has acquired an online following especially, it appears, among older Japanese, and although his activities have raised further the profile of the pilgrimage, they have also, quite clearly, enhanced his own status, given him the aura of a pilgrimage expert and teacher, and been central to a promotional campaign designed to benefit him and his grandmother (Shultz 2011b: 110–112).

Yokkun, Akimoto and Shinzaki are striking examples of the widespread contemporary tendency of foot pilgrims in Shikoku to publish accounts of their journals either as books or online.[6] Indeed, it often appears that the wish to walk the Shikoku route is not unconnected to the desire for self-promotion, in which the personalised pilgrimage becomes a media production and performance. That there is a market for such writings is shown by the continuing interest of publishing firms to commission and publish such works, and this in its turn provides increased exposure for the pilgrimage and potential opportunities for future pilgrim-authors to join in with this process and seek heightened exposure, status and personal advancement for themselves.

EXPECTATION, DESIRE AND IMAGINATION

In Chapter 2, I discussed how religious authorities have frequently built up shrine complexes to construct a form of visual emotional magnetism that inspires and attracts increasing numbers of pilgrims. In this, they are not acting unilaterally so much as in conjunction with and in response to the wishes of pilgrims, who bring with them various expectations of what they expect or want to see at the sites they visit and who thus serve as a potent force in building and shaping the physical landscape of pilgrimage. As Ivakhiv (2001: 136) indicates in his study of Sedona and Glastonbury, pilgrim expectations are an important factor in the ways that such sites have developed and in how their landscapes have been shaped in the modern day. Although Sedona and Glastonbury have past associations as pilgrimage sites associated with older traditions (the Amerindian for the former, the Christian for the latter), their development as contemporary centres of pilgrimage with New Age orientations has been accompanied, as was seen in Chapter 2, by people from the New Age milieu who have harnessed their wishes of what they wanted to see as pilgrims with their motivations as entrepreneurs. In so doing, they have built up the image of these places as 'power spots' and have engraved on an already striking physical terrain, a pilgrimage infrastructure and series of symbols that reflected what they envisioned as appropriate signs that should be present at a sacred place. Whatever attractions Sedona and Glastonbury might have had because of their past associations and their physical environments, they also required the addition of appropriate monuments and structures in order to shape them visibly as pilgrimage centres conforming to the expectations of the new waves of twentieth- and twenty-first-century pilgrims motivated by New Age ideas and beliefs (Ivakhiv 2001). Thal (2005: 97–110) underlines this point as well in her examination of how the landscape at Konpira was constantly reshaped not just by its entrepreneurial priests but by its demanding pilgrims, who reinterpreted their needs in line with changing concerns over the ages and who left behind lanterns and other votive objects as markers of their visits, to the extent that their influence alongside the activities of the priests ensured that Konpira's visual landscape continued to change and develop in line with the needs of the ages.

The early pilgrims who travelled to the Christian Holy Land also brought with them visions of what they expected to see there- visions and expectations that were instrumental in reshaping the Biblical physical landscape. Georgia Frank (2000), for example, discusses how Christian pilgrims in antiquity had read or heard about the places they were visiting and about the sacred events associated with them before embarking on their pilgrimages. In such terms, their imaginations were primed prior to travel, providing a paradigm for their pilgrimages and for their expectations of what they would see on their travels. Such imaginings and expectations were a factor in how the built landscape of the Christian Holy Land developed (Frank 2000: 81). As Glenn Bowman (1992) observes, the Middle Eastern landscape that Western Christian pilgrims encountered was, with its Muslim cultural influences, very different from their own. However, because such pilgrims believed that places such as Jerusalem belonged to their tradition, they also expected and wanted them to look like they did so. Hence, they wanted churches built in the places they visited so that they accorded architecturally with the built landscapes they were familiar with and thus looked like Christian places. Christian pilgrims also wrote pilgrimage accounts that portrayed places such as Jerusalem in the ways that Europeans wanted to see them, and their writings linked the 'alien' territories of Palestine (alien because they had long been under Muslim rule) to a 'mythical ground of Christian scriptures' through which a 'Jerusalem of the pilgrims' was created as a new Christian city framed by pilgrim rhetoric (Bowman 1992: 156–160). Such writings also helped those who were unable to go to places such as Jerusalem in medieval times to imagine what the pilgrimage might be like and kept alive the image of the pilgrimage for later generations (Howard 1980).

Michael Tavinor (2007: 29) has suggested that 'to the medieval mind sacred space had to be created and also built'; natural settings alone did not suffice, for pilgrims wanted the sites they visited to be overlaid with appropriate buildings that spoke of grandeur and significance. This is not solely a medieval perspective, of course, as my discussions in Chapter 2 on the ways in which Bodh Gaya was reshaped in the late nineteenth and early twentieth centuries in accord with the wishes of reformist Sri Lankan Buddhists, indicate. Barry Stephenson (2010: 21–23) has further demonstrated this point in his discussion of how Luther's Wittenberg has been shaped in modern times to meet with visitor expectations. Similarly, Philip Taylor (2004: 137) has observed that pilgrimages are fashioned anew by new waves of pilgrims who bring new aspirations, attitudes and values, which, in the case of the Vietnamese pilgrims he studied, were especially centred on pragmatism, convenience and consumerism.

Priests in Shikoku have often spoken to me about the wishes of pilgrims to see new developments at their temples, such as new statues and halls of worship, that signify the dynamic nature of the sites they are visiting. They also expect the sites to reflect contemporary religious trends and practices, a point illustrated by the development of statues and prayer sites for the practice of *mizuko kuyō* at Shikoku pilgrimage temples between the 1980s and the late 1990s. *Mizuko kuyō* refers to the performance of memorial services (*kuyō*) for the spirits of babies who died in the womb (*mizuko*), most commonly as a result of abortions. The practice of performing memorial services for such spirits began to develop at Japanese Buddhist temples in the 1950s, initially at just a few temples, and becoming gradually more widespread from the 1960s through to the 1980s (LaFleur 1994, Harrison 1996, Hardacre 1997). Initially it was highly controversial, because it appeared (because of the rituals performed for aborted spirits) to condone abortion and the taking of life and because it appeared in the eyes of some to be exploitative of women (Hardacre 1997). Such controversies were initially, at least until well into the 1980s, a limiting factor to its wholesale acceptance at Buddhist temples. A common feature of the practice is the erection of Buddhist statues—most commonly of Jizō, a bodhisattva commonly venerated as a protector of children, but also of Kannon in her guise as a compassionate mother—that serve as guardians of such spirits, and at which offerings to the spirits of the deceased babies are offered.

When I first went to Shikoku in 1984, I noted such statues at just three of the eighty-eight temples—a reflection of the degree to which it was, in the first half of the 1980s, a fairly marginal practice. Over the next decade or so, however, it became increasingly widespread and normative in Japan and *mizuko* statues, of either Jizō or Kannon, became quite ubiquitous at temples throughout the country. They were increasingly visible from the 1990s onwards at the Shikoku temples, until by the late 1990s *mizuko*-related statues could be found at most of the Shikoku temples. I commented on this fact during a visit to one Shikoku temple in April 1997, remarking to the wife of the temple priest that the temple had installed a *mizuko Jizō* statue since my last visit a few years before and that it seemed to have plenty of offerings in front of it. She replied that the statue was a response to pilgrim wishes, because more and more pilgrims wanted, while on pilgrimage, to make ritual offerings to the deceased spirits of babies whom they or their families had lost or had aborted. Over the years, I have heard similar stories; pilgrim demands (which reflected the general spread of the *mizuko* practice in Japan in the latter part of the last century) have led to most of the temples offering scope for this practice. In other words, pilgrims in Shikoku, like those cited earlier in the medieval Christian Holy Land and 'New Age' pilgrims at sites such as Sedona, can serve as pressure groups influencing the shape of the sites they visit and encouraging those who run them to continually reshape them and provide them with new adornments that accord with the changing wishes and feelings of their visitors.

MULTIPLE PERFORMANCES AND REPETITION

On essay deadline day in 1993 while working at the University of Stirling in Scotland, I received an essay faxed to me by a student from a ferry crossing the English Channel. The accompanying note said he had gone home for the Easter break but that before he could finish his essay, he had had to go with his family on their annual pilgrimage, done always at that time of year, to Lourdes, and that this was the first opportunity he had had to send the essay to me. This incident emphasised to me that something I had observed as a feature of pilgrimage in Japan—that many people who perform pilgrimages do so often and may make them into regular normative events within their lives—was a phenomenon found elsewhere as well. Many Shikoku pilgrims do the pilgrimage many, and even hundreds of, times (Reader 2005: 249–266) and the same is true for some of Japan's regional pilgrimages. I have, for instance, met pilgrims in Shōdoshima who have done the pilgrimage hundreds of times, and several groups I have met have done it on a regular, often annual basis.

I have discussed elsewhere (Reader 2001) the example of Japanese pilgrims who perform multiple pilgrimages, including the example of a couple who, besides doing various pilgrimages (notably Saikoku, Shikoku and pilgrim ascents of Ontake, a prominent mountain in central Japan that is the focus of a pilgrimage cult) in Japan, had visited numerous pilgrimage sites in China, Japan and Europe and who saw pilgrimage as an embedded feature of their everyday lives. Conversations with pilgrims on various Japanese pilgrimage routes indicate that such multiple performances are common practices, a theme identified also by Satō's (2004) analysis of pilgrimage survey data in Japan. On pilgrimage tours, I have heard pilgrims discussing with each other which route they planned to do next. Those who run pilgrimage tour companies or societies in Japan also emphasise that such 'repeat and multiple performance' pilgrims (whom they identify most commonly as people who have retired and who are in their sixties or older) are a significant element in the pilgrimage market, a mainstay of their pilgrimage tours, and a likely potential market for new pilgrimages that may develop or be invented. Normally, such sources say, people start with more local or regional small-scale pilgrimages, as a form of 'entry-level' introduction to pilgrimage, and then move on to larger pilgrimages such as Shikoku. The priests I have spoken to who have been instrumental in developing new pilgrimages in Japan have similarly said that an element in their expectations for their new routes was that they could tap into this community of pilgrims who performed pilgrimages regularly and appeared keen to try various different routes.[7]

Japan is not an isolated case. Taylor (2004: 5) identifies such repeat and multiple performances as a feature of the Vietnamese pilgrim community too, stating that the country has a number of shrines that 'are linked in an annual itinerary of pilgrimages, attracting a core of widely travelled pilgrims, most notably women who market and trade'. The pilgrim family mentioned earlier who repeat Lourdes visits every year as a form of regular event are not alone as an example of multiple or regular Christian pilgrimage performers who return time and again to the same place. As Simon Coleman (2000) comments, some pilgrims visit Walsingham so regularly that it becomes a form of second home to them. The practice of doing numerous pilgrimages is a recurrent theme historically in Christian contexts, as with the example of Margery Kempe who undertook many pilgrimages to collect indulgences in the fifteenth century and figures such as the palmer in John Heywood's sixteenth-century play *The Four PP* who regales listeners with accounts of multiple pilgrimages to dozens of shrines (Duffy 1992: 193). The potential multiple nature of Christian pilgrimage performance was evident at Knock, where I heard people engaging in the sort of 'have you been to . . .' and 'where will we go next' discussions I have heard repeatedly at pilgrimage

124 *Pilgrimage in the Marketplace*

sites in Japan. Other signs at Knock suggest the potential for (and indeed encouragement to) people to visit multiple sites; on the back wall of the old shrine chapel at Knock, there is a rosary wall relief in which each rosary bead contains the name of other pilgrimage sites in Europe focused on Mary. Linked in a rosary, there is an implicit connection between them—one that, from conversations heard at Knock, is something that many pilgrims make as well.

I take up this issue again in Chapter 6, when I discuss how such multiple performers of pilgrimage help create a demand for new forms of pilgrimage souvenir and goods. The point to make here is that there are numbers

Figure 5.1 Rosary sculpture at Knock shrine with beads indicating other Marian pilgrimage sites.

of people who perform multiple pilgrimages as well as repeatedly making visits to the same pilgrimage places and who, in so doing, not only make pilgrimages into something highly familiar—a second home perhaps—but also stimulate interest groups such as religious authorities and tour agencies involved with the pilgrimage market, to respond to their interests by creating new pilgrimage sites for them to visit.

PILGRIMS ARE NOT ASCETICS (AS A RULE)

One key point to make here is that, whether they are performing repeated pilgrimages or just taking part once or very occasionally in the practice, pilgrims are not, as a rule, ascetics. Nor are they in general seekers after solace and detachment from the hubbub and noise of the world. Although hardship and asceticism may be seen by some as an intrinsic element to pilgrimage—a point at times emphasised in Hindu contexts, where pilgrims are expected to return home 'thinner and poorer' (Gold 1988: 266)—this does not mean that they are essential elements in pilgrimage. For example, no regulations or pilgrimage texts state that a Shikoku pilgrim must walk and perform austerities or that pilgrims to Mecca must undergo severe hardships to get there or that they cannot use aeroplanes. Even when there is a notion that hardship ought to be an element within pilgrimage, this has not blocked the development of services that have made pilgrimages more amenable for greater numbers of people. Pragmatism (often fuelled also by the competition of those offering services for pilgrims) has generally won out over asceticism in pilgrimage contexts. When opportunities for quicker modes of travel and the avoidance of ascetic foot pilgrimage have arisen, they have been quickly been taken up by pilgrims and legitimated by religious authorities, as was evident in the examples cited in the previous chapter of the readiness with which Buddhist and Hindu authorities accepted rail travel and the eagerness with which Tibetan Buddhist pilgrims stopped walking and started riding trains.

The tendency for pilgrims to move from ascetic to more worldly modes of pilgrim travel when such opportunities arise has been evident across the spectrum. To be sure, some commentators suggest that, at least in early Christianity, asceticism and hardship were essential to pilgrimage. This is the line taken by Edwin Mullins (1974: 52), for example, when he states that medieval Christian pilgrims embraced an ethos that favoured hardship and that viewed life as a struggle against the temptations of the Devil and that, hence, they were not so interested in comfort. Yet it is clear that as the potential for easier travel and greater comfort grew, pilgrims readily opted for such things; comfort trumped hardship as pilgrimage shifted away from the penitential and austere. Jonathan Sumption (1975: 94–105) argues that such a change occurred during the eleventh and twelfth centuries, with the development of better organised and secure routes that made pilgrimage more feasible for greater numbers of people. As a result, one began to see pilgrims beginning to travel in a 'comfortable, sometimes luxurious manner' (Sumption 1975: 123). Whether in the ships that enabled English medieval pilgrims to avoid much of the overland route to Santiago (Childs 1999) or the Venetian package tours mentioned in the previous chapter that removed many of the dangers and difficulties of the pilgrimage to Jerusalem, Christian pilgrims began to vote with an eye to convenience and comfort and against obligatory austerity.[8]

Likewise, the various means—most recently the growth of air travel—that have helped Muslim pilgrims avoid the dangers of traversing deserts to get to Mecca have been widely embraced by pilgrims, for whom getting safely and quickly to the places they regard as holy and avoiding the dangers that were once so prominent on the way, clearly is an issue of primary concern. Although it is imperative for hajj pilgrims to perform a set routine of rituals and to wear specific pilgrimage clothing that indicates purity and makes all pilgrims ostensibly the same, this does not make ascetic travel to the Meccan region obligatory or necessitate arduous and painful practices either on the way to or while there. The Saudi hajj authorities have, indeed, done much to make the pilgrimage more comfortable and to alleviate any hardship by, for example, constructing air-conditioned tunnels to enable certain parts of the hajj that otherwise would have to be performed in the searing heat of the desert and that in past ages had caused deaths and discomfort, to be carried out safely and comfortably.

Penitence and austerity, it appears, were modes of choice when there was no option, when facilities were rudimentary and going on foot was the only choice for all but the very wealthiest. The more choice pilgrims have had, however, the less central asceticism has become. This does not mean that pilgrims universally reject asceticism and solace as the potential for comfort and convenience increases. There are still those nowadays who choose to perform pilgrimages as an austerity and who find the noise of crowded sites to be disturbing. In Shikoku, for instance, the ascetic tradition has not disappeared, and there are a very small minority of foot pilgrims who perform austerities such as sleeping out and/or existing solely on alms (Reader 2005: 83–85). Many of those who walk do express unease at encountering crowded sites, a theme expressed in many walkers' diaries in Shikoku that focus on the quiet of mountain paths and display angst at leaving them to enter noisy temple courtyards full of bus pilgrims (e.g., Harada 1999: 25). However, one cannot take these as representative of general pilgrim attitudes. Walkers and others who perform austerities may be significant figures in the wider pilgrimage picture, and they frequently are given most emphasis in the academic literature,[9] but they are in general a minority in the overall pilgrimage population. In Shikoku, for example, where walkers have become more common in the past decade and a half, they still constitute at most less than two per cent of all pilgrims and probably less (Hoshino 2001: 353–360, Hoshino and Asakawa 2011: 144–158). And if walkers are thus not representative of pilgrims as a whole, ascetic walkers are also hardly representative of all walking pilgrims. Most of those who now walk the Shikoku pilgrimage do not treat it as a religious austerity so much as a challenge and a form of long-distance hiking (Hoshino 2001: 353–365, Kobayashi 2003)—something that is also evident among those walking the Santiago Camino (Frey 1998). Many walkers do the Shikoku pilgrimage in short sections of a week or so at a time before going home to rest up (Reader 2005: 19–20) as is the case also for the Santiago Camino (Frey 1998: 20–28). Most stay overnight in hostels and lodges and eat regular meals, too, and as such, they hardly engage in extended travails or separate themselves in any major way from their normative home structures. Moreover, for modern walkers—certainly in Shikoku—home comforts and communications appear to be highly important. Foot pilgrims are now are as likely as not to carry with them various modern conveniences such as Japanese cell phones, often along with apps and online guidebooks, iPods, laptops and other devices to keep them in touch with their families and the wider world, to listen to music and to enjoy whatever other luxuries of the modern computerised world they aspire to (Kobayashi 2003, Shultz 2009).

Instead of seeking out quiet and solace, it has been more common for pilgrims to seek and be drawn to places thriving with crowds, excitement and noise, all of which, as was pointed out in Chapter 2, are potent attractions for pilgrims rather than the reverse. As the priests of Shōdoshima, cited in Chapter 2, observed, the quietness of sites can be put off pilgrims rather than attract them. I remember also a visit to Walsingham in its off-season, on a bitterly cold and snowy late winter's day, with a Japanese academic friend who specialised in the study of pilgrimages. There were hardly any visitors, and we could wander around the site unbothered, but as my Japanese companion commented, this meant that there was a lack of atmosphere that made it hard to find the place compelling. It is perhaps little wonder that some sites have off-seasons and that we resolved that if we were to visit Walsingham again, we would go at a time when it received plentiful pilgrims rather than when it was so eerily empty.

By contrast, the allure of places thronging with people, markets and entertainment is evident in many pilgrim accounts, such as that of the Chinese pilgrim and writer Zhang Dai (1597–1689) about his visit to the pilgrimage site of Tai Shan. Although Zhang Dai was gripped by the beautiful scenery of mountain, he was especially drawn by the crowds, hubbub and carnival atmosphere of the place, with 'numerous hawkers, wrestlers and story-tellers' in the temple courtyard (Brook 1993: 45–46). There are striking resonances here with the experiences of pilgrims at Konpira, drawn by its noise and attractions, and with the crowds who flock to mass *kaichō* events or to Catholic pilgrimage sites when indulgences have been declared. Knowing that a site will be crowded and noisy because large numbers of

Figure 5.2 Pilgrimage party in Shikoku washing hands before entering a temple.

other pilgrims will be flocking there, is more of an allure than a detraction for pilgrims as a rule.

THE LUXURY OF CHOICE AND THE SEDUCTIVENESS OF TRANSPORT

The example I mentioned in Chapter 2 about how the railways were central to the rise of Hardwar as a major pilgrimage site and about how, in the period when the railway was closed for a time, pilgrim numbers declined to almost nothing, is telling, as are the correlations between better, faster modes of transport and rising pilgrim numbers in Mecca, Shikoku and elsewhere. As we saw in the previous chapter, transport organisations such as railway companies have promoted pilgrimages as a way of increasing the numbers who use their products, while rail, bus and air travel have become accepted parts of the pilgrimage industry and infrastructure. Religious authorities and associations, too, from the Catholic Church, welcoming French Railways assistance in making Lourdes into a national pilgrimage, to Buddhist and Hindu groups embracing the help of Indian Railways and Japanese temple associations working with bus and train companies to promote pilgrimages, have avidly legitimated and engaged in the promotion of such conveniences.

Pilgrims have rarely provided a counterargument to such conveniences but the reverse in their readiness to embrace the services available.

Shikoku provides a good example again here. Mori, writing about how the development of new modes of transport—trains, buses and then private cars plus also new motorised ferries—in early twentieth century transformed the face of the Shikoku pilgrimage, has spoken of the 'seductiveness of transport conveyances' (*norimono no yūwaku*) for pilgrims (2005: 41). Such seductiveness has been a feature of Japanese pilgrimage development very much in evidence in Shikoku, where the growth of a modern motorised transport network became a feature of the pilgrimage landscape from the 1920s, affecting how people performed the pilgrimage and how easily they could become pilgrims. It also, as was seen in Chapter 4, led to the Shikoku pilgrimage being featured in travel and tourist magazines as a modern tourist and travel opportunity and as a means of reaffirming concepts of national identity and cultural pride. The first railway lines opened in Shikoku in the late 1880s, and by the 1930s, much of Shikoku was accessible by rail. The development of good roads and bus services, along with boat services that speeded up travel between some of the coastal temples, meant that by the 1930s, one could do practically the whole pilgrimage by public transport—an issue emphasised by the guidebooks and maps that started to appear in increasing numbers from the 1920s on and that increasingly drew attention to the variety of choices and convenient ways in which pilgrims could do the route. Cable cars, too, proved popular among pilgrims, and by the 1930s, pilgrims could make use of a number of these new facilities to access several of the mountain temples. It was not just those who preferred to ride rather than walk who benefitted, for better roads also made walking and finding one's way easier (Mori 2005: 33–34). Pilgrims could also combine walking with the use of different forms of transport—something that has become a common method of doing the pilgrimage, in which people may walk the sections that are largely rural and in quieter mountain areas while taking public transport along sections that follow the highway for long distances.

Pilgrimage naturally speeded up as a result, because pilgrims were able to choose from an increasing variety of means to get around the route. And as choices became available, pilgrims made use of them, as is illustrated by Mori (2005: 35) in a fascinating table in which he outlines this process. The first pilgrim whose journey we know much about, the Buddhist monk, Chōzen, did the pilgrimage in 1653, took ninety-one days, travelled by the only viable option of the era, foot, save when he came to rivers and inlets. When ferryboats were available to save him the lengthy time it would take to go circumvent the river or inlet, he would use them, and in all Chōzen, did this five times. Through the Tokugawa era, bridges progressively reduced the need for ferries, and the emergence of new forms of transport from the late nineteenth century onwards provided pilgrims with new choices and possibilities to facilitate their travels. Mori cites a pilgrim in 1907 who used ferries, trains, horse carriages and even, at one point, a sedan chair.

By the 1920s and early 1930s, the time spent on pilgrimage had dropped significantly and the number of different forms of conveyance had risen; in 1926, Tomita Gakujun, a prominent Buddhist priest, took thirty-five days for the whole route and used five ferries, ten trains, eighteen cars or buses and one horse carriage. In 1932, the travel writer Miyao Shigeo took just eighteen days and rode on seven ferries, thirteen trains, twenty-eight cars or buses, one cable car and one rickshaw. By the late 1930s, rickshaws and horse carriages had disappeared from pilgrim itineraries and ferries became less widely used, whereas the use of trains and motorised vehicles, including cable cars, continued to rise (Mori 2005: 35). Since the development of bus package tours in the 1950s and with better roads and faster train services, the speed of the pilgrimage has increased further; now car and taxi pilgrimages as well as bus package tours are commonplace, enabling pilgrims to complete the whole journey in ten days or less.

Although such changes have been encouraged by the pilgrimage service industry's marketing and provision activities, they have clearly been impelled by the choices and wishes of pilgrims, who have for the most part opted to take advantage of the opportunities that new modes of transport offer. Their wishes have been a driving force in this process, spurring religious authorities and commercial interest groups to be ever ready to respond to their changing desires and needs and to produce new ways of getting around and of enhancing their travel experiences. The popularity of cable cars provides a good example here, and many of the mountain temples of Shikoku have taken steps, in conjunction with transport firms, to have such facilities built. Unpenji (Temple Sixty-six) is the highest temple on the Shikoku route at more than one thousand metres. When I first visited it in 1984, it was approached by narrow winding roads for buses and cars or by steep paths for walkers. By my next visit in 1991 a cable car led up to the temple, which by then also had a Buddhist statue in its courtyard donated by the cable car company that had, according to the pilgrimage guide (*sendatsu*) in whose party I was then travelling, entered into an agreement with the temple to help support and promote visits there. Although the group I was with did not use the cable car and drove up the narrow and tortuously winding road instead, we were in a tiny minority. We came across few vehicles on the ascent and when we reached the car park at the top, we found it was almost empty. The temple courtyard, however, was full of pilgrims disgorging from the cable car, while the parking lot at the cable car station down below that we had passed on our ascent was full of cars and buses. Bus tour itineraries regularly now involve parking there so that the pilgrims go up and back on the cable car, and most pilgrims who travel by car seem to do likewise. It makes for a dramatic scenic ride, cuts out some winding roads and time and is, bus company officials have informed me, what the pilgrims who book their tours want. This has led to many companies amending their itineraries to include such 'seductive' means of conveyance in accord with the wishes of Shikoku pilgrims who appear to have similar desires to the pilgrims mentioned in Chapter 2 who flooded to the Mansa Devi temple in Hardwar after temple authorities built a cable car up to it in 1984.

Contemporary pilgrims in places such as Shikoku have something unimaginable for those who lived in eras when walking was the only possibility: the luxury of choice. They are able to select various modes of transport to make their journeys more attuned to their personal wishes and convenience. They commonly, as the preceding examples indicate, go for what is most comfortable, scenic and speedy. Such expressions of pilgrim desire have not just led to progressive eradication of hardship in pilgrimage but also to an increasing individualisation in and adaptation of pilgrimage practices to fit with personal aspirations, comforts and modern circumstances. This constant reshaping of the ways in which pilgrims undertake their journeys has continued in recent years. In Shikoku, the inception of bus package tours in the 1950s—and the competition brought about as different companies sought to get into the market—led to this mode of travel dominating the market within a very few years (Osada, Sakata and Seki 2003: 166–174) as it has in so many other parts of the world.[10] This trend, highly evident in Shikoku in the second half of the last century, is now, however, being supplanted by a shift, closely aligned to an increasing emphasis on personal autonomy and to rising levels of car ownership, towards a more individually organised pilgrimage process in which people are travelling either in small units—familial, as husband and wife units and/ or with friends—or individually by car. Such journeys have been facilitated by the three bridges that were built across the Inland Sea and linking Shikoku to Japan's main island of Honshu from 1988 onwards. The bridges have enhanced car access to Shikoku and have made it easier for people from the mainland to make quick visits there, as a result of which has been an increase in people breaking the pilgrimage up into a series of short journeys by car and completing the route over a number of visits and perhaps even years (Hoshino and Asakawa 2010: 25, 162–163).[11]

ACCOMMODATION AND COMFORT

In an article in *The Guardian* on July 31, 1999, about contemporary pilgrimage trends, Father Liam Griffin, an English chaplain based in Lourdes was quoted as follows:

> The pilgrims have changed over the years. People going on holiday are so used to going to resorts and the luxuries available that they're beginning to expect it from pilgrimage sites as well.[12]

Griffin's comment resonates with my observations in Shikoku and with what I have heard from temple priests and pilgrimage lodge owners there. On my first visit to Shikoku in 1984, when my wife and I walked the pilgrimage, we stayed at a number of small pilgrim lodges run by ladies who (as they told us) came from families that had been running pilgrims' lodges for generations. Each told a similar story of how they would likely be the last person to do so. As one lodge owner put it, nowadays (and she was speaking in 1984) pilgrim expectations were rising and the facilities she could offer, in a small lodge capable of housing only a few people, were too basic for most pilgrims. She could in no way match the newer and more luxurious lodges that now catered to bus parties that wanted space and rooms for thirty or more people at a time or provide facilities—including karaoke, large baths and opulent menu choices rather than a simple rice-based meal and individual rooms—for which pilgrims were asking. Her wonderful (in our view) lodge had an ancient round Japanese bath and basic yet (to us as hungry walkers who had just trekked many miles across mountain paths in cold weather) very tasty meal of rice, soup, vegetables and pickles. Yet she told us that she was unlikely to continue for much longer because there were few walkers at that period and because a more modern and bigger inn with a sizeable hot-spring bath, plentiful food choices and the capacity to take in bus parties was now available only a short drive away. It had become the overnight place of choice in the area. A few years later, when I visited the area again, the inn was gone. We had similar conversations with other people running small, simple lodges in 1984 that, by the 1990s, had disappeared.

A recent rise in the number of walkers in Shikoku has led to the development of new lodges catering to walkers (but usually with such modcons seemingly essential to the modern pilgrim-hiker, such as Wi-Fi, that older-style lodges had not provided), but overall the pattern has been of increased comfort and the upgrading and modernising of accommodation facilities. Although bus companies seeking to make their packages more comfortably attractive for would-be customers have been instrumental in this process, they have not acted unilaterally. As company officials in several prominent bus companies have informed me, the demand for more opulent and upmarket modern accommodation and facilities comes from pilgrims who, after many hours in a coach, want a spacious bath, good beds, and individual rooms (rather than as pilgrims of yore did in Shikoku, all sleeping cheek by jowl in common rooms) as well as quality food and other luxuries. From simple rice with pickles, local vegetables and tea, they had graduated to sashimi, tempura, meats and other more sumptuous dishes, as well as beer and other drinks. Philip Taylor points to similar attitudes among Vietnamese pilgrims. When he asked a female pilgrim whether it was appropriate to make the pilgrimage to of Bà Chúa Xú in an air-conditioned vehicle and drinking beer, she responded 'Why shouldn't one do whatever one can to make doing this was comfortable on a long trip?' Drinking beer, she said, was fine (if one did not overdo it) because it would be good for relaxation, and although it was not right to do so at the shrine itself, there were plenty of bars around it where one could indulge (Taylor 2004: 141).

Pilgrims in the Marketplace 133

In Shikoku, pilgrim demand has also been instrumental in the improvement of facilities at the temples themselves. In 1984, when I first visited Shikoku, the toilet facilities available were, to put it mildly, somewhat on the basic side. Most temples only had ancient, nonflush Japanese-style toilets that were built over cesspits, seemed generally to come with hordes of flies around them and almost always were bathed in an aura of what I could only describe as 'essence de stale urine'. They were, by the mid-1980s, leading to complaints from pilgrims, who felt that if they were spending a fair amount of money on package tours and were contributing, by offerings and fees, to the well-being of the temples, they ought to be provided with better facilities as well. Several priests informed me that pilgrim complaints meant that improvements had to be made, and after surveys into pilgrim attitudes conducted in the late 1980s reinforced this view, the temples engaged in a mass renovation campaign. Through the 1990s, I noted a progressive improvement in the toilets available at the temples. Now, the temples invariably offer pilgrims spacious, clean, ultramodern toilets with waterjets, blowers and all the most modern comforts that any modern city dweller would aspire to in his or her homes.[13]

DROPPING BY AT THE SHRINE AND HAVING A HOLIDAY WITH MARY: ENTERTAINMENT, ENJOYMENT AND SIDE TRIPS

The popular and cryptic Tokugawa era saying at the start of this chapter (cited in Hoshino 1987: 11) about how pilgrims to Ise also just dropped by for a moment at the great shrines there indicates something striking not just about popular perceptions of pilgrims but about pilgrim behaviour and expectations relating to their travels and to the shrines and sites they visited. Ise, home to Shinto's most prominent shrines, attracted more pilgrims than any other place in Japan in the Tokugawa period, partly because it had developed a vibrant entertainment quarter full of bars and brothels (Nishigaki 1983, Vaporis 1994: 240). In Tokugawa, Japan, pilgrimage was the only way that commoners could travel, and hence, it was the only way in which they could escape temporarily from the restrictions of everyday village and feudal morality and have any sort of vacation. It is clear that many pilgrims were far more interested in such things than in actual worship and that their obligatory visit to the shrine itself (necessary so as to get the shrine's imprimatur that showed to the authorities back home that one had fulfilled the requirements of one's permit to travel and in order to acquire shrine talismans to bring back as souvenirs) was a fleeting event compared to their indulgences in Ise's pleasure quarters (Breen and Teeuwen 2010: 58). Similarly, Konpira pilgrims readily enjoyed the entertainments used to attract them to the shrine, to such an extent that priests worried that the town was descending into profligacy, even as they came to accept that pilgrim demands for prostitution and other such diversions were so intrinsic to the pilgrimage's popularity that they could not realistically ban them. Pilgrims, it was clear, would interact with site in ways they saw fit and appropriate to their needs, whereas pilgrimage confraternities saw their visits not just as occasions to pray to and seek blessings and boons from the deities, but as a form of socially sanctioned vacation in which they could get away from everyday morality (Thal 2005: 103–114).

Susanne Formanek (1998) has similarly shown how the desire for entertainment and travel was important in the development of pilgrimage in Japan from Tokugawa times onwards, often serving as much (or more) as a pretext for tourism as for piety. She discusses how pilgrims to Tateyama, a mountain pilgrimage site in central Japan, would spend much of their time and money on diversions along the way, often stopping off at hot spring resorts, while staying just two days at Tateyama itself. As such, Formanek shows how entertainment and amusement became a dominant theme as Tokugawa pilgrimage moved away from the more clearly ascetic orientations of earlier times. As this happened, the descriptions that Tateyama's pilgrimage guides (*oshi*) gave of the site also became more oriented towards entertainment (Formanek 1998: 174–183).

Hot springs—one of the great pleasures of Japan and, once enjoyment-focused travel became widespread, one of the main foci of internal Japanese travel and tourism—can be an important element in (and diversion from) pilgrimages in Japan and a major attraction for pilgrims, to the extent that having hot springs in the vicinity of pilgrimage sites became an important factor in the allure of many sites. Pilgrims readily made use of such facilities, not just in Tateyama but also when travelling to Ise (Vaporis 1994: 240–241) as well as when on the Saikoku and Shikoku pilgrimages. In Shikoku, a particular pilgrim favourite has been Dōgo Onsen (Dōgo hot springs), one of Japan's best-known and oldest such resorts that is right on the Shikoku pilgrimage route near the town of Matsuyama. Pilgrims have over the centuries shaped their itineraries to allow for a night (or more) staying there so they can relax in the baths, and this remains so in the present day. Many bus tours stop there overnight because of pilgrim demand. Indeed, on the numerous occasions I have been in the vicinity over the past two decades I have felt obliged to go there as part of my research—not, of course, for any reasons of entertainment but purely to learn more about the Shikoku pilgrimage experience by soaking myself in the hot spring baths. I have always encountered many pilgrims relaxing there as well.

This historical patterning has influenced the cultural ambience of pilgrimage and tourism in Japan where, as has been widely observed, prayer, play and travel are deeply interconnected (Graburn 1983, Kanzaki 1990). The links between piety and play are evident in the wishes of pilgrims as evident in the itineraries of Saikoku pilgrims and guidebooks cited by Foard (1982) and discussed in Chapter 4, and in the desires of Shikoku pilgrims to stop by at places such as Dōgo. Pilgrimage tour organisers in Japan emphasise the importance of pilgrim wishes in these areas. The nationwide pilgrimage society Junrei no kai has its headquarters at the Buddhist temple Manganji in Chiba Prefecture, around two hours by train from Tokyo. The temple has miniature versions of several Japanese pilgrimage routes, including Shikoku, in its courtyard and its head priest is a well-known authority on pilgrimage and author of many guidebooks on the subject (e.g., Hirahata 1982, 1990). The Junrei no kai regularly organises pilgrimage tours in Japan to Shikoku, Saikoku and other prominent destinations and those who join these tours are obliged to wear traditional pilgrimage clothing and join in the regular prayers at every site visited. Alongside its emphasis on faith and following pilgrimage protocols the Junrei no kai tours pay heed also to the wishes of pilgrims to have diversions and to stay at hot springs and places with comfortable accommodation with good food. Well aware that pilgrimage tours offering only prayer, rituals and hard travel were hardly likely to attract many people or increase the numbers of pilgrim visiting temples, it recognises that pilgrimage should not be separated from the sorts of relaxing activities, diversion and comforts that pilgrims like to participate in and want to have included in their tours. Indeed, one of the most popular pilgrimages that the organisation runs is to the thirty-three-stage Mogami Kannon, because that region has good hot-spring resorts, excellent local cuisine and good sights to see. Thus, although the Junrei no kai imposes certain expectations (about clothing and prayers) on its pilgrims, it also shapes its pilgrimages around pilgrim desires, which have enabled the organisation to bring the practice of pilgrimage to wider numbers of people.[14] The importance of hot springs, good scenery and the like was emphasised, as was seen in Chapter 3, by the priests who established the 'prevention of senility' pilgrimage in Kyushu in 1987. Shimoyasuba Yoshiharu, a former civil servant (now deceased) and Buddhist layman who devoted his retirement to producing pilgrimage guidebooks and who served as an advisor helping temples to develop new pilgrimages in Japan in the 1980s, also emphasised to me that these features were essential (along, he noted, with good parking facilities that could accommodate several bus tour parties at once) elements in the structure of a successful pilgrimage. Although faith, prayer and the hope of receiving benefits from the Buddhist figures such as Kannon were important to would-be pilgrims, so too were opportunities for enjoyment and relaxation, which were often more vital to modern Japanese pilgrims than were tales of miracle. Indeed, the structures of modern pilgrimages and of the modern guidebooks he had helped produce, with their emphasis on sights to see along the way, were very much shaped by pilgrim wishes above all else.[15]

Pilgrim wishes also mean that diversions from the pilgrimage route are common in Shikoku. I have elsewhere discussed how a pilgrimage party I travelled with in Shikoku paid a side visit to Konpira Shrine and treated this as a tourist diversion and 'escape valve' from the pressures of their pilgrimage tour (Reader 2005: 238–240). Officials of companies that run pilgrimage tours in Shikoku have told me that pilgrims coming from places in Japan far from Shikoku tend to see their visits as possibly the only time they may get to the island, so they are keen to see the island's other attractions (such as two dramatic gorges in the island's centre and one of Japan's most famous gardens in Takamatsu, the island's largest town) as well as the pilgrimage sites themselves. Because of such wishes, companies generally include a number of 'nonpilgrimage' stops in the itineraries of some of their tours. Iyo Tetsu, for example, began incorporating tourist sites in its pilgrimage tours from 1979 onwards (Mori 2005: 165). Nowadays, for many people, sightseeing appears to be more of a factor for pilgrims nowadays than does faith in Kōbō Daishi—an issue I look at again in Chapter 7.[16] The guidebooks to pilgrimages such as Saikoku and Shikoku that, as I discussed in Chapter 4, have progressively incorporated more and more side trips and sights to attract the pilgrim's attention, are thus mirrored by the interests of pilgrims who want to see and enjoy such diversions and expand their pilgrimages to take in interesting places along the way.

This is, of course, not something limited to Japan but indicative of common pilgrim attitudes that have historical resonances, for example, in the early package tours to the Christian Holy Land, which offered pilgrims opportunities to enjoy various excursions in the region and to take in other sites on their way home that they would never otherwise have had the chance to see, such as visits to Egypt (Chareyrou 2000: 158–159). They are reflected, too, in more modern periods, in the opportunities the newly developed pilgrimage to Lourdes offered pilgrims to shop and sightsee as well as perform their religious devotions (Kaufman 2004: 44–45). Jill Dubisch's (1995) discussion of the pilgrimage on the island of Tinos in Greece shows that although this is suffused with issues of emotional pain, sadness, vows and stories of miracle, pilgrims do not spend their whole time focused on such things. As Dubisch (1995: 105–106) notes, in Greek life, the spheres of the religious, the social and the recreational are 'closely bound' so that trips to Tinos, although religious, are also recreational, with pilgrims supplementing their penitential acts at the shrine with visits to other nearby, nonreligious, places as they went swimming and shopping and moved back and forth between the penitential and the playful.

Indian pilgrimages manifest similar themes. Christopher Fuller (1992: 205), discussing the expansion of Hindu pilgrimages in the modern period, states that pilgrims tended to combine their holy travels with what he terms 'ordinary tourism' such as visits to monuments and museums, a point also affirmed by Gladstone (2005). Anne Gold provides a striking example of this when describing how, in the long-distance pilgrimage made by Rajasthani villagers to numerous important Hindu sites including Gaya (where they performed rituals for their deceased kin and immersed their ashes in the river) and the holy town of Puri, the pilgrims also took time out to enjoy other clearly nonreligious attractions. As she comments, for many of the pilgrims, the high point of the trip, the one many of them later talked about and remembered most vividly, was seeing and bathing in the ocean at Puri Beach (Gold 1988: 281–283). One is reminded, too, of the Tibetan pilgrims discussed by Huber (2008) for whom the train journey became the most memorable aspect of their pilgrimages.

The close links of pilgrimage and tourism evident in pilgrim attitudes and intentions have, at times, caused concern for religious authorities, even as they have contributed significantly to this process. Kaufman (2004: 84), for example, reports about how priests at Lourdes (who had done much to encourage large numbers of visitors there) began to express concerns that 'pilgrims seeking penance too often became tourists on holiday'. However, the recognition of the therapeutic value of holidaying has, for the most part, been recognised as an element in the dynamics of pilgrimage. Dutch insurance companies, for example, at times send infirm Dutch people on pilgrimages to Lourdes to help them get better, through the process, as a pilgrimage coordinator working with these insurance companies put it, of giving pilgrims a 'holiday with Mary' (Notermans 2007: 5). Notermans's (2007: 5) description of the pilgrimage tour she observed shows the therapeutic values of such holiday-pilgrimages in ways that reaffirm the value, cited earlier, of diversions and side trips that provide a break and a release valve to help people better deal with the intensity of pilgrimage journeys:

> On the third day we took a day trip to the Pyrenees to distance ourselves from the sanctuary, to get a breath of fresh air, and think and deal with the emotions that had been released during the previous days.

NEW PATTERNS, NEW CHOICES AND DAY TRIPS: CASUALISING THE PILGRIMAGE?

The aforementioned transport developments (from foot to bus tour to car pilgrimages) in Shikoku and on other Japanese pilgrimages have enabled pilgrims to readily break their pilgrimages up into short, manageable sections; many Shikoku pilgrims do a few days at a time on the route and then return home to rest up and wait for the next opportunity that they can get away from home and/or work. Santiago pilgrims also may engage in similar patterns of pilgrimage (Frey 1998: 20–21). This process of fragmentation—in which doing the pilgrimage no longer constitutes one whole journey but may be divided up into several parts—has led to what are known in Japan as 'day return' (*higaeri*) pilgrimages. This pattern had already become common in the Saikoku pilgrimage by the 1980s, by which time the large majority of pilgrims came from the Kansai (western Japan) region where the thirty-three temples are located (Satō 2004: 175–176). It was especially convenient for them to do the pilgrimage in short sections, either spending a weekend or, more commonly, doing a series of day trips to different temples and doing the pilgrimage over an extended period. By the 1990s, many Saikoku pilgrims were doing it as a series of day trips (Satō 2004: 183–184). Among pilgrims

I have interviewed and surveyed in Saikoku from the mid-1980s onwards, perhaps the most prevalent pattern is for the pilgrimage to have become a family-oriented day-trip affair. According to a survey a colleague and I did in 1987, husband–wife combinations constituted some 55 per cent of Saikoku pilgrims (Leavell and Reader 1988: 114–116). My interviews with pilgrims and priests at Saikoku sites over the last quarter of a century indicate that this pattern persists and that the main day for such trips is on Sundays (the most common day for leisure activities in Japan). There is also a seasonal dimension to such day trips, with two periods of the year being especially common: the cherry blossom season in spring and the period when autumn leaf colours are at their best. They are also climatically the most pleasant times to travel in Japan. By travelling at such times, pilgrims in Saikoku have progressively constructed their pilgrimages to fit with their home routines and convenience as well as to take advantage of the best weather conditions and the most striking natural physical delights around the temples. Many of the pilgrims I have met at Saikoku temples over the last quarter of a century have said that they not only tailored their travels to the seasons but abandoned planned days out if the weather turned bad. They might be on pilgrimage, but they did not want to get wet and cold; they wanted to do the pilgrimage as a series of pleasurable trips to scenic temples framed by autumn colours or cherry blossoms and admire their art treasures, without the risk of rain or other inconveniences.[17]

The development of high-speed communication networks and the bridges that have made Shikoku readily accessible by bus or car from much of western Japan have led to the *higaeri* practice developing also in Shikoku in the last two decades. I have met several people travelling in this way. Two women I met at one of the temples in April 2000 lived in Matsuyama, one of Shikoku's main towns, and they were doing the pilgrimage around their home island by car on a day-trip basis over several months, setting off early on Sunday mornings when the season and weather were both amenable and coming home late in the evening if going to a distant temple and part of the island. The bridges (the first of which was opened in 1988) that link Shikoku to the mainland by road and rail have facilitated the potential for those from outside the island to similarly do day trips, and I have met many people who have come over on the bridges to Shikoku to do either one-day or weekend trips and who are doing the pilgrimage over extended periods. The pilgrim interest in such types of pilgrimage is now also reflected in bus tour schedules, as prominent companies in Shikoku such as Iyo Tetsu have in recent years instigated *higaeri* pilgrimage tours to cater to this new wave of pilgrim demands. One can, for example, now do the whole pilgrimage in a series of fifteen *higaeri* trips and/or 'Sunday pilgrimage' (*nichiyō henro*) journeys by Iyo Tetsu bus tours over several months, whereas other companies, including several from heavily populated areas on the mainland, are also now providing similar services. By contrast, with the recent tendency towards such *higaeri* tours, interest in doing the pilgrimage all in one go on

Iyo's tours appears to be declining. As a result, the company is amending the structure of its tour schedules to meet with this more recent pilgrim demand and is increasing its focus on *higaeri* tours.[18] Thus, pilgrimage patterns are being refashioned in Shikoku, with the pilgrimage, like Saikoku starting to acquire something of a 'day-trip' orientation in accord with the wishes of many pilgrims.

The same patterns are seen elsewhere in the Japanese pilgrimage world. One Sunday in early September 2011, for example, I made a day trip to the Chichibu region from Tokyo and walked a short section of the pilgrimage route there. Descending from the train were several people dressed in hiking gear. One man, in his fifties, whom I chatted to said that he was walking the pilgrimage route bit by bit on Sundays out, not, he stressed, for any religious reasons but because Chichibu was a lovely area, readily accessible from Tokyo, and the pilgrimage provided him with a good hiking route to this end. Over the years, I have made several trips to Chichibu, and in talking to those who are visiting the pilgrimage sites and to those looking after them, I have heard similar attitudes expressed on many occasions. Many of those visiting Chichibu have also talked about the scenery and about how good it is to get out of the city for a few hours and to look at some fascinating temples. Not everyone, of course, views the pilgrimage simply as a nice hiking route, and I have encountered various pilgrims travelling either individually or in groups who engage in extended devotions and who have expressed deeply pious comments about their relationship with Kannon. However, as one lady taking care of one of the temples said to me, the hikers and 'Sunday trippers' make up a sizeable number of those now visiting Chichibu temples (a point also made by Satō [2004: 193–194]); other site officials have similarly said that, although such enjoyable excursion-type pilgrimages have long been part of Chichibu's makeup, the proportion of people now doing it in such a manner is on the rise.[19]

AUTONOMY AND THE PILGRIM

In such ways day-trippers have emerged as powerful forces shaping aspects of pilgrimage in Japan today; they are also reminders of the autonomy of pilgrims to do pilgrimages in the manner in which they wish. Pilgrims, as this chapter has indicated, may readily perform multiple pilgrimages while weaving their pilgrimages into their everyday lives; they have particular expectations about the sites they visit and play a pertinent role in the construction of the physical environment of sites, while readily using the most convenient means available to visit the sites and keenly enjoying the surroundings, the entertainment, the markets and the pilgrimage goods that they encounter there. They may be motivated by deep faith, an enthusiasm for miracle tales, a sense of being drawn to places they deem as special and/ or the desire to leave the mundane world behind and encounter what they perceive as the holy. For the most part, they do so also with a ready acceptance and enthusiasm for the dynamics of the marketplace and all it entails, for the potential that pilgrimage sites offer for travel, tourism, entertainment and ways of escaping from the restraints of everyday life and their normative social environment, and because of what such places appear to offer them in terms of such diversions and attractive images. Furthermore, what is found around shrines and pilgrimage sites may well occupy more of their focus and time than the supposed sacred centre to which they travel. The presence of such modes of entertainment has—as the successful use of prostitutes, wrestling and other spectacles to draw pilgrims to Konpira; the attraction of the entertainment quarters around the Ise shrines in Tokugawa times; and the recurrent popularity of hot spring resorts all indicate—proved magnetic, to the extent that the magnetism places of pilgrimage might possess is not solely of the spiritual variety.

Although priests and others may, as they have done at Lourdes, Konpira and many other places, at times bemoan the tendency of pilgrims to view their journeys through the prism of holidays or shudder at the profligacy that arises when hordes of pilgrims are drawn to their sites, they tend to have little real influence over pilgrims in such contexts. Pilgrims as a whole are clearly relaxed about such things, finding accessibility, convenience and entertainment to be appropriately commensurate with their expectations of pilgrimage, to the degree that their absence may be more problematic. Although prayer, piety and related intentions may form a notable element in the journeys of some, they are not necessarily the most evident aspects either of pilgrim motivations or of behaviour for large swaths of the pilgrim community compared to the pragmatics of comfort, the potential for social engagement, status advancement, entertainment and the chance to engage with supposedly mundane attractions and see new places and things. These are all critical aspects of the pilgrimage market and of pilgrim actions and motivations that should always be considered in any accounts of pilgrimage. They suggest also that, as opportunities for increased consumer comforts, diversions and other means of engaging in pilgrimage activities grow, and as chances for self-promotion offer themselves, pilgrimages may increasingly become focused on such themes. I examine such issues in more detail in Chapter 7, but before that, I turn to another important area in which pilgrim wishes and consumer choices play a significant role in shaping pilgrimage dynamics: the souvenirs, relics and talismans that are found on sale at and around pilgrimage sites, and it is to this area that I turn next.

6 Scrolls, Singing Toilet-Paper Roll Holders, Martin Luther's Socks and Other Sacred Goods of the Marketplace

> If you're a peasant from Calabria and you see a toilet-paper roll holder that plays Ave Maria when you pull out a sheet you think 'Fantastic!'
> —Monsignor Vladimir Felzmann, pilgrimage director for the Catholic diocese of Westminster[1]

> it's easy to see without looking too far that not much is really sacred
> —Bob Dylan, 'It's Alright, Ma (I'm Only Bleeding)', from *Bringing It All Back Home*

INTRODUCTION: SOUVENIRS AND THE SACRED

Few aspects of the pilgrimage landscape have been more vilified than the trinkets and souvenirs sold at and around places of pilgrimage. The quotation from the *bmibaby* website with its disdainful comments about the 'tacky trade industry' and 'fluorescent Virgin Mary statues' and the comments in the *Rough Guide to France* about the 'indescribable kitsch' of Lourdes, both cited in Chapter 1, sum up a prevalent perception of such things: cheap, crass commercialism that contrasts with the holy aura of sites and detracts from their 'magic'. The 'fluorescent Virgin Mary statues' of the website accord with the manufacture for monetary gain of the 'flesh colored Christs that glow in the dark' that Bob Dylan refers to in his 1965 song 'It's Alright, Ma (I'm Only Bleeding)' when he says that 'not much is really sacred'.

Similar disparagement occurs in academic literature too. Michael Stausberg (2011: 210), for example, says that 'souvenirs tend to be kitsch of the worst kind', while, as was also seen in Chapter 1, David Sox (1985: 195) refers to the items on sale at Lourdes as 'garish' and 'tasteless'. Alan Morinis (1992: 6) uses terms such as 'tawdry' to describe pilgrimage souvenirs even as he argues that their innate links to the realms of the holy mean they need not be of any great cost or aesthetic value. Such comments reiterate the views, cited in earlier chapters, of those who lament the apparent ways in which the 'sacred' has been perverted by the depredations of the market and of materialism. The sale of souvenirs is something that, according to Eade

142 *Pilgrimage in the Marketplace*

and Sallnow (1991), most annoys those who run pilgrimage shrines. They state that such religious officials find souvenirs to be 'distasteful' and that they are especially hostile to 'the petty traders of shrine souvenirs' because they threaten the

> fragile boundary between religious devotion and workaday commerce, and by extension between the sacred and secular realms, which they are obliged to maintain. (Eade and Sallnow 1991: 26)

Yet, although there may be tensions between religious sites and souvenir sellers, I would argue that these might well be as much to do with competition over the selling of souvenirs as about any actual condemnation of or disdain for souvenirs that may be held by religious officials; as will be seen later in this chapter, pilgrimage sites and those who run them often themselves are heavily engaged in the sale of such items. And perhaps no aspect of pilgrimage serves as a sharper warning against the sort of moralising condemnation evident in the words of those who bemoan how sacred sites are being undermined and disturbed by commercialism than does the subject of souvenirs. Such condemnation misrepresents souvenirs as somehow antithetical to the sanctity and 'real' meaning of pilgrimage. It is also implicitly demeaning to pilgrims, portraying them as gullible, manipulated and as little more than awestruck 'peasants' beguiled by singing toilet-paper roll holders, fluorescent Virgins, plastic Buddhas, Kōbō Daishi keyrings and other of the souvenirs and objects that will appear in this chapter. They also are muddled in confusing assumptions about aesthetic quality (or apparent lack thereof, although one must always realise that these are issues very much in the eye of the beholder), with issues of sanctity. As Cynthia Hahn (1990) points out in her study of the souvenirs that medieval pilgrims brought home from shrines in the Christian Holy Land, the aesthetic was not necessarily a quality that pilgrims sought when looking for something to bring home from their travels. The ampoules of oil and water that were common souvenir fare for medieval pilgrims might have been simply made from cheap materials, but they had importance, value and meaning because they signified the potency and energy of the places the pilgrims had visited, were repositories of the blessings gained there, marked their possessors out as being among the elect who had visited them, and were efficacious reminders of the pilgrims' visits and experiences there (Hahn 1990: 86–91).

These are all points that will come to the fore in this chapter, which argues that souvenirs illustrate clearly how problematic it is to make divisions or differentiations between the putative notions of the sacred and the profane- an artificial division that has led to some aspects of religion being neglected or marginalised. Colleen McDannell (1995: 8) makes this point in her study of material Christianity in the United States, in which she demonstrates the importance and significance of material objects (many of which would doubtless be labelled as kitsch or as tacky by some) in the study of religion while criticising the field for paying little attention to what she sees as the recurrent 'scrambling' of the sacred and the profane throughout U.S. Christian history. Much the same can be said for the study of religion in Japan, where a similar scrambling occurs (Reader and Tanabe 1998).

Souvenirs are an integral part of the pilgrimage process, and a cardinal element in their construction and popularity. They are examples not so much of the 'fragile boundaries' that Eade and Sallnow suggest exist between devotion and commerce but of the porous nature of these spheres of activity, which readily overlap and flow into each other. As has been discussed earlier, how pilgrimages accord with the desires and wishes of pilgrims, for whom the hubbub and attractions of the marketplace are likely to be more enticing than is tranquillity or separation from the everyday world, is a key element in how or whether they will flourish, and a critical component in this is their potential to allow would-be pilgrims to acquire goods and reminders of the places they are visiting. Indeed, such goods and souvenirs (a category that, as I argue later, includes amulets and relics) form an important part in pilgrim motivations, experiences and memories, whereas those who purchase such items are not being manipulated by religious authorities and marketplace merchants so much as they are (as was indicated in the previous chapter) avid consumers who may visit many different sites wishing not just to pray, experience spiritual benefits and see splendid sights but also to get souvenirs and other material reminders of such places. As consumers, they stimulate the marketplace of pilgrimage souvenirs, which serve not as signifiers of the corruption of the sacred but the reverse: as an emphatic reaffirmation to pilgrims of the sanctity of the places they are visiting.

BRINGING IT ALL BACK HOME: SOUVENIRS, MEMORIES AND CONNECTIONS

When the journalist Tom Adair visited Knock, he initially was disdainful of the souvenirs on sale there, describing them as 'garish fripperies'. However, when he attended a mass at the shrine at which the priest invited the congregation to raise up the souvenirs they had bought for a blessing, Adair quickly realised that his earlier dismissal was off the mark. As forests of holy pictures, rosaries, medals and the like were lifted up:

> It occurred to me then that what I had seen as dross had become for others uniquely, harbingers of something inexpressible. The shoddiness of these goods had rendered them cheap and thus attainable. The democracy of universal access. (Adair 1998: 18)

Adair realised Hahn's point made earlier, that the importance for pilgrims was in the meaning, not the aesthetic nature, of the items they had bought. What he initially dismissed as shoddy 'fripperies' were for the pilgrims repositories of Knock's potency that could be taken back home as reminders of its aura and as a means through which they could express their love for their families and friends and connect them to the place itself. Indeed, many items sold at Knock serve as media through which pilgrims can interact with those back at home, such as the water bottles that are inscribed with the message 'Holy Water from Knock: I prayed for you at Knock'.

Such messages along with the uses of pilgrimage souvenirs draw attention to a critical issue that often gets overlooked in pilgrimage studies—the importance of home. Studies of pilgrimage have frequently focused on such themes as movement and on the importance of journeys, of people in transit and of escaping and getting away from everyday frameworks and constraints. Such a focus on movement is clearly understandable when studying pilgrimage, but it has its downsides in that emphasising transience and being away from normative routines tends to deflect attention away from concepts of home. This is a point I have already made, in Chapter 2, where I drew attention to the quotidian dimensions of pilgrimage and the ways in which it serves to rearticulate and strengthen the values of one's home culture. Souvenirs and the messages embedded in them—such as the words written on Knock water bottles—powerfully reinforce this point while emphasising how central the idea of home is to the pilgrimage process. It is not just that journeys are normally (although by no means always) temporary[2] or that pilgrims return home and then may (re)interpret and view their journeys via the context of home. Concepts and imaginings of home—and of those left behind—are often intrinsic to the thoughts of pilgrims when they are physically on pilgrimage as well.

Souvenirs are significant in this context. Not only are they a tangible means of bringing back memories and symbols of the site(s) visited, both for one's own consumption and to share with or give to friends and family, but they are also a means of thinking of home while on pilgrimage and mechanisms for homemaking when one returns and for incorporating into one's home thoughts, signs and symbols of the places one has visited. This became clear to me through listening to pilgrims at various Japanese sites talking about why and for whom (including themselves and their homes) they might be acquiring various items on sale such as amulets, rosaries, pilgrimage scrolls, trinkets with images of Buddhist icons, and so on. Many of the Japanese pilgrims I have met and talked to have, for example, emphasised the importance of getting a completed pilgrimage scroll that could be later hung in their house, and have indicated that it was a central element in their motivations as pilgrims (see the following discussion) as well as serving as a decorative object that could enhance the ambience of their home and heighten their sense of pride in it.[3]

When I visited Knock, I was similarly struck by the discussions among pilgrims in the shops around the shrine; although the language (English) was different from what I had heard around Japanese temples, the content was remarkably similar. The pilgrims were not complaining that the shops were

Scrolls, Singing Toilet-Paper Roll Holders, Martin Luther's Socks

Figure 6.1 'Holy water from Knock. I prayed for you at Knock'.

146 *Pilgrimage in the Marketplace*

Figure 6.2 Souvenir shop window in Knock (including assorted Marys and Padre Pio).

spoiling the sanctity of Knock or deriding their goods as tawdry. Rather, they were talking about their value as items to take home, about which item (a rosary, a Virgin Mary statuette, a cross, a picture) would be most appropriate for which friend or relative; two middle-aged women I overheard spoke about how inspiring particular items were and of how such-and-such a statuette would be just perfect for a (named) cousin and/or friend. Catrien Notermans (2007) has drawn attention to the importance of such social considerations for Dutch pilgrims to Lourdes, who may purchase candles and statues to be brought home and placed on the graves of deceased kin. Notermans speaks of how such pilgrims use Lourdes's souvenirs to make connections between their living kin and the site itself. Pilgrims on returning home do not talk much to their family and friends about their experiences; rather, they pass on to them 'the material memories'—that is, the souvenirs—they have bought there (Notermans 2007). Kaufman (2004: 71), too, comments on how Lourdes's pilgrims 'considered the buying and selling of religious souvenirs to be a normal part of the pilgrimage journey'.

Souvenirs certainly have immense social importance in Japanese pilgrimage contexts. Tokugawa-era pilgrims were socially obliged to bring home souvenirs for those who were unable to travel, often in return for donations made in advance to assist the pilgrim in his or her travels (Kanzaki 1990: 70–92, Vaporis 1994: 222–224, Formanek 1998: 166). Pilgrims would thus come back 'loaded down with gifts', sometimes spending much more on souvenirs than on travel expenses, especially as their journeys were very often a once-in-a-lifetime event (Vaporis 1994: 223). Frequently, too, pilgrims' journals indicated that they were more interested in what they could purchase as souvenirs than they were in the sites that were the purported focus of their travels (Vaporis 1994: 240). In the modern day, too, the parties of pilgrims I have travelled with or observed in Shikoku have spent plentiful time seeking out and buying such items for those they had left behind, to the extent that buying such items played an integral part of their pilgrimages.

Such 'material memories' thus reaffirm the bonds (and obligations) between pilgrims and those left behind at home. They can also play a significant part in creating bonds with fellow pilgrims and building a sense of common belonging within pilgrimage parties, as I discovered when travelling with a party of pilgrims in Shikoku who bought souvenir items for each other during the journey. Some of the pilgrims formed close links together through such means, notably two women in their late sixties, both travelling alone (one widowed, one whose husband was unable to travel), who shared a mutual interest in going around the stalls and temple shops looking for new items to purchase, and who spent much of their time in such pursuits and in discussing the items on sale, comparing prices and commenting on potential purchases. They also at times wanted the tour to be slowed a little so that they could spend more time on such pursuits at some of the temples. At the end of our pilgrimage, when we reached our final temple, one of them, who had also had been very friendly towards me, said she wanted something to remind her of me and vice versa. Thus, she had two commemorative photographs taken of us and made into souvenir telephone cards (this was in the pre–mobile phone days when phone cards were widely used in Japan, and when one could have personalised cards made), giving one to me and keeping one for herself as mementoes of our trip together.

SHOPPING AND PILGRIMAGE

Shopping in such ways is an integral part of pilgrimage itineraries. It can also (similar to the side trips and tourist diversions mentioned in the previous chapter) have a cathartic and therapeutic role during pilgrimages, enabling pilgrims especially in parties to deal with the intensities and tensions that may arise when people are travelling together and have to exist at close quarters with others for extended periods. It is unsurprising in such terms that pilgrimage schedules frequently provide time and opportunities for such activities, as was the case with the above-mentioned Shikoku pilgrimage tour. The schedules of pilgrims at Knock, too, clearly allowed them time for souvenir buying, while the conversations they had in shops indicated how central such activities were to their pilgrimages. The service provided by the priest to bless such items in the church further emphasised how important this was to the

148 *Pilgrimage in the Marketplace*

wider framework of their pilgrimages. I was reminded, through observing pilgrims at Knock, of a visit many years earlier, in 1988, to Chikubushima, an island in Japan's largest lake, Lake Biwa, and the location of one of the Saikoku pilgrimage temples, Hōgonji. Alongside the temple complex, the only other thing of note on the island was a row of souvenir stalls where the ferries arrived. Ferry schedules meant that pilgrims normally only had one hour on the island, and in that time, the pilgrims managed to do a number of things. They hurried up the steps to the temple, made a round of its halls of worship praying and making offerings, got their pilgrimage scrolls or books stamped at the temple office and found time to rummage through the stalls to purchase souvenirs. Temple visiting, getting scrolls stamped, praying and buying amulets and souvenirs were part of an integrated whole rather than separate acts with potential contradictions among them.[4]

Abdellah Hammoudi's description of his hajj pilgrimage indicates similar scheduling structures allowing pilgrims plenty of time—which they happily used—to visit the markets of Medina, which were lavishly stocked with consumer items. As he observed, 'Medina's beating heart had two chambers: the mosque and the marketplace' (Hammoudi 2006: 100). Although he is personally discomfited by the commercialism on display, and complains of a binary tension in which he 'could be only a worshipper or a customer', this does not seem to be the case for his fellow pilgrims, who, he observes, came to do their religious duty *and* to engage in commerce and buy things without seemingly considering there to be any conflict between the two (Hammoudi 2006: 84–86).

RELICS, SOUVENIRS AND OTHER SACRED OBJECTS

At this point, I wish to emphasise that I consider that it is not helpful to make distinctions between items purchased at shops and stalls adjacent to a shrine and those acquired within them that might be purveyed as amulets, relics or other forms of sacred objects. I regard all these as belonging to a similar category in that their significance as objects is grounded in their association with particular places and/or holy figures venerated there. Stausberg (2011: 209) in effect says something similar in indicating that, if souvenirs are seen as possessing a 'special agency' because of their associations with sacred places, they would be on the 'same footing as relics'. He initially speaks of an 'ideal-typical' division between pilgrimage and tourism, in which the former is associated with religion, faith, spiritual matters and asceticism, and the latter associated with pleasure, the secular world, commerce and materialism (Stausberg 2011: 20). If that were the case, he says, then there would be differentiations between relics and souvenirs, with the former being associated with pilgrimage and the latter with tourism. However, he recognises that such 'ideal-typical' differentiations are not workable, that in reality there is far more of a continuum between these spheres (as he represents them) and that souvenirs have been long associated with pilgrimage sites to the extent that souvenir buying is as much a natural element in pilgrimage as it is in tourism (Stausberg 2011: 209). For Stausberg, therefore, there is in effect a continuum between relics and souvenirs just as there is also, in his view, between pilgrimage and tourism.

However, the very idea of a continuum implies some form of differentiation—as indeed Stausberg's ideal-typical binary notion indicates. This is where I part company with him, for I do not find such differentiations between, for example, a relic or an amulet acquired at a shrine or temple, and a souvenir depicting a religious icon or figure, or even playing a tune associated with a sacred figure as it dispenses sheets of toilet paper, that has been bought at a shop outside a shrine, to be workable even if located within the framework of a continuum. This is especially so when, as with the scenario Adair viewed at Knock, souvenirs can themselves be blessed at a shrine. In such contexts, any potential differentiation, and hence any sense of a continuum, disappears. The same holds true when one considers the reality that items that are sold within shrine precincts and are depicted as sacred in nature (such as the amulets that Japanese shrine and temple visitors commonly buy) may be purchased for social reasons and as souvenirs (Reader 1991: 189).

Relics may also be souvenirs. Relic collecting was an important part of the pilgrimages of medieval Christians who went to the Christian Holy Land and sought to bring back items redolent of the places they had been (Bowman 1992: 150). Because these items were associated with memories of the places concerned, they could therefore serve as souvenirs. Relics were also produced in great numbers to satisfy the demands of pilgrims seeking something tangible to take home with them as reminders of their journeys and of the places they had visited. Such was the flood of relics that came from the medieval Holy Land, such as the countless relics of the 'True Cross' that logically could not all have been from the cross on which Jesus was crucified, that they could not all have been 'genuine' or 'authentic' in the sense of being the actual objects or items they were purported to be. Mass production of some sort was clearly involved, just as it is with the Virgin Mary water bottles found in the souvenir shops of Knock. In such terms, it is hard to differentiate between the two: between the purported relic (of, for instance, the 'True Cross') and the mass-produced statuette or water bottle on sale in a souvenir shop. Both are material representations of the hopes, aspirations and the consumerist desires of the purchasers intent on acquiring and bringing home some tangible reminder of a shrine and/or a figure of worship.

Relics can certainly be mass produced, as the example of the tongue relic of Saint Anthony sold at Padua Cathedral, indicates. Pilgrims go there to seek the grace of St. Anthony, and they file by and touch his tomb in the cathedral, invoking prayers as they do so. They also can pay homage to his tongue, which is preserved in a reliquary on display in the cathedral and which serves as a vital remnant and signifier of the saint's physical presence there. At the cathedral shop, alongside the usual array of souvenir objects, crosses, postcards and books, they can also purchase and take home with them what is described by the cathedral as a 'relic' of the tongue. This is not an actual, physical piece of tongue, but a tiny piece of linen in a paper sachet. The sachet provides the explanation that on occasion the reliquary is opened so that strips of linen can be passed across the actual tongue relic, thereby imbuing the linen with Saint Anthony's holy power. The linen is then cut into tiny pieces, each of which is placed in a sachet to become a 'relic' that is sold to pilgrims. The linen may not be a physical trace of Saint Anthony's corporeal body, but for devotees and for the cathedral's ecclesiastical authorities, it is portrayed as such, as a relic of Saint Anthony that pilgrims can take home. Of course, sold as it is in the cathedral shop alongside various souvenirs, there is no guarantee that everyone who purchases one does so because they believe it is an efficacious relic or to use it as an object of veneration. I, for example, bought one as a souvenir from Padua and as an exhibit to use in my teaching. Others appeared to buy tongue relics along with other seemingly more overt souvenir items such as postcards and the like. I also bought (at a stall outside the cathedral) a snow shaker depicting the baby Jesus, Mary and Joseph. The stall also sold candles and a variety of votives that could be lit at or placed in the shrine, and several people I saw seemed to buy these, presumably for such use, along with items such as the snow shakers. The point I am making here is that people appeared to purchase the relics (and other items such as votives and candles) along with objects that appeared to be more overtly of the 'souvenir' variety. Yet there was no way in which one could necessarily discern whether they were making clear differentiations between these different mass-produced artefacts, all of which stood for the cathedral and its saint and all of which could be taken home as reminders (i.e., souvenirs) and representations of a special place and person visited.

Some people also appeared to rub items they had purchased or had carried into the cathedral, against the saint's tomb as if to infuse them with the saint's aura. This sort of activity was remarked on by the curator of the *Treasures of Heaven* exhibition (a display of relics and sacred items from medieval Europe held at the British Museum in 2011), in an academic paper about the exhibition, in which he described how some people visiting the exhibition bought Saint George badges at the British Museum shop and then went into the exhibition and rubbed them on the exhibition cases containing relics, as if to transfer the sacred power of the relics into the souvenirs (Robinson 2012). This example suggests that one cannot make any real differentiations in terms of the end result—what is taken back and why—between relics and souvenirs; the one can become or simply be the other. Relics can be purchased and taken home as souvenirs, which in turn may be acquired and 'made' into relics and items deemed holy through blessings (as at the church in Knock) or by the process of rubbing them against 'real' relics or saint's tombs. It is not just that the boundaries between them are porous, but also how they are viewed—as sacred objects, 'authentic' relics or souvenirs—is highly contingent and dependent on individual perceptions.

As I noted, at Padua I bought a 'tongue relic' from the shop inside the cathedral and a Jesus, Mary and Joseph snow shaker from a stall outside; to me, they were no different, just objects that could be used in my teaching on pilgrimage, as well as, in my view, rather striking examples of pilgrimage memorabilia that I just had to bring home to show to my family and friends. Others might have bought them as souvenirs, whereas for others, still they might have signified something different.

Pilgrimage sites and shrines may themselves conflate souvenirs with supposedly 'sacred' items. When promoting the items that can be bought at shrine shops, for example, authorities at the Shri Mata Vaishno Devi Shrine in Jammu, India, appear to manifest very little conceptual distinction between souvenirs, sacred objects and offerings to the gods. Pilgrims are informed on the shrine's website that the deity Shri Mata Vaishno Devi can grant all manner of boons to pilgrims and that 'no-one goes home empty-handed from Her Great Pilgrimage'. To this end, pilgrims are informed that the shrine owns several 'souvenir shops' (this is the term used by the shrine) where pilgrims can purchase items such as shawls and saris that have been previously offered to and blessed at the shrine. These can be taken home as souvenirs or as items to be put in a home shrine or 'place of worship inside their houses'.[5] Shrine offerings that have been blessed can thus be taken home as souvenirs or be used as items for continued worship, depending, it would seem, on the views of the purchaser. Later in this chapter, when I discuss Japanese pilgrimage scrolls a similar ambivalence and multiplicity of meanings—in which such items may be treated as religious objects that are used in rituals at home and/or as resplendent souvenirs to be admired, depending on the personal perspectives of those who acquire them—will be evident.

This glossing of seemingly religious and secular perceptions with regards to souvenirs is evident in the Japanese word *miyage*, which is commonly translated as 'souvenir' in standard Japanese–English dictionaries. Nowadays it is written with two ideograms 土産 that signify 'something produced/made in the locality', but in earlier times, as the Japanese scholar of tourism Kanzaki Noritake (1990) emphasises, it was written with different ideograms 宮笥, the first of which (*miya*) means shrine and the second (*ge*) signifies a special box for food offerings at shrines. The souvenir, in origin, was thus something brought back from or associated with offerings at shrines (Kanzaki 1990: 82–92). In such terms, a souvenir may be also implicitly or explicitly of a very similar ilk to a relic or other purported sacred object—a point evident in the following discussion of items such as pilgrimage scrolls and Catholic medals.

PILGRIMAGE SCROLLS, MOTIVATIONS AND MEANINGS

The acquisition of souvenirs that can serve as reminders and signifiers of places visited is, as I have noted earlier, often an important motivating factor for pilgrims. To illustrate this further, here I turn to Japan and the pilgrims'

152 Pilgrimage in the Marketplace

books (*nōkyōchō*) and scrolls (*kakejiku*) mentioned earlier in this book. The books (*nōkyōchō*) are usually simple concertina-like books of plain paper with a pilgrimage inscription that the pilgrims have stamped (and on some routes the priest also adds some ink-brush calligraphy as well) at each temple they visit; a completed book (and the same is true for scrolls) is evidence of a completed pilgrimage. Initially the book served a practical function. In the Tokugawa period, when would-be pilgrims needed a permit to travel, and when pilgrimage served as the main reason for such permits to be granted, pilgrims would carry such books to be stamped at the temples as proof that they had fulfilled their obligation of actually doing the pilgrimages they had permits for. Indeed, the Tosa feudal authorities who controlled the southern part of Shikoku, where sixteen of the Shikoku pilgrimage temples are located, prohibited pilgrims not in possession of this book from entering their domain (Kouamé 1998: 61). Although it was thus a practical document proving that one had fulfilled the conditions of a permit, in popular pilgrimage lore, the book (and subsequently, the scroll, whose use became widespread among pilgrims in the postwar era) came to take on a different meaning for pilgrims. It was viewed as a testament of the merit they had gained through doing the pilgrimage, one that wiped away their transgressions and earned them rebirth in the Buddhist Pure Land at death. Hence in effect it served as a passport to the Pure Land (Maeda 1971: 56, Shinno 1980: 52).

Pilgrimage scrolls are similar to, albeit more costly and more cumbersome to carry than, *nōkyōchō*. They too are stamped and inscribed at each temple one visits. They have become exceptionally popular among more affluent pilgrims in the postwar era, especially among those who travel by bus and car. (Walkers rarely carry them because they do not readily fit in a backpack). They are generally beautiful and striking ornaments that shatter any assumption that pilgrimage items are always cheap and unaesthetic; their cost is high, for pilgrims generally pay at least 15,000 yen (more than 160 U.S. dollars) for the basic scroll plus a fee (currently in Shikoku 500 yen or 5.5 dollars) to get it stamped at each temple, plus a fee of at least 800 dollars to have the completed scroll properly mounted after completion.[6] The scrolls also represent the cumulative pilgrimage process and are (like the Compostela acquired by pilgrims who have completed the pilgrimage to Santiago de Compostela [Frey 1998: 159–162]) a testimony of completion.[7] The scroll manifests (and hence replicates) the main image of the pilgrimage; Saikoku scrolls normally have Kannon, and Shikoku scrolls Kōbō Daishi, at the centre. Around the images of these central figures in the pilgrimage are spaces for the thirty-three (or eighty-eight) temples to inscribe their stamps and add ink-brush calligraphy, an act done by the priest or a designated temple official. Often, those who carry out this task have inherited a tradition of stamping and inscribing scrolls from earlier generations of their families. When the pilgrimage has been completed, the scroll will be taken or sent to a specialist scroll mounting firm to be affixed onto an embossed backing; pamphlets and signs advertising the services of such firms (which also often emphasise their long tradition

Figure 6.3 Temple official inscribing calligraphy on a Japanese pilgrim's book at a Saikoku temple.

of performing such services for pilgrims) can readily be found at pilgrimage temples and now, also, online.[8]

There are many people involved in the production of the completed scroll: those who made the initial scroll, those who stamped it at each temple, those who mounted it—and of course the pilgrim who carried it around the route and ensured that it was stamped at each place. In such terms, the scroll is a cumulative artefact that encapsulates and, via the image of the holy figure at the heart of the pilgrimage and the stamps that represent the sites, replicates the entire pilgrimage. For some pilgrims, it serves as a ritual object. Maeda Takashi (1971: 171) describes how Saikoku pilgrimage scrolls may be used as ritual objects in funerals, with the spirit of the dead 'led' around the pilgrimage via the chanting of each pilgrimage temple's sacred song (*go-eika*) in turn, thereby symbolically taking the spirit to each site on the route and enabling it to enter the Pure Land.

Hence, the scroll also serves as a marker of spiritual attainment and as a ritual object to be used in religious rites. Yet it also remains highly popular because of its aesthetic qualities as an artefact of beauty and as a souvenir of one's travels. Many of the pilgrims I have interviewed at Saikoku temples have made this point to me. In a survey of 449 pilgrims that a colleague and I conducted at Mimurotoji, one of the Saikoku temples, in November 1987, 72 per cent said that they regarded the scroll as a souvenir and reminder (*kinen*) of their pilgrimage.[9] Encounters with scroll-carrying pilgrims at various pilgrimage sites have confirmed this view. Thus, a middle-aged couple I met at Kazanin—the temple where Emperor Kazan took the Buddhist tonsure, and which, although it is not officially one of the thirty-three temples, is able to stamp Saikoku scrolls and which is often visited by Saikoku pilgrims[10]—in September 1987 said that they saw the scroll as a wonderful souvenir and memento of their travels together. For many pilgrims, the beauty of the scroll is paramount, and many regard getting such an item as a prime motivation for their own pilgrimages. One Japanese lady, who was a family acquaintance, said that she had seen a completed Saikoku pilgrimage scroll in her sister's house and was so taken with its beauty that she wanted one herself. On being told that the scroll had been acquired through visiting the Saikoku temples, she immediately resolved to do so herself—becoming a pilgrim, in other words, because she wanted to acquire a visually splendid souvenir. Although scrolls may, for some pilgrims, be representations of the graft and sweat of pilgrimage, and of its symbolic structures and meanings, they are also important aesthetic objects to be desired, consumed and displayed to adorn one's home and to impress visitors. It is perhaps little wonder that some of the visitors to the Saikoku pilgrimage exhibition at the department store described in Chapter 1 were persuaded to do the pilgrimage as a result of seeing the scrolls there and thinking that they also would like to own such beautiful and desirable items.

I have met numerous Japanese people who could be described as scroll collectors who have done multiple pilgrimage journeys in order to pursue

Scrolls, Singing Toilet-Paper Roll Holders, Martin Luther's Socks 155

Figure 6.4 Completed Saikoku pilgrimage scroll.

this hobby. Two examples should suffice. One was when my wife and I lived in Tarumi, a suburb of Kobe, between 1985 and 1987. We became friendly with one of the local rice and beer merchants, a man in his mid-fifties, who, on finding out I was interested in pilgrimage, invited us around for an evening in October 1986, during which he brought out a number of completed scrolls. His hobby, he said, was doing different pilgrimages in Japan—always by bus or car and never, he stressed, on foot—and getting scrolls from each of them. This was not, he emphasised, for any religious reasons but because he liked the scrolls and wanted them as beautiful keepsakes. He had done the Saikoku pilgrimage four times, at different times of the year to get a feel for the temples in different seasons, and had a scroll from each trip. Although he felt that visiting temples gave him a good and peaceful feeling, he viewed his travels as largely touristic and focused on going to nice places while collecting beautiful objects to bring home. Similarly, I was once invited to visit the house of a farmer in rural Mie Prefecture whom I had met through mutual friends. He wanted to meet me because of my interest in pilgrimages, and he spent the evening proudly showing me the various scrolls and other memorabilia he had brought back from Saikoku, Chichibu and other pilgrimages. He, too, stressed that this was not something concerned with prayer or religion but was, rather, a hobby carried out with three friends who similarly collected scrolls. Together they would select new pilgrimages to do together, taking account of such things as good scenery and facilities (including nearby hot spring resorts) that would help make their journeys enjoyable, but always with the aim of getting new scrolls. They, like the beer merchant, did not see them as items of religious significance, nor did they use them in rituals; they viewed them as aesthetic objects and motivating factors in their hobby of visiting pilgrimage sites.

SCROLLS, CHANGING PRACTICES AND INNOVATIVE SALES

Not all priests appear wholly enthusiastic at the contemporary interest in scroll acquisition. A priest at Kami Daigoji, one of the Saikoku temples, complained to me during a recent visit there in March 2008 that the temple, which is set in the hills to the southeast of Kyoto and offers scope for some lovely hikes, had become little more a point on a hiking route and a place where people just dropped by to get their scrolls stamped. Most people, he said, do not even bother to pray or make any offering; they just come to the temple office, proffer their scrolls for stamping and then head off again. I heard similar complains when visiting the Sasaguri pilgrimage route in April 2007. Many of Sasaguri's eighty-eight pilgrimage sites are small, unmanned wayside halls; although pilgrims are supposed to visit them in order to complete the pilgrimage, the scrolls are stamped only at the small number of temples with resident officials who stamp the appropriate sections of the scroll or pilgrims' book for the unmanned sites as well. Yet I heard from officials there that in recent times, many pilgrims appeared only to visit the sites where one got the stamps and skipped the rest. Priests in Shōdoshima, where there are twenty-nine temples where one can get scrolls and books stamped and which do the stamps for the remaining sites, which are wayside halls of worship that are not always manned, have said much the same. Pilgrims will visit the places where they can get their books or scrolls stamped, and having got the stamps for the unmanned sites, often skip them if it makes the journey quicker and easier. As such, the material signifier of having done the pilgrimage has become transformed into a desired object and motive for the pilgrimage. It has become such an overriding concern that some people feel they need not do the whole pilgrimage as long as they can get the stamps that (symbolically) signify completion.

Such is the allure of scrolls and books that a trade has developed in surrogate pilgrimages (Japanese: *dairi sanpai*) in which commercial firms offer the service of providing people—for a substantial fee—with a completed scroll or pilgrim's book from pilgrimages such as Saikoku and Shikoku. Advertisements for such services suggest that many people may not, because of ill health or other difficulties such as not having time or living too far from Shikoku or Saikoku, be able to do these pilgrimages, and they offer them the alternative of purchasing completed scrolls or books that have been carried around the pilgrimage by company representatives. The enterprises concerned assure would-be customers that their representatives who follow all the appropriate rules and etiquette of pilgrimage, dressing in pilgrimage clothing, praying at each temple, lighting candles and so on. Some sites even suggest special surrogate plans whereby one can get two stamped pilgrimage books as a present for (for example) one's parents, a suggestion made on the website of Ippoippodō, an online company specialising in pilgrimage goods and services that also sells pilgrimage DVDs and all manner of pilgrimage equipment.[11]

Such services, along with scrolls in general, also are a reflection of the inventiveness of those in the pilgrimage service industry in responding to the needs and demands of pilgrims while finding new ways to attract their custom. Pilgrimage temples, priests and associations likewise recognise this issue. In October 1987, I was at one of the Saikoku temples when I noted a group of pilgrims with scrolls that had at their centre an image not of Kannon, the central figure in Saikoku, but of Amida, the main focus of worship in Pure Land Buddhism, numerically the largest Buddhist tradition in Japan. The scrolls also had the *nembutsu*, the Pure Land Buddhist recitation of praise of and faith in Amida, inscribed on them. I was surprised that Kannon appeared to have been removed from the central place in a scroll of her own pilgrimage, so I asked a Saikoku temple priest about this. His response was that the scrolls had been produced in order to encourage a wider clientele; Pure Land followers should, according to their sectarian teachings, only venerate Amida, and so many would feel uneasy about engaging in a pilgrimage whose focus was another figure of worship such as Kannon. By producing an Amida-centred pilgrimage scroll, the Saikoku

158 *Pilgrimage in the Marketplace*

temples were making it easier for Pure Land followers to engage in the pilgrimage and get their scrolls without compromising their religious teachings.

SHINHATSUBAI: NEW GOODS AND MARKET DEMANDS

The need to constantly keep abreast of pilgrim demands and produce goods to attract them is widely felt in the Japanese pilgrimage market. I have noted a constant flow of new items and styles of goods as well as amulets at the shops and temples of Shikoku over the years, and people in the pilgrimage business I have interviewed have emphasised the need to ensure such a flow is maintained. In April 2000, I visited a well-known shop, Inoue Shinichi Shoten, that sells pilgrimage and other goods and that is located near the gates of Tatsueji (one of the Shikoku temples). There I talked with the people overseeing the shop and was given a key-ring holder with a small Kōbō Daishi figurine at its centre and the names of the eighty-eight temples inscribed around it. It was a *shinhatsubai* ('new product', a popular buzzword and marketing term in Japan) that the firm had developed that year, and I was told that they had high hopes that it would attract the attention of pilgrims. The people associated with the shop were clear that to make a living off the pilgrimage in a business such as theirs required a constant flow not just of pilgrims but also of new goods. Pilgrims demanded such things, especially those who repeat pilgrimages regularly (as is the case with many in Shikoku) and who are always on the lookout for, and want, new items every year to commemorate each pilgrimage they make. Undermining the notion that temples and shops outside their precincts necessarily exist in a state of tension the people at shops such as this have emphasised to me numerous occasions that they had good relations with the temples and cooperated with them in various ways, such as by sharing with them the same suppliers of goods and by helping them develop new items for sale.[12] Recently, as if to reinforce this point about the need for a regular and distinctive new pilgrimage goods, amulets featuring the popular figure Hello Kitty have been sold at shrines and temples throughout Japan; the Shikoku temples have their own special *henro kitty* ('pilgrimage Kitty') version of this amulet (Hoshino and Asakawa 2011: 149). The cooperative campaign that I mentioned in Chapter 4 between Japan Rail and the Saikoku temples that was initiated in 2008 to attract new pilgrims (and new rail customers) used, as a key element in its appeal, the offer of combined reduced price train tickets that included admission to the temples (some of which charge a *haiken* or entrance/worship fee) and special pilgrimage souvenirs produced for the campaign and distributed to ticket holders by the temples.[13]

SHRINES AND THE SALE OF SOUVENIRS

The trade in the infinitely reproducible relics described early in the context of Saint Anthony's tongue at the cathedral at Padua, is indicative of a recurrent pattern in which pilgrimage sites readily engage in the sale of goods. The almost ubiquitous engagement of shrines in selling such items—whether they are regarded as souvenirs, religious charms or relics—suggests that if souvenirs and related modes of commerce are a key area of tension and contest between religious authorities and stall vendors, it may not so much because shrine authorities consider what is being sold outside their gates to be distasteful, but because of concerns about market share and competition over selling the same goods. Rather than deploring the sale of souvenirs and portraying them as demeaning the sanctity of a shrine, religious authorities have, as I showed earlier, proved highly adept at creating and selling such items themselves. Indeed, souvenirs, whether in the guise of objects such as the aforementioned Saint Anthony's tongue relic, of Shikoku pilgrimage scrolls and 'pilgrimage Kitty' amulets, or of more seemingly prosaic souvenirs such as Archbishop of Canterbury teddy bears (sold by Canterbury Cathedral in England[14]) are often an important element in shrine economies. The fees for stamping scrolls and books are a mainstay of the economies of pilgrimage temples in Shikoku and elsewhere in Japan, as are sales from the temple shops they run. Shikoku pilgrimage sites certainly encourage pilgrims to acquire scrolls, books and other such goods from their shops to signify that they are pilgrims. Even though there is historically no injunction to say that Shikoku pilgrims should wear particular forms of pilgrimage regalia such a pilgrims' hat, shroud and staff or carry a book or scroll to be stamped, Shikoku pilgrimage authorities emphasise that this is what bona fide pilgrims should do (Shikoku Hachijūhakkasho Reijōkai 1988: 144). When pilgrim numbers decline, the loss of income, whether from a decline in fees from stamping scrolls or the loss of sales from temple shops, can be very damaging. This has, for example, had a heavy impact on the Shōdoshima temples in recent times, causing them further worries about their future and serving as another spur to their attempts to find new ways of promoting their pilgrimage.

The sale of pilgrimage goods and souvenirs was important also to medieval Christian shrines. As Diane Webb (2002: xiv) comments, objects such as pilgrim badges and souvenirs were both a product of and a stimulus to pilgrimage. By the twelfth century, the making and marketing of souvenirs was widespread across the Christian world, whereas objects such as pilgrim badges not only identified people as pilgrims but also helped publicise the shrines they represented. At times, too, pilgrim demand for them was so high that it outstripped supply (Webb 2002: 35–36). Some saints proved especially profitable and their shrines were able to sell large numbers of items -notably pilgrim badges—related to them. In this context, few in medieval times were more successful than was Saint Thomas à Becket, whose shrine at Canterbury generated more souvenirs than did any other in Europe at the time (Robinson 2012).

A good example of the engagement of shrine authorities in the sale of goods and in the provision of opportunities to buy souvenirs is provided by the Shri Mata Vaishno Devi Shrine. As I mentioned earlier, it has a number of shops that provide pilgrims with shrine offerings that can be taken home as souvenirs or as offerings for their own household shrines. The shrine also

160 *Pilgrimage in the Marketplace*

offers pilgrims various 'exclusive items' only available at its shops and not, it emphasises, at any rival stalls nearby, such as

> audio cassettes, CDs, various publications of Shrine Board, laminated photos of the Holy Pindies, Jute Bags, Bangle Chura etc. Yatries may take notice that all these items are exclusively available at the Souvenir Shops of Shrine Board and are not available at any of the private shops.[15]

Moreover, well-to-do pilgrims are encouraged (and perhaps buoyed by the shrine's promise that no one goes home empty-handed) to go beyond just purchasing souvenirs:

> If the budget is on the higher side, one can always donate in cash or in kind and obtain a proper receipt for the same. All the donations to Shri Mata Vaishno Devi Shrine Board enjoy tax benefits under section 80-G of the Income Tax Act.[16]

Such attempts to monopolise the market or to offer exclusive items only purchasable through shrines, are commonplace. Japanese pilgrimage temples are able to do this in terms of amulets and lucky charms, for example, because these are only considered to carry any form of religious significance if blessed by and acquired from a shrine or temple (Reader and Tanabe 1998). Most pilgrim items, however, from scrolls to pilgrims' shrouds and key rings, can be bought either at the temples or at shops nearby (or, increasingly in recent times, online). There is little difference or separation in such contexts between temple and commercial shop, and no clear boundary between the supposedly sacred and profane; a scroll purchased at a shop in the 'profane' streets outside the temple and one purchased within the 'sacred' grounds of the temple are regarded equally and may be every bit the same.

ATTRACTING PILGRIMS AND CREATING NETWORKS: THE MIRACULOUS MEDAL OF PARIS

Souvenirs can serve not only as advertising and marketing tools but also as key formative elements in pilgrimage cults and their popularity. Such is the case with the 'Miraculous Medal' sold at the Chapel of Our Lady of the Miraculous Medal (Chappelle Notre Dame de la Medaille Miraculeuse) in the Rue du Bac in Paris. This provides us with an example of a pilgrimage that has at its core a souvenir item imbued with religious meanings and that is only available through and within the precincts of its specific pilgrimage site.

The Rue du Bac chapel owes its significance as a Marian pilgrimage site to three apparitions of the Virgin Mary said to have been seen there by a twenty-four-year-old novice nun, Catherine Labouré (later canonised as Saint Catherine Labouré) 'in flesh and bone' shortly after she joined the convent in 1830. According to Catherine, Mary entrusted her with a mission to have a medal made bearing the words 'O Mary, conceived without sin, pray for us who have recourse to you'. The medal would, the Virgin informed her, bring 'great graces' to its wearers. Thereafter, the convent had such medals—'designed' according to shrine literature, by Mary and bearing her image—made. Known as the Miraculous Medal, the convent has been distributing them ever since. Rapidly reports of 'numerous graces of conversion, protection and healing' began to circulate, including claims that it had stemmed an outbreak of cholera in Paris in 1832. As a result the archbishop of Paris ordered an inquiry into the phenomenon and subsequently pronounced that the plethora of medals being struck, and the 'astonishing benefits and graces' that they bestowed on the faithful, indicated the veracity of the apparition, a judgement ratified by Pope Gregory XVI in 1846. Thus, the medals served as testimony to the truth of the apparition in whose name they were struck. The subsequent declaration by Pope Pius IX of the doctrine of the Immaculate Conception in 1854 further advanced the status of the medal; shrine leaflets claim that Pius was referring to it when he stated that 'through her Immaculate Conception, Mary came into the world like a splendid dawn that spreads its rays everywhere' (Rue du Bac, nd-a: 4).[17]

The medal rapidly became linked to other Marian pilgrimage sites. At the Shrine of Our Lady of Einsiedeln in Switzerland, which enshrines a Black Madonna and has been a pilgrimage site since around 1000 CE, Mary was said to have appeared, holding the medal, before a Benedictine nun in 1835. Such apparitions and the Miraculous Medal itself paved the way for the later apparition at Lourdes in 1858; shrine literature claims that Bernadette was wearing a Rue du Bac medal when she saw Mary, who looked just as she did on the medal. The link between the two shrines was reaffirmed in the 1950s when the papacy had a commemorative medal struck for the centenary of the Lourdes apparitions, in which the Miraculous Medal of the Rue du Bac and the Grotto of Lourdes were depicted together (Rue du Bac, nd-b).

The shrine in Paris has since produced vast numbers of medals—50,000 in March 1834 alone, and millions distributed ever since to the approximately two million visitors it attracts every year, many of whom purchase large numbers of them. The medal, as the shrine notes, is very simple and 'costs next to nothing', but it serves as 'an icon for the poor. . . . anyone can possess one.' (Rue du Bac, nd-c: 32). Shrine literature tells of miraculous events that have occurred to people who wear the medal and of pilgrims who bought large numbers of them to give to family members (Rue du Bac, nd-c: 7). Wearing the medal is a sign of faith in Mary and an acceptance of the gift (the medal) she has bestowed.

In the shrine literature and in the activities at the shrine, two things stand out for me. One is that nowhere in the accounts provided is there any mention of the aesthetic qualities of the medal. It is proudly portrayed as cheap—and hence accessible for the poor. Its significance is not in its beauty but in what it stands for, as a representation of Mary, as the product of a particular holy place and as a facilitator of the presence of the holy in this mundane world. The medal is clearly perceived by the nuns, ecclesiastical authorities and pilgrims alike as something special, a provider of graces and benefits, and a means of accessing Mary's benevolence. It is an item created by the shrine in commemoration (and signification) of a special event that serves to link pilgrim, site and object together.

The other striking thing for me is that although the literature and messages talk of the medal being 'distributed', it is in fact *sold* within the shrine precincts in its gift shop—for a small fee certainly, but one that ensures a steady flow of income to the shrine.[18] In such terms, although it may be a miraculous medal, it is also a purchased commodity and souvenir that may be taken home for others. The chapel has a monopoly on sales of the medal, which is available in a variety of forms, and can be purchased individually or in larger numbers; their prices in April 2012 ranged from around 1.5 dollars to just more than 5 dollars[19] for single medals, whereas one could buy bags of ten, twenty or fifty medals, either in gilded or silver-metallic forms, at reduced bulk rates. The shop was doing a good trade when I visited, with plenty of visitors purchasing a variety of booklets, postcards, rosaries, statuettes and medals—often, in the case of the latter, in sizeable quantities. The Miraculous Medal of the Rue du Bac, in other words, is both a souvenir of the chapel and a means of spreading the message (inscribed on the medal itself) central to its Marian cult. The medal has, through stories linking it to other Catholic pilgrimage shrines such as Einsiedeln and Lourdes, thereby augmented and enhanced the standing of the shrine in Paris, while contributing to the growth and vitality of Marian pilgrimages in general. As such the souvenir (which I am sure some would call tacky) is an integral element and driving material force in the Rue du Bac pilgrimage cult and a staple element in the economic well-being of the shrine that 'distributes' it.

The production of goods and souvenirs has helped spur the popularity of Lourdes as well. As Kaufman (2004: 47–50) notes, mass-produced goods such as Mary statuettes and Pastilles de Lourdes—lozenges made from sugar and grotto water that were claimed to have same power as shrine water—were, from soon after the pilgrimage cult started, available at economic prices to be taken home for family and friends who were unable to go to Lourdes. Lourdes authorities, indeed, encouraged pilgrims to buy souvenirs for the well-being of their families so that they too could participate in the cult. Other goods including postcards (with epithets such as 'I am thinking of you at Lourdes') and phials of Lourdes water also helped draw attention to the site and make it widely accessible. As such, mass produced items took on the guise of sacred objects used in the promotion of Lourdes as well as becoming central aspects of the pilgrimage itself (Kaufman 2004: 54–56). During the latter part of the nineteenth century, the cult of Lourdes spread overseas also via such means. Phials of Lourdes water were, for example, shipped to the United States, where U.S. Catholic priests such as

Father Alexis Granger oversaw their import and sale to U.S. Catholics while using the water as a means of spreading Marian devotion. Replica Lourdes shrines (amongst the first of which were on the campus of the Catholic Notre Dame University in Indiana, but which later included also the Bronx Lourdes shrine mentioned in Chapter 1) and Catholic shrine shops at these replicas that sold models of the Lourdes grotto and statuettes of Our Lady of Lourdes, further helped spread the Lourdes cult among a U.S. Catholic populace unable, in the nineteenth century, to travel abroad to Lourdes itself (McDannell 1995: 132–160).

SELLING BEADS AND SELLING PILGRIMAGES

Souvenirs that are also depicted as sacred objects may even be a factor in the formation of pilgrimages, as in the case of *Juzu Junrei* ('Rosary Pilgrimage') in Japan, which developed in the region around Kyoto in Japan in 2008. Currently (as of 2012) there are sixty-three shrines and temples involved in this pilgrimage, which has a rather fluid structure. One need not visit every site but can pick and choose how to shape one's pilgrimage while deciding how many and which sites one wishes to visit. At each site, the visitor/pilgrim acquires (i.e., purchases) a rosary bead inscribed with the name of the shrine or temple visited. By collecting the beads of specific numbers of temples, one can make rosaries that have symbolic numerical value—for instance, of 108 beads, a standard Buddhist rosary length symbolising the 108 evil passions and their eradication or significant numerical divisions of the 108, such as thirty-six beads representing the thirty-six evil passions in this realm. Pilgrimage promotional leaflets, along with the *Juzu Junrei* website, suggest a variety of forms in which the beads can be used, such as making rosaries, bracelets or other items according to one's wishes.[20] Rosaries and rosary beads are an important item in Buddhist prayer and worship (Tanabe 2012), but the beads can also be used as attractive, decorative commodities for everyday use, for example, in the form of bracelets (one of the possibilities suggested by the website and promotional pamphlets) and as souvenirs of temples visited. The bead is thus simultaneously holy object, souvenir and decorative item, depending on pilgrim wishes, and is designed to publicise a pilgrimage whose focus is on the acquisition of its souvenirs.[21]

MARTIN LUTHER'S SOCKS: OR IS THERE A LINE TO BE DRAWN?

In his study of the German town of Wittenberg where Marin Luther nailed up his ninety-five theses that helped give birth to the Reformation, Barry Stephenson (2010) shows how the town has made cultural and economic capital out of 'performing the Reformation' and through linking pilgrimages

Figure 6.5 Poster advertising the *Juzu junrei* pilgrimage.

to Luther's home with festivities aimed at celebrating the town's heritage—thereby boosting its modern economy through contemporary tourism that interweaves themes of religion and play. Stephenson describes how Wittenberg's Marktplazt (marketplace) is a setting for events and festivities infused with religious, cultural and historical motifs that help entice visitors to spend their cash. The town naturally attracts members of the

Lutheran church, many of whom come from North America to visit what is for them a spiritual homeland associated with the origins of their church. Unsurprisingly, they like to take home with them reminders of the place, yet, perhaps mindful of the origins of Protestantism as a reaction to the Catholic Church's selling of indulgences and religious commodities, some of them may find what is on sale troubling. This was clearly the case with a Canadian pastor who said,

> Luther socks . . . It's nice to go home with a Luther mug or something, but it has gone to the extreme. (Stephenson 2010: 175)

The quotation raises interesting questions. We have already seen how at Lourdes, Catholic authorities can accept and even be exuberant about singing toilet-paper roll holders that might instil wonder in visiting 'peasants' and how Kōbō Daishi key rings and Hello Kitty charms are by no means anathema to Shikoku temples or pilgrims. (I also on one occasion acquired a bottle of saké in Shikoku, in the shape of Kōbō Daishi in which his monk's hat served as a saké cup, and which I shared with a prominent Buddhist scholar). Yet the Canadian priest's unease indicates that, even if people want some souvenirs and signs of the special place, they might still feel the need for such commodification to be restrained and limited. The question, however, is whether, where or if such lines should or could be drawn. The Lutheran Protestant minister appears, even in a theology that is restrained about religious commodities, to accept that pilgrims should be able to buy objects redolent of the special place and linked to the significant religious instigator of their tradition, and he was able, as such, to feel that a Luther mug was a reasonable item in such terms. Yet socks seemed troubling; for the pastor, there was clearly a dividing line between the apparent reasonableness of a mug and the worrisomeness of Luther's socks. One might, of course, be able to find other ministers for whom socks are acceptable but mugs are not.

Such ambiguities have concerned (some) religious authorities too, as various discussions by Catholic Church authorities over the items on sale at Lourdes indicate. Catholic authorities, Kaufman (2004: 71) writes, were at times frustrated by what they saw as the inability of the Catholic masses to resist what nineteenth-century church officials saw as 'foolish and fraudulent goods'. Their concerns were to a degree a reaction to the criticisms raised in nineteenth century French secular circles against what was going on at Lourdes; criticisms of the 'superstitions' at play there formed part of liberal secular discourse at the time, and led Catholic authorities to try to police the shrine and draw a line between what might be viewed as legitimate and illegitimate commerce (Kaufman 2004: 68–70). Yet, although such concerns clearly affected the church in an age of powerful state-driven secularism, statuettes and pastilles, along with other trinkets, continued to be sold and avidly bought by pilgrims who, no matter what church authorities said, lapped them up and saw them as integral to their pilgrimages. And even if Catholic authorities might have tried to make distinctions about what might and might not be reasonable souvenir items at that time, a century or so later, when Lourdes had become a truly international mass pilgrimage centre, such distinctions appear less in evidence judging by the readiness of senior Catholic figures to laud the sale of toilet-paper roll holders that play Ave Maria. In Japan, where the same temple can sell or inscribe a beautiful scroll and sell a garishly pink 'pilgrimage Kitty' and where there has been a long tradition of creating innovative and visually striking artefacts that serve as religious items and souvenirs (Reader and Tanabe 1998), there is far less of a hard and fast conceptual line of the sort posited by the Lutheran minister and his worries about Martin Luther's socks. It may simply be that such distinctions and worries are more prevalent in a protestant theological context than in a Japanese (or Catholic) one. Overall, though, it would appear that the conflation of souvenirs and relics as commodities infused with the meaning of place and as links between it and home pertains across the pilgrimage spectrum and serves as yet another example of the problems inherent in trying to uphold a sacred–profane dichotomy and in viewing the items on sale at pilgrimage sites and stalls as disjunctions to the wider meaning of pilgrimage.

SOUVENIRS, MARKETPLACES AND THE 'REALLY SACRED'

Souvenirs are a commodity whose purchase and acquisition is integral to and deeply embedded in the pilgrimage process. They are not disjunctions that mar the pure realms of the sacred but parts of its environment. The material, visible, collectable, purchasable world of goods and souvenirs taken home as reminders of and links to the sacred, and as gifts to loved ones to remind them of the thoughts of the pilgrim, are important and integral elements in the makeup of pilgrimage and in the construction, shaping and vibrancy of the pilgrimage landscape.

Elsewhere I have suggested, when speaking about the Shikoku pilgrimage, that pilgrimages are framed and shaped by an 'emotional landscape' that draws in pilgrims. In that context, I argued that although Shikoku's dramatic scenery and fusion of mountains and coastal splendour, along with its often-imposing temples, present a dramatic picture that is alluring to potential pilgrims, this landscape should not just be thought of as being just physical. Rather, the legends and stories, along with the images shaped by publicity literature, posters and the like that project the pilgrimage as a manifestation of cultural tradition, are also aspects of its landscape—ones that intensify the potency of the physical and help create an emotional frame of reference for pilgrims (Reader 2005: 39–74). I would here take this notion a step further by suggesting that the issues outlined in this chapter—the trinkets, the stalls, the potential souvenirs to take home and the signs and symbols of the sacred that are on offer to pilgrims—are also aspects of that emotional landscape, aspects that help shape it while performing vital functions (such as allowing pilgrims therapeutic release valves from the intensity of travel) within it. In this emotional landscape in which the materiality of souvenirs plays an integral part, the seemingly sacred realm of the pilgrimage site is the fertile soil in which the apparent profanity of the commercial realms of souvenirs and amulets is rooted and flourishes. Likewise, the seemingly profane souvenirs—the singing toilet-paper roll holders, the flesh-coloured Christs and the plastic water-bottle Virgin Marys—are steeped in the sacred dimensions of the places where they are sold; they represent it and are taken home as such. The pilgrims who eagerly purchase such goods—and who may even, as with the Saikoku pilgrims I have cited, be motivated to go on pilgrimages because of them—appear not to find a disjunction between praying and purchasing souvenirs. They are pilgrims and consumers of goods at the same time.

In such contexts, the flesh-coloured Christs and their ilk are really sacred, insofar as they are part and parcel of the construction and representation of the idea of the sacred. They are also profane if one wishes to view them as products of a material culture and as commodities produced to draw money from pilgrim pockets. More realistically, they are exemplars of the problems of using terms and concepts such as sacred and profane and of thinking that they might be mutually contradictory rather than inhabiting a somewhat unclear and porous overlapping area in which an object can both be a profane and tacky fluorescent plastic Virgin Mary sold for a small price in a souvenir shop and a sacred reminder of Knock for those who bring it home.

As I argued earlier, there is no innate category of the sacred that is separate or marked out from the profane or mundane everyday world. Places are made sacred (or, more precisely, made into pilgrimage sites) in the popular imagination through a variety of means, from miracle stories and the coming of pilgrims to the use of material signifiers such as churches, relics and statues, and to the actions of mercantile and other agents who create the mechanisms that make such places accessible and attractive. The souvenirs, scrolls, amulets and other material goods acquired at pilgrimage sites are a further part of that construction of the sacred and part of the allure and attraction for pilgrims.

As such, they remind us that the sacred in itself is not necessarily bounded or restricted by concepts of cheapness, aesthetic (un)worthiness or material shoddiness; in the pilgrimage marketplace a plastic Virgin Mary is as worthy and sacred as an artistic scroll. When the 'peasant from Calabria' says, 'Fantastic', at the sight of a singing toilet-paper roll holder from Lourdes, he or she is not expressing the naïve and gullible wonder of an unsophisticated, backwoods ignoramus duped by the commercially astute vendors and the manipulative Catholic overseers of Lourdes, so much as he or she is displaying an underlying and sophisticated grasp of the deep connections between religion and material culture and an awareness of how closely embedded in the marketplace pilgrimages and pilgrimage sites are. To dismiss the items they collect as tacky and lacking in meaning or to decry them as anomalous, out of place or antithetical to the 'true' meaning of pilgrimage and of the sacred is to misunderstand and misrepresent those terms and to be locked into an artificial, overly idealised and conceptually muddled perspective.

To that extent, if concepts such as the 'sacred' are to have any meaning or viability in terms of pilgrimage, they should be extended to include the material manifestations and commercial goods on display at and around pilgrimage sites. It is such items that bring the perceived or believed sacred power of a site within the ambit of ordinary people, and creating avenues through which they can engage with, experience, consume, take home and make familiar that sense of power. Such material dimensions are indications that the sacred is not something set apart from the mundane or dissociated from the world of materialism and goods but the reverse. Indeed, to be truly successful a pilgrimage site needs such material goods and a thriving market of souvenirs, which serve as evidence of its essential meanings for pilgrims. As such, the seemingly shoddy (and the occasionally exquisite) goods of pilgrimage, including its flesh-coloured Christs are, in a real sense (with apologies to Mr. Dylan), 'really sacred'.

7 Strawberries, Camel Coolers and Luxury Hotels

Heritage, Hiking, Holidays and the Consumer Rebranding of Pilgrimage

INTRODUCTION: ABANDONING CRUTCHES AND SANITISING THE PILGRIMAGE

Iyataniji (Temple Seventy-one on the Shikoku pilgrimage) is a mountain temple with a long history of miracle tales related to healing. Physical reminders of such stories on display at Iyataniji provided pilgrims with a visual reminder of the temple's reputation in this area, and a collection of crutches, leg braces, corsets and similar items left behind by previously infirm pilgrims who had, it was claimed, been healed there and who had been able to walk on thereafter unaided, could be seen arrayed along a wall at the temple. Pictures of these items featured regularly in popular pilgrimage guidebooks (e.g., Hirahata 1982: 419) and in my own (Reader 2005: 68) study of Shikoku. I first saw them in 1984, and on subsequent visits, I always noted how they created a buzz of interest among pilgrims. In 1991, for example, the leader of the group I was travelling with regaled us, as we approached Iyataniji, with tales about the leg braces and crutches we would shortly see and the miracles they reflected. In so doing, he created such a sense of expectation that, by the time we climbed the steep steps to where they were displayed, the pilgrims were excitedly talking about the possibility of miraculous happenings.

Yet when I returned to Iyataniji in April 2005, I was surprised to see that they had disappeared and that the wall had been repainted. I asked a temple official what had happened (assuming that they had simply been removed temporarily while the wall was repainted) and he replied (in Japanese), 'Oh, we took them away'. Further enquiries established that the removal was permanent and that it had happened a few months earlier. It transpired that temple officials felt the items were old and a remnant of a past era in which superstition, rumours and miracle tales were paramount. As such, they were out of kilter with the modern day ambiance of the pilgrimage. Other contacts in Shikoku later told me that the removal was part of a conscious effort to eradicate items associated with premodern superstitions and to develop a more modern orientation to the pilgrimage.

Not long afterwards, in 2007, the Shikoku temples banned *takuhatsu*, begging for alms, at or around their precincts. *Takuhatsu* has been common among Shikoku pilgrims over the centuries and is linked to the custom of alms giving (*settai*) outlined in Chapter 5. It is based in Buddhist monastic concepts, in which monks were supposed, as a mark of humility and to sustain themselves in an austere lifestyle, to beg for alms as part of their Buddhist practice. Pilgrims in Shikoku sought alms because for many it was an economic necessity but also because, as pilgrims, they identified with Kōsbō Daishi in his guise as a mendicant and because it made them akin to Buddhist monks while they were on pilgrimage (Kojima 1989, Shinno 1991: 29). Although begging had declined in modern times as Japan's economy grew, as pilgrims became better off and as organised bus tours changed the tenor of the pilgrimage, it became more prominent again after Japan entered into economic troubles and recession from the 1990s onwards. This threw many people out of work and led to an upsurge in unemployed men becoming pilgrims in order to deal with the emotional trauma of losing their jobs. Such pilgrims have often been in financial straits and have turned to begging as a means of helping support their pilgrimages (Hamaya 2009). Yet, although beggar-pilgrims might have been an accepted part of pilgrimage in earlier times, they clearly did not fit in with the temples' vision of what modern pilgrimage (one whose main clientele was based around tour buses) ought to look like. An official of one of the publication relations (PR) agencies involved with the Shikoku campaign to get the pilgrimage accredited as a UNESCO World Heritage site (see the following discussion) told me that the contemporary presence of pilgrims who begged or slept out was a 'problem' (*mondai*) for the temples.[1] Indeed, the authorities running the temples were so concerned that mendicant pilgrims might put off other visitors, that they put up notices banning pilgrims from doing *takuhatsu* in their environs (Hamaya 2009: 108). Although, as has been discussed earlier, the Shikoku Reijōkai has emphasised the image of tradition as a key selling point in its promotional materials, this has been an idealised and photogenic image of tradition centred around such things as white-clad pilgrims on rural paths, rather than on destitute foot pilgrims, who might be part of the pilgrimage's historical tradition but who clearly do not manifest the sorts of ambience the temples want to project nowadays. Faced with the possibility that begging pilgrims might put off the urban seekers after 'tradition' that they have been attracting so successfully in recent times, the temples have chosen to proscribe a Buddhist practice that was for much of the pilgrimage's history an intrinsic element in pilgrimage life.

The Shikoku temples are by no means the only pilgrimage authorities to downplay miracles. As Catrien Notermans (2007) has noted, shrine authorities at Lourdes have removed any physical signs hinting at the miraculous, by taking away objects such as crutches left behind by pilgrims who claim to have been healed. They have also announced that the shrine's waters have no therapeutic or healing elements to them, have been notably reluctant to affirm miracles there, only ratifying sixty-seven cases (the last taking fifty years to do so) since 1859, and have been keen to present a more modern face to the shrine, and to avoid accusations of superstition and irrationality there (Notermans 2007: 219). This does not mean that miracles and hopes of healing are not important to pilgrims (see A. Harris 2013) so much as that the authorities concerned are cautious and inclined to restrain pilgrim fervour in order to guard against the accusations that Lourdes faced in its early history, of pandering to 'superstition'.

In Shikoku, the impetus to reduce pilgrim expectations of miracles and to remove signs associated with past stories of healing is clearly grounded in the desire to attract well-heeled pilgrims whose interests are centred on comfort and heritage rather than on asceticism and miracles. To that degree, the pilgrimage is being sanitised to make it accord with the contours of the modern world and to increase its potential appeal beyond the boundaries of the religious faithful. This process is not limited to Shikoku but has resonances with patterns in a number of other significant cases worldwide, at times leading to a 'rebranding' of pilgrimage that makes it more appealing to people in higher income brackets and heightens its consumerist potential by projecting it increasingly through the lens of holidays and leisure, and transforms into something akin to a theme park spectacle—issues that are the focus of this chapter.

FROM POVERTY TO STRAWBERRIES, ICE CREAM AND GOURMET TOURS

In earlier chapters, I have discussed how the Shikoku pilgrimage developed in the modern era, as various interest groups including tourist and travel agencies, transport companies and media concerns, along with the Shikoku temples, helped transform its image from a marginalised and largely ascetic affair into a mass pilgrimage associated with Japanese cultural traditions and heritage. In this process, the pilgrimage became a highly photogenic and scenic commodity appealing to people seeking to 'discover traditional Japan' and has been highlighted in the mass media as such. It has also become regularly featured in exhibitions at department stores and museums, often in conjunction with sponsoring media agencies such as NHK. Such events have also helped increase public knowledge of and interest in the pilgrimage, while making it ever more into a media-ised commodity in which (at least in museum displays) the items on display are depicted predominantly as aesthetic objects, rather than as objects of worship (Reader 2007a).

The apparent shying away from notions of miracle and asceticism identified earlier, in the removal of the leg braces at Iyataniji and the banning of begging around the temples, is a further step in this process of transformation, sanitisation and image recalibration. It seems to fit with the changing attitudes of pilgrims as well, as identified by Osada, Sakata and Seki (2003) and by Hoshino and Asakawa (2011: 66–68), who discuss how traditional religious motivations such as miracles and benefits have become weaker among modern pilgrims, compared to issues of cultural heritage, encountering an idealised image of a Japan that differs from their everyday urban lives, and reenergising oneself and improving one's health through escaping the city to enjoy the rural environment of the island. Hoshino and Asakawa (2011: 83–84) also show that people walking the Shikoku pilgrimage (a category that has grown in recent years) are nowadays generally not focused on faith or on performing religious activities or austerities; rather, they are doing the pilgrimage because they are looking for new challenges and are keen on hiking, self-reflection and on refreshing themselves and becoming healthy.[2] The intentions, discussed in Chapter 4, of travel writers such as Iijima and of tourist magazines and agencies from the 1920s onwards to remove the 'religious' from the pilgrimage so as to widen its appeal, are clearly coming to fruition in the present day. As I indicated also in Chapter 4, guidebooks and other media representations of the pilgrimage (often produced or endorsed by the temples) have also focused on entertainment, convenience and the like. Such patterns of representation, along with the work of those in the travel and tourist industry seeking to make the pilgrimage more accessible to new clienteles who are not concerned about faith, have contributed to the public transformation of the pilgrimage's image. Their influence can also be seen in the conscious attempts of pilgrimage authorities to excise from the pilgrimage landscape some of its more traditional religious dimensions, as outlined previously.

This process is also evident in the ways in which, in recent years, the pilgrimage has started to appear in a number of new media outlets devoted to a sector of society that was certainly not present among pilgrims in earlier eras: fashion-conscious young women interested primarily in clothes, leisure and consumerism. In several glossy magazines designed for young well-off females in the past decade, the Shikoku pilgrimage has been depicted as a fascinating means of seeing Japan, and as a modern mode of leisurely travel full of consumer delights and culinary experiences, rather than as a practice involved with miracles, faith and austerities. One such magazine will give a flavour of this.[3] *Savvy* is a glossy magazine geared towards young Japanese women and is largely concerned with fashion, consumerism, travel and food. In September 2005, it ran a special feature on the Shikoku pilgrimage, portraying it as a fashionable culinary tour through the Japanese landscape suitable for well-off young women. Following the standard trope for guidebooks and other pilgrimage promotional materials that I have mentioned in earlier chapters, the magazine article depicted two young ladies dressed in white pilgrimage clothing, carrying pilgrims' staffs and wearing pilgrims' bamboo hats set against the background of the pilgrimage path as it wound through forests or rice fields, while neglecting the modern features and highways so widespread along the route. The young pilgrim-models were primarily, however, shown eating and making their way through the foodstuffs and delicacies to be found along the way. Besides the usual food delights of Japan, from sushi and sashimi to regional dishes, all of which are found in abundance in Shikoku, there were, the magazine informed readers, plentiful opportunities to indulge in all manner of delightful sweetmeats that young Japanese women appear to find especially attractive. The young female pilgrim-models were depicted as eating their way through all manner of such delights along the way, such as ice cream sundaes and strawberries with ice cream. *Savvy*'s portrayal in effect turned Shikoku into a food pilgrimage, and contained also accounts of various restaurants along the route where one could partake of local foods and seasonal delicacies (*Savvy* 2005: 29–51).

It is not just trendy young women's magazines that portray the pilgrimage in gastronomic terms. Bus tour pilgrimages, too, have been advertised in such terms; in July 2011, I came across online advertisements for 'gourmet bus pilgrimage tours' that offered two-night, three-day excursions to the Shikoku temples combined with the promise of 'delicious cuisine' (*oishii ryōri*).[4] Various Shikoku pilgrimage-related websites offering advice and pilgrimage tours also emphasise the 'gourmet' delights of Shikoku as an element in pilgrim travels.[5] One can also find other related pilgrimage package tours oriented towards those with an interest in art and visual culture and which are advertised with phrases that inform potential customers that the Shikoku pilgrimage is not just about worshipping (*sanpai*) at temples but about art, beautiful Buddhist statues, paintings and gardens.[6] In such ways the pilgrimage has continued to move, in advertisements and public representations, further and further from an ascetic endeavour associated with miracle tales and the presence of a wandering Buddhist holy man and towards being a fashionable and consumer item, and as a gourmet and/or artistic and cultural tour in which faith, miracle and the like take a backseat.

FROM EXHIBITIONS TO WORLD HERITAGE: IN THE FOOTSTEPS OF SANTIAGO

This emphasis on heritage and culture has been further augmented by attempts to get the Shikoku pilgrimage accredited with UNESCO World Heritage status. In December 2007, the regional government agencies of Shikoku, along with the representatives (mayors and councils) of fifty-eight towns and cities in Shikoku, along with the representatives of the eighty-eight pilgrimage temples, and supported by various Shikoku media, transport and commercial agencies, petitioned the Japanese Ministry of Culture to nominate the Shikoku pilgrimage as a UNESCO World Heritage site.[7] Oyamada Kenshō, head priest of one of the temples, was an early advocate of this idea, and although his proposal initially provoked opposition from some of his fellow priests, it was subsequently supported by the Shikoku Reijōkai and taken up enthusiastically by the island's political and tourist authorities and various Shikoku commercial groups and educational institutes.[8]

174   *Pilgrimage in the Marketplace*

The UNESCO World Heritage campaign came about in part because of concerns at the island's economic decline, because it has been hit badly by depopulation and the erosion of formerly important industries such as shipbuilding. Local business concerns, represented especially by regional chambers of commerce and rotary clubs, were worried that population decline and a falling economy would undermine their businesses. Authorities in Shikoku, concerned about this, worried about the potential loss of tax revenues as the economy declined and pressed by the national government in Tokyo to find ways of regenerating the region, have found the pilgrimage to be especially important in this context because it is one of the few, if not the only, things that unites the island. Regional government agencies thus viewed the pilgrimage, already an important item in the region's modern economy, as a vital mobilising element for the island in a period of uncertainty. It already brings large numbers of Japanese people to the island—people who are liable to spend money and help sustain local businesses such as restaurants and the like. In the plans initiated in 2000 by Endō Toshio, the then governor of Tokushima Prefecture (where twenty-three of the temples are located), to revitalise the local economy, special emphasis was placed on forms of tourism centred on themes of cultural heritage and healthy activities. The pilgrimage featured significantly in Endō's plans, which in turn helped generate momentum for the UNESCO campaign. Government sponsorship of a variety of education activities, including public conferences, lectures and studies by scholars (especially those based at universities in Shikoku) discussing the pilgrimage's role in Shikoku's history and culture, and designed to raise regional awareness of its significance, served to further these visions.[9] Acquiring UNESCO World Heritage status would, it was believed, make the pilgrimage and island attractive to an international audience while increasing its appeal among Japanese people—both of which are often the case when places are awarded UNESCO World Heritage status (Hoshino and Asakawa 2011: 159–168).

The Shikoku Reijōkai, after overcoming some initial reservations (see note 8), joined in this campaign as part of a long-term strategy for survival. Although the pilgrimage was doing well, many priests were worried about its longer-term future. Priests I have talked to in Shikoku have invariably been conscious of the general decline in interest in pilgrimages in Japan in very recent times, and several referred to the problems faced by pilgrimage temples in Saikoku, Shōdoshima and other areas. They knew that historically their pilgrimage had had periods of severe decline, and that periods of success could be transitory, and hence, they were well aware that the decline facing other routes in Japan could spread to Shikoku, especially as Japan's population decline, economic problems and a rising tide of indifference to Buddhism, were all impacting on temples throughout Japan (Reader 2011a).

Thus, they saw UNESCO accreditation as a means of safeguarding their future by securing an international profile and clientele for the pilgrimage, and were thus ready to capitalise on the interest in the issue evident in Shikoku government, business and tourist circles.

In this context an important strategic example has been provided by another pilgrimage on a different continent—the Camino of Santiago de Compostela, which, because of its focus on a long-distance pilgrimage way and its sharing of a similar imagery to Shikoku (in which the sacred figure of the pilgrimage, Saint James, like Kōbō Daishi in Shikoku, is depicted as a pilgrim and guards over pilgrims on the way), is seen by people in Shikoku as bearing many similarities to their pilgrimage. The Santiago de Compostela pilgrimage, whose revival in modern times is well documented (Frey 1998, Roseman 2004), is seen by Shikoku authorities as a model example of how to bolster the long-term viability of a pilgrimage in an increasingly secular age.

Although the Santiago de Compostela pilgrimage was one of Catholic Europe's great pilgrimages in the medieval period, it had become moribund, with virtually no pilgrims by the mid-nineteenth century. In all of 1836, just thirty-seven pilgrims stayed at the Hospital Real (the place where pilgrims traditionally lodged on arrival at Santiago), and this number fell further to a mere twenty-five by 1840. This may have been the pilgrimage's nadir, but numbers remain very low for the rest of the century; only 965 pilgrims came in 1897. However, the pilgrimage underwent something of a revival spurred initially by papal and regional ecclesiastical authority campaigns from the late nineteenth century, followed by support from political powers, notably General Franco, who promoted it as a symbol of his brand of nationalism and orthodox Catholicism, in ways that helped revive pilgrim numbers in the earlier twentieth century. Franco's regime reconstructed the ancient city of Santiago, and from the mid-1960s on, a period when Spain began to develop a mass package tourism industry as a way of reviving its economy, his regime put resources into rebuilding the old pilgrim's way that had fallen into partial abeyance (Davidson 2010).

After Franco's death and Spain's emergence as a modern democracy, efforts to promote and 'reanimate' (Frey 1998: 250) the pilgrimage have continued apace, and they have transformed it into a highly successful international pilgrimage route and destination. Since the 'reanimation' of Santiago has been widely discussed elsewhere (Murray and Graham 1997, Frey 1998, Roseman 2004, Davidson 2010, Gonzalez 2012), I shall here only summarise some key themes that have emerged from existing studies. It is evident that a crucial factor in this reanimation was that various political, tourist and religious agencies cooperated and strove to promote the pilgrimage in the modern day and increase its participation rates, often eschewing any overt emphasis on faith as they did so (Frey 1998: 243–244, Roseman 2004: 70–71). The Catholic Church, through declarations of Holy Years (most recently in 1993 and 2010) and via high-profile visits by Pope John Paul II in 1982 and 1989, placed the pilgrimage firmly back on the Catholic map, whereas Spanish and Galician government agencies have thrown their weight behind the pilgrimage, promoting it as a manifestation of cultural

176 *Pilgrimage in the Marketplace*

heritage and as a focus of cultural tourism from the 1960s onwards. Sharon Roseman (2004: 77–80) has described how government agencies provided funds to help promote the pilgrimage internationally in ways that have transformed it into a cosmopolitan, ecumenical phenomenon and locus of cultural transformation. Nancy Frey (1998: 251) talks of how regional government agencies used the pilgrimage as a magnet to attract visitors to Galicia and to persuade them to then visit other parts of the region and how they produced various guidebooks on the region's gastronomy and cultural sites to this end. Murray and Graham (1997) have discussed how the Spanish national government included the Camino in its portfolio of places to develop as sites of heritage tourism and how it perceived the Camino as a cultural resource central to the tourist development strategies of the regions it passed through. Regional governments played a significant role in this context, by developing what has become the de facto and well-signed 'official' pilgrimage route that was designed to avoid built-up areas and take pilgrims through the most aesthetically pleasing areas possible along the way (Murray and Graham 1997: 516). Linda Davidson (2010) has discussed how local communities in Galicia played a major role in developing support structures that made the pilgrimage appealing to a modern clientele, while noting that the heavy marketing of the pilgrimage carried out by regional

Figure 7.1 Xubi, the 2010 Holy Year pilgrimage mascot, along with other pilgrim badges in a shop window in Santiago de Compostela.

authorities and the state avoided any real mention of its religious content. In the church-designated Holy Years of 1993 and 2010, regional authorities also created official mascots (in 2010 a mascot named Xubi, badges of which could be found everywhere in the city) to help promote the pilgrimage and enhance the Holy Year campaigns.

City and regional authorities have applied for and acquired a series of cultural imprimaturs and international marks of recognition from bodies such as UNESCO and the Council of Europe that have enhanced the status of the city and pilgrimage and made them more attractive to visitors. Santiago de Compostela was designated by UNESCO as a 'Cultural Patrimony for Harmony' site and as a UNESCO World Heritage City in 1985. The Council of Europe then declared the pilgrimage route to be a 'European Cultural Itinerary'—the first such under the auspices of the European Union. In 1993, UNESCO awarded World Heritage status to the pilgrimage route whereas Santiago de Compostela was proclaimed as European City of Culture in 2000. Such designations have helped increase international interest in the city and the Camino, leading to increasing numbers of visitors whether by foot or by various modes of transport. They have also given added weight to the marketing given to each by regional and state government agencies, which have eagerly seized on these cultural designations to further promote the city and pilgrimage.

What is evident in this growth and its associations with such cultural designations, however, is that it has led to a diminution of emphasis on religious themes within the pilgrimage. I noted earlier that the marketing by regional government and tourist agencies made little mention of the pilgrimage as a faith-based religious activity, and the activities of those who have been drawn to Santiago by such campaigns appear to reflect this. Murray and Graham, writing in 1997, for example, have stated that many of the rituals held in the Cathedral at Santiago had become largely tourist events because of this. As such they suggest that the UNESCO and other heritage-related designations would in the future make the pilgrimage even more oriented towards 'secular cultural tourism' (Murray and Graham 1997: 520).

Their predictions appear to be accurate. Although the Catholic Church may have played its part in publicising the pilgrimage and trying to increase pilgrim numbers via papal visits, Holy Years and special indulgences, it has been less prominent in such terms than regional and national political and tourist authorities, which have been the main driving forces in publicising the pilgrimage in recent years. These agencies have used the pilgrimage as a means of boosting regional tourism while distancing it (and Spain) from its problematic past associations with Franco and nationalistic Catholicism and, instead, promoting it as a means of enhancing a new Spanish ecumenism and sense of trans-European identity. These dynamics have increased in the last decade or so since the publication of Murray and Graham's article. When I visited Santiago in late 2010, I was struck not only by the plethora of posters and publicity materials emphasising the cultural aspects of the pilgrimage and by the ubiquity of Xubi mascot images and badges, but also

178 *Pilgrimage in the Marketplace*

by the crowds at a pilgrims' Mass I watched in the cathedral, where much of the audience (and I use the term *audience* rather than *congregation* deliberately) appeared more intent on taking photographs than on participating in the service. As will be noted in the following, also, the pilgrimage has become increasingly presented in recent times in the public domain as a holiday experience. It has also accumulated numerous of the signs and phenomena associated with heritage and cultural status, such as museums and exhibitions—phenomena likewise found increasingly in Shikoku and which, by their very nature as museums and exhibitions, help to transform an avenue of practice such as pilgrimage, into a manifestation of visual culture, art and aesthetics.

All of these activities have certainly increased the flow of visitors to Santiago and the numbers walking the Camino. They have also reoriented the pilgrimage in many respects, with tourism and European cultural heritage, along with a variety of New Age ideas that have become part of the milieu of many walkers on the Camino (Frey 1998: 34), becoming prominent in recent years. Murray and Graham (1997: 519) cite a study by the British-based Confraternity of St. James that indicates that for 70 per cent of Anglophone pilgrims 'cultural' issues (including interests in art, architecture, aesthetics and Spanish language) are their main motivation; only 9 per cent cited 'religious-spiritual-faith' reasons. Such developments have in effect weakened any control that Catholic authorities may have had over the pilgrimage. With public images of the pilgrimage now being shaped so much by political and tourist agencies whose prime concerns are regional and national regeneration and economic growth, rather than the advancement of the Catholic faith, it appears that Catholic authorities are now worried that their influence in the pilgrimage has waned and that they are considering ways to reclaim it as a Catholic enterprise.[10]

TAKING THE LEAD FROM SANTIAGO: THE SHIKOKU HERITAGE CAMPAIGN

The Santiago de Compostela pilgrimage's acquisition of UNESCO World Heritage status has been integral to the Shikoku heritage campaign. It is seen as setting a precedent in the eyes of the officials and priests I have interviewed in Shikoku, because it shows that an entire pilgrimage *route* can be awarded the UNESCO heritage label. Civic authorities, commercial-interest groups and priests alike in Shikoku are very much aware of the success of the Santiago pilgrimage since it was designated as such by UNESCO, and this also is a factor in their wish to acquire similar recognition for Shikoku. Various interest groups from Shikoku—from priests and academics, to regional government functionaries and those running nonprofit organisations (NPOs) funded by local businesses and whose purpose is to promote the Shikoku UNESCO campaign—have been to Santiago in order to see what ideas they can draw from the Santiago experience. I became aware of this (and of the extent to which businesses in Shikoku were involved in the heritage campaign) when I contacted the Omotenashi Network—an NPO funded by Shikoku business interests and local activists to promote the Shikoku heritage campaign—in late March 2008 while visiting Shikoku. I was invited to join them on a day out in which members led a group of local children and their parents along a section of the route to get them to learn more about the pilgrimage and its role in local culture, and to enable group members to distribute leaflets and put up posters and stickers promoting the pilgrimage. I was especially struck by the presence of a representative from Coca-Cola's Shikoku branch who at one point made a short speech that reminded me of Wright Mills's comments, cited in Chapter 4, about rotary club members assigning altruistic meanings to activities associated with company interests, and in which he pledged Coca-Cola's support for the heritage campaign and its commitment to Shikoku's cultural traditions. In so doing, he announced that the company was allowing the Omotenashi Network to put its promotional stickers on Coca-Cola's ubiquitous drinks machines throughout the island. The pledge made in front of such a drinks machine and accompanied by a short ceremony in which one of the youngest members of the party, a girl of about eight, was asked to duly affix such a sticker onto the machine. During the walk, members of the organisation informed me that they were planning a visit to Santiago, asked me what I knew about that city and pilgrimage, and later followed this up by sending me e-mails asking if I could provide any references to literature about the Santiago pilgrimage. They later let me know they had accomplished their plan by visiting the city later in 2008. The Omotenashi website promoting Shikoku's world heritage cause invokes the example of Santiago to justify its campaign—a claim also articulated by the websites of other Shikoku NPOs involved in the campaign.[11]

The application for UNESCO World Heritage status submitted by the Shikoku temples and regional political agencies to the Japanese Ministry of Culture,[12] refers on a number of occasions to UNESCO's accreditation of the Camino of Santiago de Compostela and uses it as a means of validating the application (Ehime-ken et al., 2007: 42–44). The application itself and the rhetoric surrounding the campaign are interesting in that they pay very little attention to concepts often associated with pilgrimage, such as religion, faith, practice, sacred icons, apparitions or miracles. On one level, this may not be surprising because the application is about heritage status as a cultural treasure, not as a centre of religious faith; is directed at an organisation, UNESCO, whose interest is in heritage rather than religious promotion; and needs to be endorsed by the Japanese government, which is constitutionally disbarred from promoting religion and religious institutions. Yet, even so, the paucity of comments about the pilgrimage's associations with Buddhist traditions, faith and even local religious customs is quite striking, given the importance of such things in the context of Shikoku pilgrimage history. The forty-four-page application document does give a brief introductory history of the pilgrimage, noting that it has roots in faith in a Buddhist figure and mentioning that Kūkai, known in folk-faith terms as Kōbō Daishi, was born in Shikoku in 774, travelled around Shikoku performing austerities in his youth and, in his guise as Kōbō Daishi, was central to the origins of the pilgrimage. After this brief mention, however, the document thereafter avoids talking about Kōbō Daishi and eschews any use of terms such as *shūkyō* (religion) or *shinkō* (faith). Words such as *reigen* and *kiseki* (both of which are commonly used in Japanese to refer to miracles) do not feature at all. Instead the application emphasises the pilgrimage's location in the natural surroundings of Shikoku (pp. 14, 22), the old streets and traditional buildings found along the route (p. 14), the cultural assets and artistic treasures of the temples (pp. 10–13) and the fact that the route passes through a large number of towns and districts throughout the island, thereby providing a focus of unity and identity for it (p. 14). The pilgrimage is described as a 'living cultural property' (*ikita bunkashisan*, p. 9), whereas references are made repeatedly to the 'pilgrimage culture' (*henro no bunka, henro bunka*) of Shikoku (e.g., p. 40) and of the need to conserve this heritage for future generations.

Such terminology has pervaded the Shikoku heritage campaign. There is a clear expediency here in that the UNESCO focus is on 'heritage' and because of Japanese political and legal factors. Regional government officials in Shikoku, for example, informed me of their need to avoid any activity that could be perceived as promoting religion or using public funds for the support of religious institutions because such activities are prohibited under Japan's secular constitution of 1946. As such they had decided, in consultation with the temples and other interested agencies, on the concept of *henro bunka*—pilgrimage culture—and with the emphasis on *bunka* while eschewing any mention of 'religion' (*shūkyō*) or 'faith' (*shinkō*). As such, although the pilgrimage and its associations with the faith-centred cult of Kōbō Daishi have long been central elements in the religious lives of people in Shikoku (Kaneko 1991), such themes have been set aside in the UNESCO application and campaign. Although legal considerations have played their part in this, this portrayal has also been shaped by the recognition of temple authorities that, in the present day, there has been a striking turn against religious activities in Japan (Reader 2012a, Baffelli and Reader 2012: 5–13) that they think is having an impact on pilgrim numbers elsewhere in Japan and that could impinge on the standing that their pilgrimage has attained. The actions of the temples in removing signs and symbols of miracle at places such as Iyataniji, and their banning of practices such as *takuhatsu*, further illustrate the view that, in the changing context of the modern day, people are more likely to be attracted by images of heritage and culture (as well, perhaps, by the prospect of strawberries and other delicious foodstuffs along the way) than by those of faith, miracle and asceticism.

In August 2008, the Japanese Ministry of Culture decided not to nominate the pilgrimage (or a number of other Japanese applicants) to UNESCO at

Strawberries, Camel Coolers and Luxury Hotels 181

Figure 7.2 Poster from the Shikoku campaign to gain recognition as a UNESCO World Heritage site.

that time, saying that, although it felt that the pilgrimage manifested appropriate qualities to fit with the universal heritage standards required, more work was needed on aspects of the application first.[13] As a result, the campaign has continued and remains at the forefront of contemporary Shikoku cultural politics. Many Shikoku universities have signed up to the campaign, putting on courses that depict the pilgrimage as a key element in island culture and history, requiring their students to engage in pilgrimage-related activities (including walking sections of the pilgrimage) and sponsoring pilgrimage exhibitions. Naruto Kyōiku Daigaku (Naruto University of Education), in eastern Shikoku, for example, has established a project titled 'Henro bunka wo ikashita chiiki ningenriki no ikusei' ('Nurturing the Regional Human Cooperation that Has Given Life to Shikoku's Pilgrimage Culture'), which promotes the pilgrimage as an aspect of local culture and supports its designation as a UNESCO heritage site. The project's publicity materials describe the pilgrimage as 'a nationwide tourist brand' (zenkoku kankō burando), but they also note that this is a 'brand' set in a region suffering from rapid depopulation and serious economic decline. Hence, the university, according to its publicity materials, wishes to address this problem by using Shikoku's pilgrimage culture (henro bunka) to generate a special Shikoku identity and to nurture the human potential needed to maintain regional society. To do this, the university has developed courses on the pilgrimage, sends its students out on walking tours and encourages them to volunteer as guides for local schoolchildren, taking them along what it depicts as Shikoku's cultural route. In so doing, students are encouraged to foster a sense of local identity in the schoolchildren and teach them the importance of the pilgrimage as part of their identity and heritage. The university also has plans to establish a pilgrimage-linked museum of regional culture, and to develop further pilgrimage-related educational activities, to further this campaign.[14]

Shikoku interest groups are continuing their efforts, via meetings, promotional events and symposia, to place the item on the national government's agenda and acquire its seal of approval, while temple authorities continue to upgrade facilities to make things more comfortable for pilgrims. Just as in Santiago, where an emphasis on tourism and cultural heritage has become a potent feature of the modern representation of the pilgrimage, in the Shikoku case, we can see how a pilgrimage may be transformed in terms of rhetoric and public presentation through which notions of religion are avoided and in which secular agencies from regional governments to local universities, along with the temples themselves, help (re)shape the pilgrimage through a lens of cultural heritage, tourism and aspired-for economic success.

The increasing focus in media depictions and portrayals of the pilgrimage as a form of hobby, sightseeing trip and culinary voyage is thus reflected also in the ways in which civil and religious authorities in Shikoku are projecting the pilgrimage. In eras when the practices of begging and austerities and tales of the miraculous characterised the pilgrimage, it proved less successful or popular than other competitor pilgrimages such as Saikoku; nowadays, as such activities and phenomena have been subtly excised from its public image, through a process of sanitisation and heritage-isation, the pilgrimage has acquired a larger clientele and attained modern day national and perhaps (if the aspirations of Shikoku authorities are realised) international success. In this process, it has been transformed into a heritage trail and a tourist commodity promoted not so much for any religious meanings it might have had, but for its potential to help the Shikoku economy and for its image as a symbol of heritage. The temples appear ready to embrace these transformations since they see them as the most viable means of assuring a longer-term future for the pilgrimage in a context in which religious engagement and interest in Buddhism have been on the wane in Japan. Of course, other pilgrimages in Japan, mindful also of similar pressures and aware of how Shikoku has managed to pull ahead in the competitive market while they have struggled, have themselves embarked on various campaigns and attempts—as the examples cited in earlier chapters of Saikoku exhibitions and its linkages with Japan Rail to provide souvenirs and special tickets to attract new pilgrims/passengers, indicate—to resituate themselves in ways that might prove attractive to a new clientele.

REBRANDING AND THE MECCA OPPORTUNITY

Such modern representations and rebrandings of the pilgrimage environment are not limited to Japan, to Shikoku or to Santiago but can be seen in multiple contexts globally. At times, too, such developments can make things more difficult for the less well-off, even as those with more resources can enjoy greater opportunities to perform pilgrimages in a variety of comfortable ways, from flying in to Hindu pilgrimage sites by helicopter (along with 'priority darshan') to having one's luggage carried along the Santiago Camino (see the following discussion), to having a choice of gourmet foods and being protected from the sight of beggar-pilgrims in Shikoku. In the Muslim world, too, one can see similar signs, a point illustrated by two articles that appeared in the British media on the same day, November 15, 2010, as Muslims from Britain prepared to travel to Saudi Arabia to participate in the hajj. On the BBC website, Robert Pigott (2010), the BBC's Religious Affairs editor, discussed how that there was a 'growing perception' that the hajj was 'becoming a richer person's privilege' because rising costs made it harder for poorer British Muslims to take part. Pigott quoted British Muslims who said that they had been able to afford the hajj just three or four years previously but could not now, because its costs had risen several fold. The price rises were fuelled by bureaucratic procedures in Saudi Arabia, the increasing number of 'middlemen' and agents involved in this process who acquired fees from pilgrims and because of the upgrading of Mecca's pilgrim facilities, in which smaller cheaper hotels were being replaced by larger, more expensive and more luxurious ones and in which travel companies, cashing on the popularity of the practice, had upped the prices of pilgrimage tours (Pigott 2010).

The second article, published on the same day by *The Guardian*, illustrated how upgraded pilgrimage facilities were having an impact on the hajj. Noting that the hajj appeared to be 'recession proof' due to continually high demand and high-speed travel from across the globe, the article focused on the new hotels and facilities being produced for better-off pilgrims. These included a high-speed rail line between Mecca and Medina that would cut travel times and a metro system that would enable pilgrims to move swiftly between some of the holy sites (a speeding-up process aimed, according to Saudi authorities, at 'improving the pilgrimage experience'). The article highlighted the luxurious nature of new hotels and other buildings designed to alter the face of Mecca and to make it attractive for the burgeoning upper end of the pilgrim market. Thus a complex of luxury apartments, hotels and shopping plazas, topped off by a planned 485-metre-high clocktower designed to become a 'landmark' for the city, is under way, while new hotels offer services and luxury foods—from butler services to expensive chocolate selections—aimed at the very rich who, it appears, are readily paying several thousand dollars a night for hotel suites while finding no contradiction in staying there while dressed in their hajj pilgrimage clothes. To accommodate such changes, massive redevelopments are being enacted in the region, with mountains being razed and many of the old districts of the city—and the houses of its inhabitants—swept away. Hadi Helal, a marketing agent for one of the luxury complexes involved in this upgrading Mecca's facilities, was enthusiastic about the 'the Mecca opportunity', as he termed it, and what it offered those involved in the business of providing services for pilgrims. As Helal noted, the buoyancy of the hajj market had led to large numbers of pilgrims demanding luxury and comfort when they stayed there. As such, the general trend has been for increasingly opulent facilities that privilege the rich and shut out those unable to afford the increasing costs of staying in Mecca.[15]

Certainly, facilities such as the newly built Raffles Makkah Palace (owned by the same company that runs the famous Raffles Hotel in Singapore) are beyond the reach of many. As the hotel's website informs us, it incorporates spas, beauty parlours, butler services and a dining terrace overlooking the Grand Mosque and offers guests

> a refined and elegant residential sanctuary featuring 214 suites with breathtaking views of the Grand Mosque and Kaaba, making a stay in the Islamic holy land of Makkah one of spiritual serenity.[16]

Such developments, critics say, have come at the cost not just of making it harder for poorer pilgrims, but also of damaging the local landscape. The journalist Mehdi Hasan has complained that the Saudi government has bulldozed many of Mecca's historical sites and has put up hotels and timeshares in their place.[17] Ali al-Ahmed, the Saudi director of the Washington-based Institute for Gulf Affairs, and a prominent critic of the Saudi regime, complains likewise that this destruction of ancient buildings and artefacts is a product of Saudi wishes to

> make Mecca like Dubai, it is a money-making operation. They destroy ancient buildings because they do not want any history other than their own, they see it as competition.[18]

His concern (when speaking in 2009) that these developments would increase the cost of the pilgrimage and make it an elite enterprise unaffordable for the majority of Muslims, appears borne out by Pigott's article a year later as far as British Mulsims are concerned. It also affirms some of the points made by Robert Bianchi's (2004) study of the hajj. This shows that there is a strong link between prosperity, income and performance of the hajj, with the highest per-capita rates of performance coming from wealthier nations such as Singapore and the United Kingdom and from countries with high levels of petroleum wealth (Bianchi 2004: 53–68). As Bianchi (2004: 70–71) also notes,

> pilgrimage managers have . . . virtually reinvented the way Muslims experience the *hajj* . . . *Hajj* officials tried to streamline the rituals in Mecca and Medina by discouraging customary devotions they see as hampering the orderly flow of worshipers. Pilgrim guides and police are constantly telling the crowds to keep moving and to avoid ancient but unnecessary practices such as kissing the Black Stone. . . .

Streamlining the pilgrimage and making it more amenable to an increasingly opulent clientele has also led the authorities to ameliorate the hardships earlier and poorer pilgrims faced. Now it is not just high-speed transport systems that have made the journey to and from the Meccan region faster and more comfortable; facilities are also provided by the authorities to make various pilgrimage rituals easier and more bearable. The *sa'i* ritual, which involves pilgrims running seven times (a distance of three-and-a-half kilometres) between two hills to reenact the story of Hagar, Abraham's bondswoman, in her search for water in the desert, has formerly been arduous especially in the heat of summer, but is now done comfortably because the authorities have constructed air-conditioned tunnels for the purpose. Such developments have made the pilgrimage less dangerous and easier to manage (something that helps increase pilgrim flows and profit margins) as doubtless will further innovations such as the new metro services that are planned for the region. The continued razing of Mecca's older quarters, the building of luxury hotels, the provision of butler services and the opportunities to dine out overlooking the Grand Mosque also add to this process in which facilities in and around Islam's most important pilgrimage location appear to be increasingly oriented towards the rich and their comforts.

How far this is leading to the marginalisation of poorer pilgrims or even their exclusion from the market in Mecca is a moot point. I am under no illusion that wealth did not buy privilege in earlier times or that in prior ages everyone was really equal on pilgrimage. However, as was seen in Chapter 4, the rise of mass transportation and infrastructures—and the cheapness they provided—did play a role in bringing pilgrimages within the ambit of greater numbers of people, and they certainly led to an increased democratisation of its processes. Yet alongside this has been a burgeoning growth at the top

186 *Pilgrimage in the Marketplace*

end of the market. What the preceding examples—from the marginalisation of impoverished pilgrims and eradication of signs of the 'superstitious past' in Shikoku, to the 'priority darshan' that rich Hindus can purchase with their helicopter tours, to the opulent services for the benefit of rich hajj pilgrims—show is that in the modern day, this process of democratisation and increased access is being countered by increasing levels of privilege for richer pilgrims who can enjoy increased comforts while their poorer counterparts may be marginalised or even shut out of the process.

FROM HERITAGE AND EXHIBITIONS TO THEME PARKS

If the sanitisation and transformation of pilgrimage into cultural, heritage and epicurean tours and/or luxurious affairs with butlers and gourmet foods in which unsettling signs of austerity and poverty are banished, is one contemporary trend in the pilgrimage marketplace, another, related one is the development of pilgrimage theme parks. These are not a wholly new phenomenon, because they are in many respects a continuation and extension of pilgrimage formats such as replicated pilgrimages, exhibitions and displays such as the Japanese *kaichō* and *degaichō* that have been encountered earlier. In them, the processes of sanitisation and heritage-isation have become fused together within a modern culture of convenience through which visitors can engage with an idealised version of pilgrimage locations while being protected from any encounter with the hardships, inconveniences, dust, problems and even the potentially unsettling presence of local people that have often been actualities in the pilgrimage process.

A good example of this can be seen with the Holy Land Experience, a pilgrimage theme park opened in Orlando, Florida, in February 2001. This was developed as a 'living Biblical museum' to cater for Americans who, as Yorke Rowan (2004: 250) has noted, have a 'long tradition and appetite' for images of the Holy Land and a fascination with Biblical imagery, as well as a reluctance to travel long distances overseas—partly for economic reasons but also because many Americans do not own passports, while contemporary political problems also make them reluctant to visit the Middle East. As a result, a number of replica sites have developed in the United States to enable Americans to experience the Biblical region and its pilgrimage sites without needing to actually go there. Such replication is not a new phenomenon in the United States, whose landscape has its share of replicated pilgrimage sites, from Lourdes grottoes that met the needs of U.S. Catholics especially in the nineteenth and earlier twentieth centuries when transatlantic travel was beyond the reach of most Americans, to creations of multiple-image Christian pilgrimage replica sites such as the National Shrine of the North American Martyrs at Auriesville, New York.[19]

The Orlando Holy Land Experience is an example of how the process of replication may be taken a step further by fusing it with another great tradition- the amusement or theme park, a notion epitomised in many respects by Disneyland, which has itself been compared to and interpreted as a form of modern pilgrimage site by some scholars (e.g., Moore 1980, Notoji 1990). The result is a pilgrimage theme park that replicates in an idealised form the sites of the Christian Holy Land while eradicating anything that might disturb its American visitors, who are offered the chance to experience the 'authenticity' of a Holy Land thoroughly domesticated and tailored to U.S. tastes (Rowan 2004). Not only can visitors enjoy various drinks suited to Americanised images of the Middle East such as refreshing 'camel coolers', but they can also do so without any of the hassle and problems of the real place that might spoil their experiences as U.S. pilgrims. This is a Holy Land without its dominant Jewish and Muslim populations and devoid of any vestiges of their cultural presence—a presence that might spoil the image of a sacred Christian realm of harmony—and there is no sign of the contentious issues of stewardship that are contested by different Christian orders in the actual Holy Land. Instead, and reassuringly for visitors, the inhabitants of the Holy Land Experience are U.S. staff dressed in period costumes as Jews of the first century CE, the spotlessly clean gift shops offer biblical souvenir goods without the need to haggle over prices, and the Last Supper is 'performed' ten times a day (with, according to the British journalist Tanya Gold, a Jesus with 'the glamour of a daytime TV star'). After the Passion is enacted, visitors are invited to pray and offered the chance to be born again then and there (T. Gold 2011).

The Holy Land Experience is one of a number of pilgrimage theme parks that have developed in recent times. Others include the Tierra Santa (Holy Land) park in Buenos Aires, Argentina, which has repeated reenactments of the events of Jesus's life, from Last Suppers to an hourly resurrection (Payne 2012), and a planned Hindu theme park in Hardwar, India.[20] In Japan, too, one can find similarly sanitised, idealised and native-free versions of Indian Buddhist sites,[21] whereas pilgrimage market events such as the Saikoku exhibition, discussed in Chapter 1, along with exhibitions of pilgrimage that eschew any semblance of sweat and tears while displaying the icons and treasures of pilgrimage temples within the secular context of a museum and presenting them as artistic objects to be admired for their aesthetic value also continue this pattern of sanitised representation.[22]

Although UNESCO heritage campaigns eliminate the troubling 'religious' elements of pilgrimage and make it an increasingly tourist and cultural heritage activity, places such as the Holy Land Experience—along with pilgrimage exhibitions and idealised representations of Indian Buddhist sites in Japan—strip away its sweat, inconvenience and potentially unruly local populations. As such, places such as the Holy Land Experience exhibit a continuity with heritage campaigns and luxury hotels in Mecca in purging pilgrimage of its problematic and uncomfortable dimensions, and presenting its pilgrims with an idealised and sanitised representational world that has been created to suit their idealised images of what an 'authentic' pilgrimage

188 *Pilgrimage in the Marketplace*

place should be like. It is thus a fittingly postmodern pilgrimage representation, one that replicates the idealised images encapsulated in contemporary pilgrimage publicity on Shikoku, through which reproductions of how things should be (or how the producers and promoters of pilgrimages want their potential customers to imagine how they might be) are articulated. They remove awkward realities—the crowded streets, the modern houses, highways and tunnels and the sweat and strain, as well as the poverty and hints of premodern irrationality suggested by beggars and objects imbued with the aura of miracles—to provide a sanitised, and hence readily assimilated, version of the pilgrimage suited to modern needs, in which comfort and sightseeing are paramount.

FROM HERITAGE TO HIKING AND HOLIDAYS

Pilgrimage is thus made ever more into a commodity coterminous with modern convenience and consumerism while being 'liberated' from awkward questions of faith, belief and troublesome locals that might put off prospective visitors. This enhances their potential to attract new clients (especially the well-heeled and holiday oriented), thereby not just opening pilgrimages up (in the manner to which the 1930s atheist travel journalist Iijima aspired) to those who expressly have no faith, but even making them the main focus of pilgrimages in promotional terms. In essence, what Iijima and others did in Shikoku, highlighting the pilgrimage as a secular tourist affair, writing about it in travel magazines and popularising it through a tourist medium, and what was manifest in the progressive increase in diversions and 'sights to see' along the way evident in Saikoku guidebooks from Tokugawa times on, are evidence of how pilgrimage, an early stimulus for tourism, is becoming increasingly subsumed by it.

This is not a new development, of course, as was also discussed in Chapter 4, where I looked at the ways in which various secular agencies and commercial concerns have capitalised on and helped stimulate the pilgrimage market. At various points in this book, I have pointed to the ludic and tourist dimensions of pilgrimage, suggesting particularly in Chapter 4 that as the practice has been opened, especially through the activities of secular and commercial agencies and the provision of increasingly accessible, quick and comfortable transport and support services, this orientation towards tourism is intensified. The results, as this chapter indicates, are that the intersections of pilgrimage and tourism are such that tourism has now become the overriding dynamic at large numbers of pilgrimage sites and that the ludic and touristic have become pilgrimage's most powerful public manifestations. Modernity in the shape of enhanced communications, facilities, transport and media images and representations may have made it easier for people to know about and get to pilgrimage places, but it has also simultaneously fostered the mechanisms of mass tourism and given rise to social attitudes attuned to the acceptability of relaxing and taking time off to go to other places. Pilgrimage is no longer the only avenue for escape and getting away in an era when travel for the sake of enjoyment has gained general social legitimacy. As a Japanese Buddhist priest who had previously told me that pilgrimage sites had to keep an eye on each other because they were competitors within the same market (see Chapter 2) commented, nowadays his temple faced a new level of competition. In a society in which getting away on holiday had become increasingly socially acceptable, the pilgrimage route his temple was on was not so much competing with other pilgrimages, but with exotic (and often cheaper and sunnier) holiday destinations such as Guam, Hawaii and various other Pacific islands, to say nothing of Thailand and other Asian destinations. That in itself was a factor pushing temples more towards making themselves more attractive to people who might not necessarily be motivated by faith. Portraying one's pilgrimage in engaging ways and emphasising their consumer delights are likely to become increasingly important because of such alternative competition, if the views of this priest are anything to go by. I would note also that for Japanese pilgrimage temples, the newly developed pilgrimages in Taiwan and Korea mentioned in Chapter 1, which are aimed at Japanese pilgrims and combine pilgrimage with the exoticism of tourist travel in a foreign country, represent another challenge that intensifies the need of pilgrimage sites to draw attention to their touristic potentialities.

Simultaneously, as emphasis on the surrounding environment (the restaurants, the food, the comforts, the heritage and so on) becomes prevalent in pilgrimage guidebooks and literature, and as steps are taken by those associated with pilgrimages to downplay their religious dimensions and to link them to attractive marketing ploys such as mascots, they become potentially more attractive as tourist sites. It is thus unsurprising that the tourist industry, long a player in the pilgrimage market, frequently advertises pilgrimages as an intriguing form of modern holiday experience in which pilgrimage sites and routes serve *as* holiday destinations. Interestingly, too, and in contrast to the ways in which some pilgrimages appear to have become increasingly upmarket and catering to a newly emergent rich clientele, as with the luxurious hotels for rich Muslims in Mecca or the helicopter flights for nouveau riche Indians, such advertising of pilgrimage as a holiday appears to be often aimed at a less opulent sector of the market and be depicted as a form of cheap, affordable tourism.

On October 17, 2009, for example, the Travel Section of the British newspaper *The Guardian* had a special feature on cheap holidays. These included the pilgrimage to Santiago de Compostela, which, according to the newspaper, provided a good walking route with cheap accommodation in pilgrim hostels. Being a Holy Year, 2010 presented an ideal holiday opportunity.[23] *The Guardian* returned to such themes in its list of '30 Fantastic New Trips for 2010', drawn, *The Guardian* travel writers stated, from their having scoured travel brochures advertising novel adventures and sights. Among the 'fantastic new trips' highlighted were the Kumbh Mela, the great Indian pilgrimage gathering taking place in Hardwar in 2010, and the Santiago Camino.[24] Indian pilgrimages feature widely as holiday destinations and/or are advertised in such a guise by numerous tour companies both internationally and locally. As the website of one such firm announces, 'You can cover major pilgrimage destinations of the country on India holiday packages.'[25] Indian Railways, as was noted in Chapter 4, has long been involved in ferrying pilgrims around the country and helping foment a pan-Indian pilgrimage culture, also now advertises a special pilgrimage train tour service around India that visits numerous pilgrimage sites—and that describes those it takes on the tour as 'tourists'.[26]

This representation of pilgrimage as holiday is evident also in the activities of tourist boards around the world that have seized on pilgrimage as a means of boosting local tourism—a point noted in previous chapters—as well as by private companies. Brochures advertising walking tours along the Camino that promise to 'recreate, as closely as is possible, the experience of the medieval traveller' by enabling participants to walk along what are portrayed as unspoilt sections of the route but that simultaneously promise that participants will at times be ferried in comfortable Mercedes minibuses to nearby attractions and along less-scenic parts of the route while promising that they can enjoy ' delicious local cooking and wines' are examples of this (Murray and Graham 1997: 521). Such themes are also manifest in the activities of the Galician Tourist Bureau, which has advertised the Santiago Camino as a 'rural tourism' holiday experience via its Bono Iacobus tourist service. The service promises that one can stay in rural lodges while walking part of the pilgrimage route unencumbered by one's luggage, which is transported from lodge to lodge by the Bono Iacobus service.[27] Commercial firms such as the Camino Walks Service similarly present the Santiago pilgrimage as an ideal walking holiday through which one can attain 'Quality Time & Peace of Mind on the Camino de Santiago'. The company offers various package tours to this end, with full board and lodging and a luggage service so that hikers need not carry anything.[28] Japanese travel companies also offer such package tours not just in Japan and the rest of Asia but also, in recent years, along the Camino, which is now advertised as a new guided tour holiday destination for Japanese clients. Such advertisements emphasise Santiago's status as a World Heritage site while assuring would-be Japanese participants that one does not need any religious affiliations to make the trip.[29] In such contexts, it is little wonder that (as I noted earlier) the Roman Catholic Church has begun to worry that it has lost control of the pilgrimage and is starting to talk of ways of restoring a more 'religious' dimension to what appears to be turning into primarily a long-distance hiking trail and part of a (secularised) cultural heritage tour for holidaymakers.

The emphasis on (or reinvention of) pilgrimages as hiking tourist trails is evident elsewhere in Europe, as the example of St. Olaf's (also at times written as St. Olav's) Way in Norway indicates. Based on what is cited as an ancient pilgrimage route leading to Nidanos Cathedral in Trondheim and to the tomb of King Olaf Haraldsson (later canonised as Saint Olaf), this was revived in 1997 but with very clear tourist and hiking dimensions to it under the name St. Olaf's Way. It has been promoted thereafter by Visit Norway, the country's official travel information agency, whose website promotes it as a means of discovering 'Norway's rich religious and cultural heritage as well as the spectacular landscape'.[30] The Visit Norway website draws attention to several linked pilgrimage routes associated with St. Olaf's Way that can be walked as one makes one's way to Trondheim from Oslo, with narratives emphasizing the historical sites and stunning landscapes to be seen on the way while eschewing any discussion of religious belonging or possible associations between the pilgrimage and matters of faith.[31] There are a number of hiking trails linked to the way, and these were, as a network of routes, incorporated into the Council of Europe's 'cultural routes' programme in 2010 by the Luxembourg-based European Institute of Cultural Routes, which oversees the programme. The aim of this, according to the Institute, is to further European integration, parallel to its economic and political project, by emphasising shared cultural heritage via travel and by identifying cultural routes and landscapes that help shape the 'common heritage of Europe'. Through such routes, Europeans are thus encouraged to discover a new sense of European cultural harmony and heritage via 'the tourist cultural practice' of travel along various European routes that 'influenced the history of cultural relations'.[32] In such ways, an old pilgrimage route has been revived as a hiking trail publicised by a national tourist agency as a means to explore Norwegian history, landscape and culture and adopted by the Council of Europe as part of a wider heritage and cultural identity project.

The Shikoku pilgrimage trail, too, has been promoted as a 'hiking route', a process that started, according to Mori Masato (2005), in the 1930s, the period when the travel industry was looking for ways to cash in on the phenomenon. More recently, Shikoku regional tourist authorities have established a hiking trail that almost exactly replicates the pilgrimage route, but which they can promote (because it is not the exact pilgrimage path) without seeming to support religious activities. This portrayal of the pilgrimage route as a hiking trail and hiking opportunity is now attracting the attention of the walking community in Japan. Mori (2005: 12–42, 270–274) describes how he saw posters advertising the pilgrimage in hiking gear shops in Osaka and how the pilgrimage nowadays features in hiking magazines and related media, where it is portrayed as an opportunity for trekking and backpacking. He also notes how walkers on the pilgrimage commonly nowadays emphasise their activity in such terms while saying they have no association with or interest in religion, thereby affirming Hoshino and Asakawa's (2011) aforementioned comments on this score. NHK, too, whose documentaries presenting Shikoku through the lens of culture and heritage have been discussed earlier, also now has

192 *Pilgrimage in the Marketplace*

begun to portray the pilgrimage in the guise of a hiking trail, a theme evident in a series titled *Shumi Yūyū* ('Pleasurable/Leisurely Hobbies') that featured the pilgrimage and was broadcast in autumn 2006, along with an accompanying book (NHK 2006). The book and documentaries provided practical advice (such as the best shoes to wear) about how to do the pilgrimage, advising participants to devise and keep to a specific planned schedule in so doing, and portraying it as a form of leisurely 'hobby' useful for keeping healthy and fit. There was little suggestion that it might have any religious connotations. As with Japanese advertisements of Santiago pilgrimage tours, Galician campaigns to promote the pilgrimage as a form of rural tourism and British newspaper articles about pilgrimage routes as holiday trails, the NHK programmes and book transformed the pilgrimage into a refreshing hobby and holiday activity seemingly dissociated from any notions of faith.

Such patterns are emerging, too, within the Shikoku heritage campaign, as is indicated by the website of the NPO Kokorohenro (literally 'spirit of the Shikoku pilgrimage'), an interest group supported by island businesses and that campaigns for Shikoku to attain UNESCO World Heritage status. It states that the focus of the Shikoku pilgrimage has changed in the present day so that nowadays sports, health and exercise are at its heart. Health has, the site announces, replaced faith as its main focus; moreover, continuing the rhetoric of theme parks and tourist brands outlined earlier, it describes the Shikoku pilgrimage as 'the world's greatest theme park'.[33] In such ways, the Shikoku pilgrimage is being reformulated in public representations as a 'brand', a theme park and a holiday, hiking and heritage trail—themes that appear rather distant from the Buddhist and faith-centred orientations on which it was initially founded and that had been central to it in earlier times. To what extent the temples will begin to wonder, as the Catholic authorities of Santiago appear to be doing, that they have lost control of the pilgrimage is unclear. Although some priests have privately expressed such concerns to me, and this worry was behind the reservations some priests had over the heritage campaign when it was first mooted, such concerns do not appear to have yet emerged in public to any degree, and thus far the broader trend has been towards an increasingly secularised public representation and marketing of the pilgrimage.

FUTURE DIRECTIONS?

In this chapter, I have focused on some modern trends in pilgrimage and in its promotion and public representation that are being replicated in a variety of contexts globally, but that are particularly evident in Santiago and Shikoku—two of the world's great pilgrimage routes, both of which have had long and close associations with asceticism and arduous long-distance travel and both of which have increasingly flourished while being portrayed through the lenses of heritage, hiking and holidays in the present day. None of this is intrinsically new, and the extent to which pilgrimage has historically incorporated tourist dimensions has been recurrent feature of this book. However, in the modern day, any putative boundaries between the two have been increasingly set aside, whereas the focus of pilgrimage itself is being reshaped in global terms as pilgrimages such as Shikoku and Santiago (and these, I would argue, provide us with images that will appear familiar to those who know and have visited other sites and serve as templates, models and indicators of the potential futures of pilgrimage) are being reshaped and portrayed as representative symbols of cultural heritage. Through such dynamics the unseemly, irrational and ultimately uncontrolled aspects of pilgrimage, whether in the form of leg braces and crutches somehow redolent of an irrational past, as at Iyataniji, or in the guise of anything so intrusively unsettling to the imagined and wholly Americanised Holy Land Experience as the actual inhabitants of the Middle East, are excised to help make pilgrimages conform more the idealised images manifest in publicity pamphlets and tourist brochures. Pilgrimages are thus becoming increasingly transformed into thoroughly modern events such as cultural and heritage tours and hiking holidays through which the pilgrim/tourist is able to evade any concerns about faith while entering into a world of cultural riches unencumbered by the travails of past ages and increasingly shaped by agencies such as tourist boards and related interest groups. As such, pilgrimage is being utilised increasingly as a mechanism for strengthening the strategies and interests of seemingly 'secular' agencies such as local business and government agencies that view pilgrimages as a potential means of social and economic regeneration. In this context what is happening in Japan, and especially Shikoku, whose emergence as the preeminent pilgrimage in contemporary contexts has been so well served by linking it to images of identity and cultural tradition, could serve as a potential indicator of the futures of pilgrimage in the modern world. It might be that we will see more cases in which pilgrimage authorities remove any signs of the miraculous from their sites, tidying them up to eradicate any odour of 'superstition' and to make their sites more amenable to images of heritage, pleasure, hobbies and hiking.

8 Concluding Comments

On Shōdoshima, as well as the eighty-eight-stage pilgrimage that has faced difficulties in recent years, one can also see vestiges of another pilgrimage, one based on the Saikoku route with thirty-three small temples or the wayside halls dedicated to Kannon. When I first visited Shōdoshima in the mid-1980s, there were some signboards indicating the existence of this thirty-three-stage pilgrimage, but the sites themselves appeared barely visited, and at no time when visiting the island have I heard of people actually performing this route. Similar to the pilgrimages on Awaji studied by Nakamura (1980; see also Chapter 2) that had been sidelined by other routes, the thirty-three-stage Kannon pilgrimage had become disused by the mid-1980s, although a far more popular route, the eighty-eight-stage Kōbō Daishi–centred pilgrimage was, at that time, attracting more than 30,000 pilgrims a year. The disused pilgrimage route served as a reminder to priests on the island that pilgrimages do not always flourish and that they can at times fall into abeyance, a point that has been much in their minds in recent times as pilgrim numbers on the eighty-eight-stage pilgrimage have fallen. It is perhaps unsurprising in such terms that priests on the island have taken measures to try to revitalise their pilgrimage lest it goes the way of the Kannon pilgrimage.

That they were prepared to take their pilgrimage to an airport mall in order to do this is not an indication that they have somehow 'sold out' to the world of commercialism so much as it is a recognition on their part that pilgrimages have necessary economic and pragmatic dimensions that need to be addressed if they are to flourish rather than fade. The priests know that the maintenance of their icons, figures of worship, temples and communities depend on practicalities and that the world of finance and materialism cannot be set apart from the religious world they embrace. They are equally aware that pilgrimages do not prosper simply by word of mouth, tales of miracle or seemingly magnetic settings. Practical matters of promotion and engagement with other interested parties—from local authorities to merchants and businesses whose support may be vital in helping pilgrimage sites to flourish—are also critical to such success. They are aware, too, of how other pilgrimages that have been skilfully marketed have succeeded and of the need to do similar things themselves if they are to survive in what has always been the competitive marketplace of pilgrimage. As such, they were prepared to go to a new arena, to an airport shopping mall, in order to seek new clienteles and to reorient the pilgrimage in ways that could appeal to people in the present day.

As this book has argued, actions of this sort are intrinsic parts of the pilgrimage dynamic not just in the present day but also across history. Although many pilgrimage sites may owe their origins at least in part to tales of miracle, dramatic landscapes and the historical or legendary presence of apparitional figures or religious founders, these alone are not sufficient to enable them to flourish or acquire a lasting reputation. Pilgrimage is located in and operates through the marketplace, and it is through the mechanisms of the marketplace that constructs such as the sacred are materialised and successful pilgrimage sites emerge. One cannot separate out these aspects into artificially divided camps in which pilgrimage is presented in an idealised form as devoid of commerce and market forces and in which any manifestation of the latter—whether in the shape of a souvenir, a package holiday or priestly promotions—is represented as 'inauthentic' and as a scar on the face of sanctity. The sacred, insofar as it is a viable category, is not separate from but grounded in the realms of the mundane, profane and mercantile, which are themselves integral elements in the construction and shaping of pilgrimage and thereby of the sacred. Without these dynamics, pilgrimages might still appear but, as the history of shrines that briefly attracted pilgrims because of reported miracles shows, popularity can fade fast and places can become, as priests in Shōdoshima commented, *sabishii*—sad, lonely—and facing decline.

Such dynamics inform us that the divisions that are commonly utilised in thinking about religion and in which religion and the sacred are seen as somehow set apart from the material, the moneyed and the mundane are highly questionable if not false. In pilgrimage—a thematic practice and activity normally associated with the religious—we see how deeply the sacred and the religious are embedded in the 'worldly'. If pilgrimage is about faith, miracles and worship, it is also about marketing, promotion, invention, entertainment, material consumption, the buying of goods and sightseeing. These are issues that studies of pilgrimage need to address more thoroughly in order to understand how and why pilgrimages may come about and attract clienteles.

These issues are also particularly pertinent in the present day. I have emphasised throughout this book that the seeming intrusions of the material and commercial into the realms of pilgrimage are not simply products of the modern day but are also historically recurrent. I do, however, suggest that the dynamics of the modern world have done much to intensify these themes and that in so doing they are contributing both to an increasing secularisation of pilgrimage and to an intensification of its marketing dynamics and tourist orientations. Pilgrimage, as I have argued in earlier chapters, fits well with and adapts to the changing contours of the age, and in the modern day such phenomena as mass transport systems, tourist agencies and the mass media that have made pilgrimages more accessible, that have opened new markets (notably to wider age sets and gender groups) and that have expanded pilgrims' choices have also led—as the Japanese example indicates—to a move away from the miraculous as more emphasis is placed on issues such as cultural heritage and tourist diversions. Such patterns of development are, I would suggest, more likely to continue than to be reversed, as pilgrimage sites continue to face the need that was intrinsic to their emergence—attracting clienteles not simply for a brief period after their formation but in the longer term—in an age when there is increased competition for the attention of would-be visitors.

All this means that the necessary engagement with the marketplace that has been intrinsic to the enduring nature of pilgrimage will remain central to it in the future and that the worlds of pilgrimage, religion and the sacred will remain intimately embedded in and inseparable from the realities of the marketplace and its manifestations. In such ways, the events cited at the start of this book are not disjunctions from the 'true' or 'authentic' nature of pilgrimage. Rather, they are a striking manifestation of it, for a pilgrimage in a department store or in an airport mall and surrounded by market stalls shops and special lunch offers is as much a part of the truly sacred as are miracles, remote temples and religious icons.

Notes

NOTES TO CHAPTER 1

1. *Junrei* is one of several terms in Japanese normally translated in English as 'pilgrimage'; for a fuller discussion of Japanese pilgrimage terminology see Reader and Swanson (1997: 232–237). The pilgrimage has thirty-three temples because, in chapter 25 of the popular Buddhist text the Lotus Sutra, Kannon (the Japanese name for the bodhisattva Avalokitesvara) vows to assume thirty-three manifestations to save humanity. In Japan, the chapter is also seen as a sutra in its own right, known as the Kannongyō (Kannon Sutra).
2. In the second half of the Heian (794–1185) period in Japan, it was common for emperors to retire because they could wield more power behind the scenes. Kazan, however, left court in order to pursue a religious life as a Buddhist monk.
3. On *kaichō* and on the supposed power of hidden icons, see McCallum (1994: 169–170), Reader and Tanabe (1998: 212–215), Rambelli (2002), and Hur (2009). Icons are kept hidden because they are believed to be especially powerful and because continuous display would devalue their potency; being put briefly on display is said to allow people out-of-the-ordinary access to their power. The periods between being put on display vary from icon to icon and temple to temple; some icons are displayed on a regular—for example, monthly—basis, but others may only be shown at extended intervals, sometimes only every hundred years or longer.
4. Normally Kannon pilgrimages have thirty-three temples, but Chichibu has thirty-four. This is because in medieval times Chichibu was seen to form a 'set' along with the Saikoku pilgrimage and another famous Kannon route, the Bandō route also, like Chichibu, near Tokyo. The three together consisted of ninety-nine temples, so an additional one was added to Chichibu to make a round hundred.
5. This agency, the Hoshi Kikaku Public Relations Agency, is based in Matsuyama in Shikoku and has worked with Shikoku temples in various campaigns in recent years. I visited the company in March 2008 and had a long interview with the person in charge of these campaigns.
6. I discuss such issues further online (Reader 2012b). One Saikoku hidden image had last been displayed in 1872, and another in 1925, and neither was due for public exposure for many decades hence.
7. This term was something of a buzzword in the Japanese media and was used by academics in the 1980s; see Reader (2007a: 30, note 21) for further discussion of why this was so.
8. In early April 2008, I visited ten of the Chichibu sites and two Saikoku temples; at each I spoke to priests and officials looking after the pilgrimage offices, and all spoke along similar lines as indicated here.

198 Notes

9. These figures and general information about pilgrim numbers in these pilgrimages were supplied by temple priests in Shōdoshima and Sasaguri. I have visited temples on these routes regularly over the past twenty or more years and have been provided with figures for the Shōdoshima pilgrimage by priests who have collated pilgrimage statistics at their temples over the last three decades.
10. This view was expressed by priests involved with the Shōdoshima and Sasaguri pilgrimage associations that organised the event, in discussions with me during my visits to these places in the period between 2007 and 2010.
11. This information comes from an online report of the event at http://www.centrair.jp/event/ev-title/1180345_3676.html and from follow-up discussions with the priests concerned in March 2010.
12. This information comes from a report on the website of the *Chūō Nippō* information agency (http://japanese.joins.com/article/article.php?aid=103340&servcode=400%A1%F8code=400&p_no=&comment_gr=article_103340&pn=8&o=a). How far the planned development has materialised is unclear; when I visited the Korean National Tourist organisation's Tokyo office on September 2, 2011, officials there said they had no idea how many people had done the pilgrimage that year, and there were few publicity materials for it on display.
13. http://kataragama.org/commercialisation.htm.
14. http://travelguides.bmibaby.com/sisp/index.htm?fx=event&event_id=104834.
15. This was in a BBC World Service programme titled *Reporting Religion* on July 2, 2007; the interviewer was Dan Damon. Until 2008, the broadcast could be accessed at http://www.bbc.co.uk/worldservice/programmes/reporting_religion.shtml.
16. Such themes are evident in the work of Dupront (1987:413), Margry (2008: 24–26), who focuses on 'placemaking' while claiming that the essence of the pilgrimage is located within the boundaries of the shrine being visited, Lochtefeld (2010), and several other studies by Japanese scholars such as Kondō (1982), Hoshino (2001), Mori (2005) and Asakawa (2008). My study of the Shikoku pilgrimage also draws attention to how the pilgrimage is 'made' as an entity and a place by a variety of actors and agencies (Reader 2005).
17. It should be noted that although Taylor does draw attention to the point that the Our Lady of Guadalupe shrine at Tepeyac developed beyond being a local into a national shrine and thus superseded other shrines in its region, he sees modern Mexican pilgrimage history as being far more complex than simply the rise of one dominant shrine and the marginalisation of all others.
18. Among recent books are Hoshino (2001), Osada, Sakata and Seki (2003), Mori (2005), Asakawa (2008), and Hoshino and Asakawa (2011). In addition, several major collaborative projects have been run at Shikoku universities on Shikoku pilgrimage history and sociology. By contrast, very few studies of other pilgrimages, apart from Satō's comparative study of Saikoku, Chichibu and Shikoku (which shows how Shikoku has become the dominant pilgrimage numerically) have been produced in Japanese in recent years.
19. Coleman and Eade's volume does have Middle Eastern and African examples, but it remains mostly focused on the West and has no chapters on Asian pilgrimages. Barbaro (2013: 46) also mentions Coleman and Elsner's (1995) overview of pilgrimage across religious traditions as another volume that pays no attention to academic research on Japan.

NOTES TO CHAPTER 2

1. See, for example, such Lourdes websites as http://www.bernadette-of-lourdes.co.uk/bernadette-of-lourdes.htm and http://www.wf-f.org/OurLadyofLourdes.html.

2. Such stories are found in early pilgrimage collections of miracle tales and in early guidebooks, notably those produced in the 1680s and 1690s by the ascetic pilgrimage proselytiser Shinnen. See my translation of and commentary on Shinnen's collection of miracle tales (Reader 1999).
3. See, for example, the town's tourist website and its article 'Things to do in Sedona', available at http://www.visitsedona.com/article/75.
4. http://www.sify.com/finance/even-gods-are-affected-by-global-financial-crisis-news-default-jeguNWdhfjd.html.
5. In the early 1990s, when I was conducting fieldwork on the activities of pilgrimage temple associations in Japan, I found the Shikoku temples and their official organisation to be informative and helpful. I got no response to communications with the Saikoku temple association (Reijōkai), which simply referred me to a well-known Japanese academic specialist on pilgrimage. He, in turn, said to me that the Saikoku temples as a group were so sure of their standing that they felt little need to talk to researchers or to engage in much publicity for the pilgrimage and that this latter issue was a factor in the shifting patterns of popularity between the two pilgrimages.
6. I base this comment not just on numbers for each pilgrimage but also conversations and interviews over the past twenty-five or so years in Japan with people involved in the pilgrimage travel business in Japan, who have noted this shift in pilgrimage patterns over the past two or so decades, and with priests of temples on each of these routes.
7. There have been several collections of miracle tales published by pilgrim activists, starting with Shinnen in 1690 and until the early 1980s the Shikoku temples, too, periodically published collections of miracle tales based on stories from the pilgrim community (e.g., Shikoku Hachijūhakkasho Reijūkai 1984). The last of these was produced in 1984, and since then little mention of the subject occurs in official documents, although from time to time miracle tales still circulate among pilgrims. However, based on my experiences of talking to pilgrims over the last twenty-eight years since I first visited Shikoku in 1984, it seems to me that most of these stories are old, even if they are repeatedly recycled by older pilgrims. I have not heard any new stories for some time.
8. This section on Knock is based on Shackley (2006) and Nairn (1997), along with various undated leaflets and pamphlets acquired at Knock and materials on display at the Knock Museum, during my visit there in June 2008.
9. As is often the case with places in mountainous areas, distances are better measured by time and days of walking rather than by actual kilometres and the like. I estimate two days from Pahalgam, although in 1971 (when younger and fitter than now) I did the round trip on foot in three long and rather hard walking days.
10. http://www.amarnathyatra.org/yatra.htm#top.
11. http://www.amarnathyatra.org/route.htm#top.
12. See, for example, http://www.go2kashmir.com/kashmir-tour-booking.html and http://www.india-pilgrimages.com/spiritual-amarnath-yatra-tours.html.
13. http://www.pilgrimage-india.com/north-india-pilgrimage/amarnath-yatra.html
14. See both the temple's website, https://www.maavaishnodevi.org, and that of the helicopter company, https://www.pawanhans.co.in/site/inner.aspx?status=3&menu_id=47; the former provides a link to the latter. Darshan is used in Hindu contexts to refer to viewing and venerating an icon or spiritual teacher and receiving its or his or her spiritual power.
15. The roads around Shikoku are quicker than Shōdoshima, and overall one can manage the Shikoku route in ten days as opposed to around four for Shōdoshima. In the past, the former might have taken five or six times as long as the latter; now the difference is marginal.

16. These comments are based on a series of interviews and discussions with priests, town hall and tourist office officials and local people in Shōdoshima in late March 2010.
17. I base this on visits to Varanasi in October 1971 and summer 1978; see also Eck (1982). In her account of the travels of Indian villagers who embark on a nationwide train journey around India in 1969, Heather Wood (1980) marvelously illustrates this tendency to seek out the familiar, as the villagers feel uneasy at the various differences in behaviour and food they encounter in different parts of India and how they long for the food of Bengal, their home region.
18. This person, Miyazaki Tateki, who is discussed further in Reader (2005: 259–265), died in autumn 2010 while working to clear a section of the pilgrimage path in the mountains.
19. I have noted elsewhere (Reader 2004) how the same place can be 'sacred' and 'profane' at the same time and how such (Western) distinctions fail to grasp the subtle complexities of religious concepts in Asian contexts such as Japan.
20. This is but one of many such volumes that list and provide information on Japan's myriad pilgrimage sites, especially on those with thirty-three (as with Saikoku) or eighty-eight (the Shikoku model) sites. Other examples I have collected over the years include Tahara and Misumi (1980: 217–307) and Tsukuda (1981).
21. Shitennōji in Osaka—one of Japan's oldest and most famed temples—lists fourteen pilgrimages it is associated with, in the FAQ section of its website, http://www.shitennoji.or.jp/faq.html. This is more than any other temple I know of but it is not an anomaly; many others (for example, Sumadera, a Shingon Buddhist temple in Kobe, Japan) are on half a dozen or more routes. This is not a phenomenon confined to Japan; as Toni Huber (1999: 93) notes, for example, Pure Crystal Mountain, a sacred Tibetan pilgrimage mountain, has at least half a dozen pilgrimages within its confines.

NOTES TO CHAPTER 3

1. In most shrine contexts, these proselytising pilgrim guides were known as *oshi;* at Ise, they were known as *onshi*. Both terms were written with the same Sino-Japanese characters. In this book, for sake of clarity, I use *oshi* because it is a more widely used term in general.
2. For a full account of the origins and development of the Shikoku pilgrimage, see Shinjō (1982: 479–491, 1020–1103), Kondō (1982), Reader (2005: 107–149), Yoritomi and Shiragi (2001) and Hoshino (2001: 175–186). On Shinnen, see Murakami (1987: 16–44), Shinno (1991: 118–144) and Reader (1999).
3. For example, in 966 the ascetic Shōkū Shōnin established his hermitage at Shoshasan, on a hilltop just outside the area now known as Himeji; this in time became a major temple, Enkyōji, on the Saikoku pilgrimage (MacWilliams 2004: 41–42).
4. This section is drawn primarily from my earlier research and discussed in Reader (1995, 1996), where I also cited interviews with the two priests and Mr. Ishii in Fukuoka on December 19 1990. I have also drawn on reports on this pilgrimage published in the newspaper *Chūgai Nippō* on June 17, 1988; June 22, 1988; and October 16, 1990, which include comments from Mr. Ishii and the priests concerned.
5. A report of this ritual opening can be found in *Chūgai Nippō*, September 9, 1988.
6. I spent the weekend of November 25–26, 1988, on the island and conducted lengthy interviews with the priests concerned and gathered pamphlets they and

the town hall and tourist office had produced. They were generous with their time and indicated when I met them that they were happy for me to cite them and to use the material from the interviews in my research, which was initially reported in Reader (1996).
7. In some pilgrimages, one finds mention of both *oshi* and *sendatsu*, but in many cases (e.g., Shikoku), only one term is used to cover all figures who fulfil such functions.
8. See Reader (1993), which gives histories and outlines of the lifestyles and promotional activities of some Shikoku *sendatsu*.
9. This latter figure was given to me by officials of the Iyo Tetsu Company during a visit to the company's offices in Matsuyama in March 2008.
10. Konpira (also known as Kotohira) shrine is the most prominent Shinto shrine on Shikoku. It is just a few kilometres off the Shikoku pilgrimage route itself and is often also visited by Shikoku pilgrims who include it in their itineraries (Reader 2005: 238–240).
11. On this matter, see also McKevitt (1991) who suggests that Padre Pio, when alive, was seen as a threat to the church's authority because of his apparent stigmata and hence manifestation of signs associated with Jesus. He was, however, championed by John Paul II especially after his death and swiftly canonised, and has now become 'controlled' by the church. See, also, however, Luzzatto (2007), who shows that some of the early church disquiet revolved around reasonable doubts over the authenticity of the stigmata and because of close links between the priest and local right-wing political interests.
12. This point was made in *The Guardian* G2 section, September 30, 2002, pp. 12–13, in an article titled 'In the Name of the Padre'.
13. This was reported in *The Scotsman* April 23, 1990; as a result, I contacted Monsignor Grady and visited him in Edinburgh (in late April 1990), at which time he reiterated the plans cited in the newspaper article. This long-term aim appears as yet to be unrealised, however.
14. This was reported in *The Guardian*, July 2, 2004, p.19.
15. Some Japanese temples, such as Shitennōji in Osaka and Fujiidera, one of the Saikoku temples near to Osaka, also have festival days known as *sennichimairi* (literally 'thousand days of worship') in which visitors who come to the temple on that special day are assured that they acquire the merit of a thousand ordinary visits.

NOTES TO CHAPTER 4

1. http://www.indiatours.org.uk/kashmir-tour/amarnath-yatra.html.
2. http://gulfnews.com/business/opinion/haj-vital-to-saudi-economy-1.533412.
3. *The Guardian* July 2, 2004, p. 19, gives this figure as thirty-five million pounds sterling, which I have converted into an approximate U.S. dollar rate.
4. These comments emanated from a series of meetings I had in the latter part of March 2010 in Shōdoshima with several temple priests as well as representatives of the civil administration of Tonoshō, the island's main town, and people working in the pilgrimage support industry.
5. However, see Chapter 6, where I look at Eade and Sallnow's (1991: 26) suggestion that shrine authorities often abhor the activities of those who run businesses around pilgrimage sites and where I discuss this assertion in relation to the trade in pilgrimage souvenirs.
6. These sentiments were expressed in the *Chūgai Nippō* articles of June 17, 1988; June 22, 1988; and October 16, 1990, cited in Chapter 3, as well as being articulated in discussions with me in December 1990.

7. I base these comments on discussions in Osaka with Japan Rail officials on March 24, 2008.
8. My interviews with the tour guide and bus driver of one Iyo Tetsu bus tour I met up with at Ishiteji temple in October 1990, for instance, are illustrative. The guide spoke of his deep faith in Kōbō Daishi, insisted on the veracity of various miracle tales (see Reader 2005: 61), and told me that his devotion was a key element in his work. For the driver what he was was just a job, like taking any coach tour around from A to B, and he was mildly cynical about the devotion of those whom he was ferrying.
9. See Reader (2005: 220–22) for further discussion.
10. As I have discussed with regard to Shikoku, some who went there as pilgrims in the Tokugawa era were already ill and were making 'kill or cure' journeys; many died in the first stages of the pilgrimage (Reader 2005: 133).
11. In 1970 (the year before I did the pilgrimage), eighteen people died in blizzards on the Amarnath pilgrimage. In 2012 more than one hundred pilgrims—the highest number for many years—died from high-altitude problems, seemingly because more people were seeking to do the pilgrimage, leading to an increase in the numbers of those who were physically unfit and whose lungs failed to cope with the thin air at more than 3,800 metres. See http://www.ucanews.com/2012/07/27/indian-pilgrimage-sees-rising-death-toll/. With regard to the hajj and deaths in stampedes, see http://news.bbc.co.uk/1/hi/world/middle_east/4606002.stm, which reports that 345 pilgrims were crushed to death due to a stampede during one hajj ritual in January 2006.
12. Preston (1992: 36), for example, writing at a time when Amarnath was not as well supported with infrastructure as now, suggests that the deaths that have occurred at Amarnath because of its harsh climate, have increased its spiritual magnetism.
13. Health improvements, from vaccinations to the acts of civil authorities to prevent outbreaks of diseases such as cholera, are a significant element in the ability of places to welcome large crowds of pilgrims and they have certainly been a factor in the growth of pilgrim numbers in India (e.g., Lochtefeld 2010: 73–74).
14. https://www.maavaishnodevi.org/new1/index.html and https://www.maavaishnodevi.org/planyatra-registration.aspx.
15. https://www.pawanhans.co.in/site/inner.aspx?status = 3&menu_id = 47.
16. This was the main store of the Asahiya bookstore chain in Japan, located at Umeda in Osaka. This has generally been a major store for books on travel and on religion and folk practices.
17. I base these comments on a visit to the head office of Toki Shobō in Osaka, on March 24, 2008.
18. See Reader (2005: 144) where I discuss how radio broadcasts from the late 1920s began to talk in this way about the pilgrimage.
19. Prominent in such contexts was Watsuji Tetsurō's famous 1928 study of landscape (*Fudō*) later translated into English (Watsuji 1961), which was a seminal volume in the the long Japanese tradition of exalting in quasi-mystical terms its scenery and landscapes as possessing spiritually potent characteristics.
20. He used the term *mushinron*, which could be interpreted as 'of no faith' but which translates also as 'atheist'.
21. Although I am generalising here about Shikoku guidebooks, the large majority of those I have examined follow very similar patterns as described here. See Reader (2005: 180–182) and Mori (2005: 273–274) for further discussion and description of relevant guidebooks.

22. One can, for example, get an app from the iTunes store that is downloadable to an iPhone and that guides one around the pilgrimage; see http://itunes.apple.com/jp/app/id434538359?mt=8.
23. I have not discussed here other such publicity materials (for example, posters and pamphlets) because I have focused on them elsewhere (Reader 1987b) but these too provide similar imagery, especially in terms of the depictions of the pilgrimage as a practice associated with Japanese culture and tradition.
24. See also Reader (2007a) for further discussion. I have also more recently explored these issues in discussions with people working for NHK who were involved in the production of some of the materials (books and documentaries) cited in this chapter and in Reader (2007a) in Tokyo in April 2008.

NOTES TO CHAPTER 5

1. Picaud, writing in Latin, uses the word *jure* here, which Viellard renders in French as *droit*, and which I would render (in both cases) as 'right'.
2. This website is at www.kushima.com/henro/.
3. See also Akimoto's website at www.mandala.ne.jp/88.
4. http://www.shinzakijinsei.com.
5. Yokkun's website is http://www2.kct.ne.jp/~fujita83/, and the items for sale are found at http://www2.kct.ne.jp/~fujita83/sozai/kuma2007.pdf. See also http://www.niji.or.jp/home/takesan/yokun.htm, which also features details of Yokkun's activities.
6. One might suggest that there has been a similar process relating to Santiago de Compostela where, like Shikoku, one can find numerous books and online accounts and blogs by people who have walked the Santiago de Compostela pilgrimage in recent times.
7. I am here generalising from numerous interviews with priests, tour company officials, pilgrimage guides on several routes and with pilgrims in Japan in general over the last quarter of a century or more. The interest groups such as the priests and the bus company involved in the development of the new Kyushu pilgrimage discussed in Chapter 3 also expressed such views to me.
8. On this point it is perhaps striking that the message expressed by the Marian apparitions at Lourdes offered comfort whereas those at another Marian apparitional shrine that arose in a similar period, at La Sallette, focused on the need to suffer (Kaufman 2004: 86) and that it was Lourdes whose message was most readily embraced by pilgrims and by church authorities.
9. Frey's (1998) Santiago pilgrimage study, for example, is focused almost entirely on foot pilgrims, whereas my study of Shikoku (2005) apportions one chapter specifically to walkers and one chapter to those who travel by bus—even though the latter massively outnumber the former.
10. See, for example, Bar and Cohen-Hattab (2003), whose study indicates that most of those engaging in pilgrimage travels in the modern-day Middle East prefer to do so on package tours.
11. In Japan, the concept of *maikā* ('my car') has been closely connected since the 1980s with what many perceive to be a shift from group-oriented societal perceptions to a more individualised stance. The move towards car-oriented pilgrimage has been commented on to me by officials from bus companies in Shikoku that report that this is eating into their market share, from priests at the temples and from lodge owners I have interviewed in recent years, and from personal observations at Shikoku temples, where the balance between coaches and cars has shifted perceptibly from the former to the latter in the twenty-six years between my first visit to Shikoku in 1984

and my most recent fieldtrip there in March–April 2010. See also Hoshino and Asakawa (2011: 25) for further discussion.
12. *The Guardian,* July 31, 1999, p. 1.
13. I base these comments on observations at the temples between 1984 and 2010 and on discussions with pilgrims, bus company officials and priests at various Shikoku temples in this period. See also Mori (2005: 184–185) for a brief history of this issue.
14. I base these comments on interviews with people involved in the organisation and involved with the running of the temple at Manganji, Chōshi, Chiba Prefecture, over a number of years between 1991 and 2007 and at an office the society had in Tokyo, which I visited in 1990.
15. I interviewed Mr. Shimoyasuba at his house in Kawachinagano, Japan, on January 19, 1991; on his activities, see Reader (1996).
16. I base this on interviews with interviews with officials working for the Iyo Tetsu, Kotosan and Setouchi bus companies, all based in Shikoku, at various times in October 1990, February 1991, April 1997, April 2000 and April 2008.
17. Satō (2004: 181–184) also affirms such patterns, not just in terms of the high level of day-trip pilgrimages but in the general focus in Saikoku on seasonality, entertainment and viewing the temples' art treasures as the key theme of the contemporary pilgrimage.
18. See http://travel.iyotetsu.co.jp/tour/88/2012/heinichi/index.html, which lists such services available in 2012. Discussions with company officials in Matsuyama during a visit there in March 2008 also confirm this general tendency; see also Mori (2005: 165).
19. Several of the Chichibu sites do not have priests in residence but are looked after by local residents. I have visited the sites on many occasions over the years—the first visit being in September 1981—and between April 2008 and September 2011, I visited Chichibu four times and talked to people at various sites there.

NOTES TO CHAPTER 6

1. He was speaking about things on sale at Lourdes, as quoted in *The Guardian,* July 31, 1999, p. 1, 'Package Tour Pilgrims Flock to Holy Sites'.
2. Not all pilgrims are just temporarily 'on the road'; some in Shikoku become permanent pilgrims and make the pilgrimage route into their home (Reader 2005: 255–266). Works (1976) also has looked at how Muslims from the Hausa ethnic group of West Africa can become 'permanent pilgrims' on the road to Mecca.
3. These points have emerged in numerous interviews with Japanese pilgrims in Saikoku, Shikoku and elsewhere between April 1985 and 2010. See also Leavell and Reader (1988).
4. Here I disagree with Watsky (2004: xi), whose study of Chikubushima in historical and artistic contexts makes a stark differentiation between people he terms 'pilgrims' and those he calls 'non-pilgrims' who come as tourists just to view the scenery and have an afternoon out while buying souvenirs. On the occasions I have visited the island (in 1988 and in 1991), just about every person on the boats I was on went up the steps to the temple and was carrying a scroll or pilgrim's book to be stamped.
5. See the shrine website, https://www.maavaishnodevi.org/new1/index.html, and its section on souvenir shops https://www.maavaishnodevi.org/sovenirshops.aspx.
6. I have calculated these dollar equivalents using exchange rates as of January 25, 2013.

Notes   205

7. See also the commemorative scrolls related to the pilgrimage to Mecca such as the one depicted in the British Library's online gallery at http://www.bl.uk/onlinegallery/onlineex/expfaith/islmanu/pilgcert/033add0000275 66u000000a0.html.
8. See, for example, http://www.yamato.vc/saigoku33-cyumon/saigoku33-chumon.html and http://www.shokokai.or.jp/21/2140212062/index.htm.
9. The survey was done by myself and James Leavell; some of our results were included in Leavell and Reader (1988), but others, including the 72 per cent figure cited here, are unpublished.
10. Typically scrolls have space for three additional stamps beyond the standard thirty-three that can be included on them, and pilgrims can choose of their own volition where they want to go for these additional stamps. However, the Saikoku temples themselves encourage pilgrims to visit temples such as Kazanin that have specific connections to Saikoku history.
11. See http://www.ippoippodo.com/henro/daiko_junrei.html for this company and http://www.page.sannet.ne.jp/nb_saka/index.html for another company offering this service.
12. I base these comments on a visit to Inoue Shinichi Shoten, Tatsueji, Tokushima Prefecture in April 2000 and on conversations with numerous other stallholders and proprietors of shops found at the temples. Inoue Shinichi Shoten itself now has a website through which it sells pilgrimage goods online at www.ohenro.com, where the firm is, as of January 2013, advertising new souvenir items produced in connection with the 1,200th anniversary founding (in legend) of the pilgrimage, which will occur in 2014.
13. http://www.jr-odekake.net/navi/saigoku/?kou.
14. https://www.cathedral-enterprises.co.uk/kolist/1/Toys+and+Gifts/Bears.
15. https://www.maavaishnodevi.org/sovenir-shops.aspx.
16. https://www.maavaishnodevi.org/holys_offerings.asp.
17. The information in this paragraph is drawn from leaflets, pamphlets and booklets from the shrine acquired in a visit on April 28, 2012, including the undated shrine booklets and pamphlets Rue du Bac (nd-a, nd-b, nd-c). The quotations cited in this paragraph come from Rue du Bac (nd-a). The shrine's website, http://www.chapellenotredamedelamedaillemiraculeuse.com, also contains information on the origins and development of the shrine—obviously from the shrine's own perspective.
18. Both the shop sign inside the shrine and the shrine pamphlets themselves refer to it as a 'gift shop'.
19. The prices were in euros, ranging from 1 euro and 15 centimes to 4 euros depending on the medal, and I have converted these prices to dollars using the exchange rates of January 25, 2013.
20. See http://www.jyuzujyunrei.com/juzu.html plus leaflets acquired at *Juzu Junrei* sites in Kyoto, January 2012.
21. For further discussion of this particular pilgrimage in the context of contemporary commodification and Japanese pilgrimage dynamics, see Reader (2013).

NOTES TO CHAPTER 7

1. This comment was made to me during a field trip to Shikoku in March 2008 to research the issues related to the Shikoku heritage campaign discussed in this chapter and when I interviewed numerous priests, government officials and people involved in assisting the campaign, including people working for public relations firms in the region.

2. Studies by Shultz (2009) and my interviews with walkers in recent years also indicate that Kōbō Daishi devotion, prominent in the views of older pilgrims I interviewed in the 1980s and 1990s, is largely absent among contemporary walkers.
3. I am grateful to John Shultz for bringing these magazines to my attention; see also Mori (2005: 177), who also mentions how a number of contemporary magazines for young women have focused on the pilgrimage.
4. http://henro-travel.watabi.com/?gclid=CP7J05Wo7KkCFcEd4QodiHejWw offered a two-night, three-day tour priced at 68,000 yen and was online throughout 2010 and much of 2011 (I first accessed it on July 6, 2011), but as of January 2013, it was no longer available.
5. See, for example, http://www.shikoku88.net/tour/gotouchi.html, which not only uses terms such as *gourmet* (*gurume*) but also has various tour plans plus a map of the island indicating different food specialities to be found on the pilgrimage.
6. See, for example, http://www.my-kagawa.jp/bus/53/, which offers a two-day, three-night tour of the pilgrimage temples 'for those with an interest in art'.
7. Nominations for UNESCO World Heritage status have to go through and be sanctioned by the government of the country concerned. For an excellent examination of the cultural politics of nominations along with discussions of how Japanese authorities designate cultural properties and the broader issue of heritage politics in Japan, see Russell (2011: 48–78).
8. This section on the Shikoku heritage campaign is based in part on numerous interviews and meetings with interested parties, including regional government officials, members of the business community, representatives of transport firms, public relations firms involved in the campaign and several temple priests, especially during a visit to Shikoku in March 2008 and a subsequent visit in April 2010. It is evident from my interviews and from comments by informants in Shikoku that an initial reluctance among some temples was overcome as various secular agencies and government officials put their weight behind the idea, and as a number of older priests who opposed the idea, stood down from their positions in the *Reijōkai* or passed away, to be replaced by new priests in the pilgrimage temples' hierarchy.
9. In November 2009, I was invited to deliver a public lecture at Matsuyama University in Shikoku at a conference titled *Sekaijunrei no naka no Shikoku henro* ('The Shikoku Pilgrimage in the Context of World Pilgrimage'), as part of this wider activity.
10. I base these comments on information from Ruben Lois Gonzalez of the University of Santiago and on a paper he gave at a pilgrimage workshop at University College London, London, on March 27, 2012. The papal visit by Pope Benedict XVI in November 2010 in which he followed in his predecessor's footsteps and sought to reemphasise the Catholic nature of the pilgrimage, appears to have been relatively unsuccessful, with small crowds turning out. I am grateful to Ruben Lois Gonzalez for sharing his thoughts on the matter with me and allowing me to use them in this chapter.
11. See its webpage at http://www.omotenashi88.net and http://www.wheritage.net/shikoku_reizyo88kasyo_to_henromichi.html, which references the Santiago pilgrimage and visits made by members of the group there.
12. This ministry in turn can endorse and forward the application to UNESCO, put it on hold or reject it, depending on how it assesses the applications it receives and on what other applications they receive in the same time frame. In this case, several other applications (including one seeking to have Mount Fuji designated as such) competed with Shikoku for nomination at the same time.

13. The webpage of the Ministry of Culture—http://www.bunka.go.jp/bunkashingikai/sekaibunkaisan/singi_kekka/besshi_8.html—indicates that the Shikoku pilgrimage application is one of those most strongly favoured by the ministry once it has been developed further. I have also heard, although I stress that these are unofficial comments from regional and pilgrimage officials who were prepared to talk 'off record', that the ministry felt that other applications from other historical and natural sites in Japan had a better chance of success at the time and that Japan's success in acquiring the UNESCO accolade for a number of sites just before this application meant that UNESCO wanted it to refrain from nominating more sites in the near future. Hence, there may be a cooling off period before a reapplication can be made.
14. I draw this information from pamphlets from Naruto Kyōiku Daigaku that I was given while in Shikoku in April 2008 and from its website at http://www.naruto-u.ac.jp/gp/henro.
15. http://www.guardian.co.uk/world/2010/nov/14/mecca-hajj-saudi-arabia (accessed Nov. 15, 2010; also available in *The Guardian*, November 15, 2010, p. 3).
16. http://www.raffles.com/makkah/ (accessed April 16, 2012).
17. Hasan's comments are taken from *The Guardian*, April 14, 2012, 'Pilgrimage of Muslim Visitors to the British Museum Leads to Surprise Hit Hajj Show'.
18. *The Guardian* October 16, 2009, p. 19, 'Divine Experience for Well-Heeled Pilgrims—A Spa, Beauty Parlour and 24-Hour Butler'.
19. On Lourdes replicas, see McDannell (1995: 154–161). The National Shrine of the North American Martyrs contains multiple commemorative buildings to different U.S. saints, as well as a replica of Our Lady of Fatima and other related sites; see http://www.martyrshrine.org/.
20. http://news.bbc.co.uk/1/hi/world/south_asia/4494747.stm.
21. I have, for example, been to a replica Bodh Gaya in Kurume, Kyushu, where one finds a copy of the Mahabodhi temple and its surrounds, plus murals of the Buddha's life, but without the hawkers, flies and dust that are found at the original.
22. Renzo Piano's new church and shrine to Padre Pio at San Giovanni del Rotondo described in Chapter Three could also be included in this rubric, given that it has become the focus of architectural tours of visitors who come to the shrine primarily to admire the architectural sights rather than to engage in devotions there (Mesaritou 2012).
23. *The Guardian*, Travel Section, October 17, 2009, also available online at http://www.guardian.co.uk/travel/2009/oct/17/free-travel-holiday-budget?page=all.
24. http://www.guardian.co.uk/travel/2010/jan/10/30-new-2010-trips?page=6.
25. http://www.makemytrip.com/holidays-india/pilgrimage-packages.html.
26. See http://www.tourisminindia.com/blogs/post/2010/09/22/New-Bharat-Darshan-Pilgrimage-Train-by-IRCTC.aspx.
27. http://www.turgalicia.es/portada-do-bono-iacobus?langId=en_US.
28. http://www.followthecamino.com/.
29. See, for example, http://www.eurasia.co.jp/nittei/s_europe/special/camino/ and http://www.noe-j.co.jp/snt/santiago/index.html.
30. http://www.visitnorway.com/uk/About-Norway/History/The-Pilgrims-Route-to-Trondheim/.
31. http://www.pilegrim.info/en/.
32. http://www.culture-routes.lu/php/fo_index.php?lngen&dest=ba_pa_det&unv=ed.
33. http://www.kokorohenro.org. See also Reader (2011a: 96–97) for further discussions of Internet representations of the Shikoku pilgrimage.

References

1. BOOKS, ARTICLES AND NAMED NEWSPAPER/ONLINE ARTICLES

Adair, Tom. 1998. A Visit to Knock. *Scotsman Weekend*, 12 September, pp. 18–19.
Adler, Judith. 2002. The Holy Man as Traveler and Travel Attraction: Early Christian Asceticism and the Moral problematic of Modernity. In William H. Swatos, Jr., and Luigi Tomasi (eds.) *From Medieval Pilgrimage to Secular Tourism: The Social and Cultural Economics of Piety*. Westport, CT: Praeger Press, pp. 25–50.
Ambros, Barbara. 2008. *Emplacing a Pilgrimage: The Ōyama Cult and Regional Religion in Early Modern Japan*. Cambridge, MA: Harvard University Asia Center.
Aoki Tamotsu. 1985. *Ontake junrei: Gendai kami to hito*. Tokyo: Chikuma Shobō.
Artress, Lauren. 1995. *Walking a Sacred Path: Rediscovering the Labyrinth as a Spiritual Tool*. New York: Riverhead Books.
Asakawa Yasuhiro. 2008. *Junrei no bunkajinruigakuteki kenkyū: Shikoku henro no settaibunka*. Tokyo: Kokon Shoin.
Badone, Ellen. 2004. Crossing Boundaries: Exploring the Borderlands of Ethnography, Tourism and Pilgrimage. In Ellen Badone and Sharon R. Roseman (eds.) *Intersecting Journeys: The Anthropology of Pilgrimage and Tourism*. Urbana and Chicago: University of Illinois Press, pp. 180–189.
Badone, Ellen and Sharon R. Roseman (eds.). 2004. *Intersecting Journeys: The Anthropology of Pilgrimage and Tourism*. Urbana and Chicago: University of Illinois Press,
Baffelli, Erica and Ian Reader. 2012. Impact and Ramifications: The Aftermath of the Aum Affair in the Japanese Religious Context. *Japanese Journal of Religious Studies*, Vol. 39, No. 1, pp. 1–28.
Baillie, Kate, and Tim Salmon. 2001. *The Rough Guide to France*. London: Rough Guides.
Bar, D. and K. Cohen-Hattab. 2003. A New Kind of Pilgrimage: The Modern Tourist Pilgrim of Nineteenth-Century and Early Twentieth-Century Palestine. *Middle Eastern Studies*, Vol. 32, No. 2, pp. 131–148.
Barbaro, Paolo. 2013. *La mise en discours des pèlerinages au Japon depuis l'époque d'Edo: Pour une théorie de l'interversion réciproque entre expérience et récit*. Unpublished PhD dissertation, École Pratique des Hautes Études, Paris.
Bard, Rachel. 1989. Aimery Picaud and the Basques: Selections from the Pilgrim's Guide to Santiago de Compostela. In William A. Douglas (ed.), *Essays in Basque Social Anthropology and History*. Reno: University of Nevada Press, pp. 189–214.
Bax, Mart. 1995. *Medjugorje: Religion, Politics, and Violence in Rural Bosnia*. Amsterdam: VU University Press.
Beaman, Lori. 2006. Labyrinth as Heterotopia: The Pilgrim's Creation of Space. In William Swatos, Jr. (ed.) *On the Road to Being There: Continuing the Pilgrimage-Tourism Dialogue*. Leiden: Brill Academic Press, pp. 83–103.

Bhardwaj, Surinder. 1973. *Hindu Places of Pilgrimage in India: A Study in Cultural Geography*. Berkeley: University of California Press.

Bianchi, Robert R. 2004. *Guests of God: Pilgrimage and Politics in the Islamic World*. New York: Oxford University Press.

Blacker, Carmen. 1984. The Religious Traveller in the Edo Period. *Modern Asian Studies*, Vol. 18, No. 4, pp. 593–608.

Boss, Sarah Jane. 2007. Jerusalem, Dwelling of the Lord: Marian Pilgrimage and Its Destination. In Philip North and John North (eds.), *Sacred Space: House of God, Gate of Heaven*. London: Continuum, pp. 135–151.

Bowman, Glenn. 1992. Pilgrim Narrative of Jerusalem and the Holy Land: A Study in Ideological Distortion. In Alan Morinis (ed.) *Sacred Journeys: The Anthropology of Pilgrimage*. Westport, CT: Greenwood Press, pp. 149–168.

Bowman, Marion. 1993. Drawn to Glastonbury. In Ian Reader and Tony Walter (eds.), *Pilgrimage in Popular Culture*. Basingstoke: Macmillan, pp. 29–62.

Bowring, Richard. 2005. *The Religious Traditions of Japan 500–1600*. Cambridge: Cambridge University Press.

Breen, John and Marcus Teeuwen. 2010. *A New History of Shinto*. Chichester: Wiley Blackwell.

Brook, Timothy. 1993. *Praying for Power: Buddhism and the Formation of Gentry Society in Late-Ming China*. Cambridge, MA: Harvard University Press.

Bruner, Edward M. 2005. *Culture on Tour: Ethnographies of Travel*. Chicago: University of Chicago Press.

Campo, Juan. 1998. American Pilgrimage Landscapes. *Annals of the American Academy of Political and Social Sciences*, No. 558, pp. 40–56.

Chareyrou, Nicole. 2000. *Pilgrims to Jerusalem in the Middle Age*. New York: Columbia University Press.

Childs, Wendy R. 1999. The Perils, or Otherwise, of Maritime Pilgrimage to Santiago de Compostela in the Fifteenth Century. In J. Stopford (ed.) *Pilgrimage Explored*. York: York Medieval Press, pp. 123–143.

Coats, Curtis. 2009. Sedona, Arizona: New Age Pilgrim-Tourist Destination. *Cross-Currents*, Vol. 59, No. 3, pp. 383–389.

Cohen, Erik. 1992. Pilgrimage and Tourism: Convergence and Divergence. In Alan Morinis (ed.), *Sacred Journeys: The Anthropology of Pilgrimage*. Westport, CT: Greenwood Press, pp. 47–61.

Coleman, Simon. 2000. Meanings of Movement, Place and Home at Walsingham. *Culture and Religion*, Vol. 1, No. 2, pp. 153–170.

———. 2004. From England's Nazareth to Sweden's Jerusalem: Movement, (Virtual) Landscapes and Pilgrimage. In Simon Coleman and John Eade (eds.), *Reframing Pilgrimage?: Cultures in Motion*. London: Routledge, pp. 45–68.

Coleman, Simon and John Eade. 2004. Introduction: Reframing Pilgrimage. In Simon Coleman and John Eade (eds.), *Reframing Pilgrimage?: Cultures in Motion*. London: Routledge, pp. 1–26.

Coleman, Simon and John Elsner. 1995. *Pilgrimage Past and Present in the World Religions*. Cambridge, MA: Harvard University Press.

Creighton, Millie. 1997. Consuming Rural Japan: The Marketing of Tradition and Nostalgia in the Japanese Travel Industry. *Ethnology*, Vol. 36, No. 3, pp. 239–254.

Davidson, Linda K. 2010. Reformulation of the Pilgrimages to Santiago de Compostela. Paper delivered at the Reformulation of the Historical Pilgrimages and the New Pilgrimages conference, Instituto de Estudios Gallegos, Santiago de Compostela, December 14–16, 2010.

Davies, Horton and Marie-Hélène Davies. 1982. *Holy Days and Holidays: The Medieval Pilgrimage to Compostela*. London and Toronto: Associated University Presses.

Dubisch, Jill. 1995. *In a Different Place: Pilgrimage, Gender, and Practice at a Greek Island Shrine*. Princeton, NJ: Princeton University Press.

Duffy, Eamonn. 1992. *The Stripping of the Altars: Traditional Religion in England 1400–1500*. New Haven, CT: Yale University Press.
Dupront, Alphonse. 1987. *Du Sacré: Croisades et Pèlerinages, Images et Langages*. Paris: Gallimard.
Eade, John and Michael J. Sallnow. 1991. Introduction. In John Eade and Michael Sallnow (eds.) *Contesting the Sacred: The Anthropology of Christian Pilgrimage*. London: Routledge, pp. 1–29.
Eck, Diane. 1983. *Banaras: City of Light*. London: Routledge and Kegan Paul.
———. 2012. *India: A Sacred Geography*. New York: Harmony Books.
Ehime-ken et al. 2007. *Shikoku Hachijūhakkasho reijō to henro michi*. Application for recognition as a UNESCO World heritage site, December 20, 2007, 44 pp., Matusyama, Japan. (initially posted online at http://www1.pref.tokushima.jp/002/01/0801henro/teiansho/1-mokuji.pdf, December 2007)
Eliade, Mircea. 1957. *The Sacred and the Profane: The Nature of Religion*. Orlando, FL: Harcourt.
———. 1971. *The Myth of the Eternal Return: Or, Cosmos and History*. Princeton, NJ: Princeton University Press.
Faure, Bernard. 1991. *The Rhetoric of Immediacy: A Cultural Critique of Chan/Zen Buddhism*. Princeton, NJ: Princeton University Press.
Feldhaus, Anne. 2004. *Connected Places: Region, Pilgrimage, and Geographical Imagination in India*. New York and Basingstoke: Palgrave Macmillan.
Fields, Rick. 1992 (1981). *How the Swans Came to the Lake*. Boston: Shambala.
Finucane, Ronald C. 1977. *Miracles and Pilgrims: Popular Beliefs in Medieval England*. London: J.M. Dent.
Foard, James. 1982. The Boundaries of Compassion: Buddhism and National Tradition in Japanese Pilgrimage. *Journal of Asian Studies*, Vol. 16, No. 2, pp. 231–251.
Formanek, Susanne. 1998. Pilgrimage in the Edo Period: Forerunner of Modern Domestic Tourism? The Example of the Pilgrimage to Tateyama. In Sepp Linhart and Sabine Fruhstuck (eds.), *The Culture of Japan as Seen through Its Leisure*. Albany: SUNY Press, pp. 165–193.
Foster, Georgana and Robert Stoddard. 2010. Vaishno Devi, the Most Famous Goddess Shrine in the Siwālik. In Rana P. B. Singh (ed.), *Sacred Geography of Goddesses in South Asia*. Newcastle upon Tyne: Cambridge Scholars Press, pp. 109–124.
Frank, Georgia. 2000. *The Memory of the Eyes: Pilgrims to Living Saints in Christian Late Antiquity*. Berkeley: University of California Press.
Frey, Nancy Louise. 1998. *Pilgrim Stories: On and Off the Road to Santiago*. Berkeley: University of California Press.
Fuller, Christopher. 1992. *The Camphor Flame: Popular Hinduism and Society in India*. Princeton, NJ: Princeton University Press.
Geary, Patrick J. 1990. *Furta Sacra: Thefts of Relics in the Central Middle Ages*. Princeton, NJ: Princeton University Press.
———. 1994. *Living with the Dead in the Middle Ages*. Ithaca, NY: Cornell University Press.
Germano, David F. and Kevin Trainor (eds.). 2004. *Embodying the Dharma: Buddhist Relic Veneration in Asia*. Albany, NY: SUNY Press.
Gladstone, David L. 2005. *From Pilgrimage to Package Tour: Travel and Tourism in the Third World*. London: Routledge.
Gold, Anne Grodzins. 1989. *Fruitful Journeys: The Ways of Rajashtani Pilgrims*. Berkeley and Los Angeles: University of California Press.
Gold, Tanya. 2011. Wholly Scripture. *The Guardian Travel Supplement*, December 24, 2011, pp. 2–3.
Gonzalez, Ruben Lois. 2012. Actors and Power Centres in the Camino de Santiago during the 20th and 21st centuries. Paper given at the Pilgrimage 2012 Workshop, University College London, March 27, 2012.

Graburn, Nelson. 1983. *To Pray, Pay and Play?: The Cultural Structure of Japanese Domestic Tourism*. Aix-en-Provence: Centre des hautes études touristiques.
Hahn, Cynthia. 1990. Loca Sancta Souvenirs: Sealing the Pilgrim's Experience. In Robert Ousterhoot (ed.), *The Blessings of Pilgrimage*. Urbana and Chicago: University of Illinois Press, pp. 85–96.
Hamaya, Mariko. 2009. 'Kojikihenro' no seikatsushi. *Tokushima-chiiki-bunka-kenkyū*, Vol. 7, pp. 103–117.
Hammoudi, Abdellah. 2006. *A Season in Mecca: Narrative of a Pilgrimage*. Cambridge: Polity.
Harada Nobuo. 1999. *Kanreki no niwaka ohenro: 35nichi.1200 kiro wo aruite watashi ga mitsuketa mono*. Takarazuka, Japan: Shinfū Shobō.
Hardacre, Helen. 1997. *Marketing the Menacing Fetus in Japan*. Berkeley and Los Angeles: University of California Press.
Harris, Alana. 2013. Lourdes and Holistic Spirituality: Contemporary Catholicism, the Therapeutic and Religious Thermalism. *Culture and Religion*, Vol. 14, No. 1, pp. 23–43.
Harris, Ruth. 1999. *Lourdes: Body and Spirit in the Secular Age*. Harmondsworth, UK: Penguin.
Harrison, Elizabeth G. 1996. Mizuko kuyō: The Re-Production of the Dead in Contemporary Japan. In P.F. Kornicki and I.J. McMullen (eds.), *Religion in Japan: Arrows to Heaven and Earth*. Cambridge: Cambridge University Press, pp. 250–266.
Hayami Tasuku. 1980. Kannon shinkō to minzoku: Kannon junrei no hattatsu o chūshin ni. In Gorai Shigeru and Sakurai Tokutarō (eds.), *Nihon no minzokushūkyō 2: Bukkyōminzokugaku*. Tokyo: Kōbundō, pp. 261–276.
———. 1983. *Kannon shinkō*. Tokyo: Hanawa Shobō.
Hirahata Ryōyū. 1982. *Shikoku hachijūhakkasho*. 2 vols. Chōshi, Japan: Manganji Kyōkabu.
———. 1990. *Shōdoshima henro*. Chōshi, Japan: Manganji Kyōkabu.
Hirota Mio. 1999. *Shikoku ohenro nazo toki sanpo*. Tokyo: Hōzaidō Shuppan.
Hoinacki, Lee. 1997. *El Camino: Walking to Santiago de Compostela*. University Park, PA: Pennsylvania State University Press.
Hoshino Eiki. 1987. Junrei: sono imi to kōzō. In Seishin Joshidaigaku Kirisutokyōkenkyūjo (ed.), *Junrei to bunmei*. Tokyo: Shunjūsha, pp. 3–22.
———. 2001. *Shikoku henro no shūkyōgakuteki kenkyū*. Kyoto: Hōzōkan.
Hoshino Eiki and Yasuhiro Asakawa Yasuhiro. 2011. *Shikoku henro: samazamana inori no sekai*. Tokyo: Furukawa Kōbunkan.
Howard, Donald R. 1980. *Writers and Pilgrims: Medieval Pilgrimage Narratives and Their Posterity*. Berkeley and Los Angeles: University of California Press.
Hsun, Chang. 2012. Between Religion and State: The Dajia Pilgrimage in Taiwan. *Social Compass*, Vol. 59, No. 3, pp. 298–310.
Huber, Toni. 1999. *The Cult of Pure Crystal Mountain*. New York: Oxford University Press.
———. 2008. *The Holy Land Reborn: Pilgrimage and the Reinvention of Buddhist India*. Chicago: University of Chicago Press.
Hur, Nam-Lin. 2009. Invitation to the Secret Buddha of Zenkōji: *Kaichō* and Religious Culture in Early Modern Japan. *Japanese Journal of Religious Studies*, Vol. 36, No. 1, pp. 45–64.
Iijima Makoto. 1930. *Fudasho to meisho: Shikoku henro*. Tokyo: Hōbunkan.
Ishimori Shuzo. 1995. Tourism and Religion: From the Perspective of Comparative Civilization. *Senri Ethnological Studies*, No. 38, pp. 11–24.
Itō Tadashi. 1981. *Koshima hachijūhakkasho reijō*. Tamano, Japan: Kannon'in.
Ivakhiv, Adrian J. 2001. *Claiming Sacred Ground: Pilgrims and Politics at Glastonbury and Sedona*. Bloomington: Indiana University Press.

Ivy, Marilyn. 1995. *Discourses of the Vanishing: Modernity, Phantasm, Japan.* Chicago: University of Chicago Press.
Kaelber, Lutz. 2002. The Sociology of Medieval Pilgrimage: Contested Views and Shifting Boundaries. In William H. Swatos, Jr., and Luigi Tomasi (eds.), *From Medieval Pilgrimage to Secular Tourism: The Social and Cultural Economics of Piety.* Westport, CT: Praeger Press, pp. 51–74.
Kagita Chūsaburō. 1962. *Henro nikki: mokujiki angya sanbyakuri.* Tokyo: Kyōdō Shuppan.
Kaneko Satoru. 1991. *Shinshū shinkō to minzoku shinkō.* Kyoto: Nagata Bunshôdô.
Kanzaki Noritake. 1990. *Kankō minzokugaku e no tabi.* Tokyo: Kawade Shobō.
Kaufman, Suzanne K. 2004. *Consuming Visions: Mass Culture and the Lourdes Shrine.* Ithaca, NY: Cornell University Press.
Kerr, Ian J. 2001a. Introduction. In Ian J. Kerr (ed.), *Railways in Modern India.* Delhi: Oxford University Press, pp. 1–61.
———. 2001b. Reworking a Popular Religious Practice: The Effects of Railways on Pilgrimage in 19th and 20th Century South Asia. In Ian J. Kerr (ed.), *Railways in Modern India.* Delhi: Oxford University Press, pp. 304–327.
Ketley-Laporte, John and Odette Ketley-Laporte. 1997. *Chartres: le labyrinthe déchiffré.* Paris: Editions Jean-Michel Garnier.
Kobayashi Kyū. 2003. *Route 88: Shikoku henro seishun junrei.* Tokyo: Kawade.
Kojima Hiromi. 1989. Junrei: 'meguri' to 'morai' to. In Setouchi Jakuchō, Fujii Masao and Miyata Noboru (eds.), *Bukkyō gyōji saijiki: gogatsu yamairi.* Tokyo: Daiichi Hōkan, pp. 168–179.
Kondō Yoshihiro. 1982. *Shikoku henro kenkyū.* Tokyo: Miyai Shoten.
Kornicki, P. F. 1994. Public Display and Changing Values. Early Meiji Exhibitions and Their Precursors. *Monumenta Nipponica*, Vol. 49, No. 2, pp. 167–196.
Kouamé, Nathalie. 1998. *Le Pèlerinage de Shikoku Pendat l'Epoque Edo: Pèlerins at Sociétés Locales.* Unpublished PhD dissertation, Institut National Des Langues et Civilisations Orientales, Paris.
———. 2001. *Pèlerinage et Société dans le Japon des Tokugawa: Le Pèlerinage de Shikoku entre 1598 et 1868.* Paris: École Française d'Extrème-Orient.
LaFleur, William R. 1992. *Liquid Life: Abortion and Buddhism in Japan.* Princeton, NJ: Princeton University Press.
Leavell, James B. and Ian Reader. 1988. The Saikoku Pilgrimage: A Research Report. *Studies in Central and East Asian Religions*, Vol. 1, No. 1, pp. 116–118.
Lochtefeld, James G. 2010. *God's Gateway: Identity and Meaning in a Hindu Pilgrimage Place.* Oxford and New York: Oxford University Press.
Luzzato, Sergio. 2007. *Padre Pio: Miracles and Politics in a Secular Age.* London: Picador.
MacCormack, Sabine. 1990. Loca Sancta: The Organization of Sacred Topography in Late Antiquity. In Robert Ousterhoot (ed.), *The Blessings of Pilgrimage.* Urbana and Chicago: University of Illinois Press, pp. 7–40.
MacWilliams, Mark. 2004. Living Icons: Reizō Myths of the Saikoku Kannon Pilgrimage. *Monumenta Nipponica*, Vol. 59, No. 1, pp. 35–82.
Maeda Takashi. 1971. *Junrei no shakaigaku.* Kyoto: Mineruba Shobō.
Maniura, Robert. 2004. *Pilgrimage to Images in the Fifteenth Century: The Origins of the Cult of Our Lady of Czestochowa.* Woodbridge, Suffolk, UK: The Boydell Press.
Margry, Peter Jan. 2008. Secular Pilgrimage: A Contradiction in Terms? In Margry, Peter Jan (ed.), *Shrines and Pilgrimage in the Modern World: New Itineraries into the Sacred.* Amsterdam: Amsterdam University Press, pp. 11–46.
Mason, David A. 2010. Rebranding Korean Tourism: Korea Has Religious, Spiritual Pilgrimage Destinations. *Korea Times* (Seoul), available online at http://www.koreatimes.co.kr/www/news/include/print.asp?newsIdx=32549.
Matsuzaki, Kenzō. 1985. *Mawari no fōkuroa: yugyōbutsu no kenkyū.* Tokyo: Meicho Shuppan.

McCallum, Donald F. 1994. *Zenkoji and Its Icon*. Princeton, NJ: Princeton University Press.
McDanell, Colleen. 1995. *Material Christianity: Religion and Popular Culture in America*. New Haven, CT: Yale University Press.
McKevitt, Christopher. 1991. San Giovanni Rotondo and the Shrine of Padre Pio. In John Eade and Michael Sallnow (eds.), *Contesting the Sacred: The Anthropology of Christian Pilgrimage*. London: Routledge, pp. 77–97.
Meeks, Lori. 2010. *Hokkeji and the Reemergence of Female Monastic Orders in Premodern Japan*. Honolulu: University of Hawaii Press.
Mesaritou, Evgenia. 2012. Say a Little Hallo to Padre Pio: Production and Consumption of Space in the Construction of the Sacred at the Shrine of Santa Maria delle Grazie. In Samuli Schielke and Liza Debevec (eds.), *Ordinary Lives and Grand Schemes: An Anthropology of Everyday Religion*. New York and Oxford: Berghahn Books, pp. 98–112.
Mills, C. Wright. 1940. Situated Actions and Vocabularies of Motive. *American Sociological Review*, Vol. 5, No. 6, pp. 904–913.
Miyake Hitoshi. 2002. *Shūkyō minzokugaku nyūmon*. Tokyo: Maruzen.
Moerman, D. Max. 2005. *Localizing Paradise: Kumano Pilgrimage and the Religious Landscape of Premodern Japan*. Cambridge, MA: Harvard University Asia Center.
Moore, Alexander. 1980. Walt Disney World: Bounded Ritual Space and the Playful Pilgrimage Center. *Anthropological Quarterly*, Vol. 53, pp. 207–217.
Moore, R. Laurence. 1994. *Selling God: American Religion in the Marketplace of Culture*. Oxford and New York: Oxford University Press.
Mori Masato. 2005. *Shikoku henro no kindaika: modan henro kara iyashi no tabi made*. Osaka: Sōgensha.
Morikawa Toshiyasu. 2005. Taiwan sanjūsan Kannon reijō no kankōgakuteki kōsatsu. *Bulletin of Ohkagakuen University Faculty of Humanities*, Vol. 7, pp. 97–116.
Morinis, Alan. 1984. *Pilgrimage in the Hindu Tradition: A Case Study of West Bengal*. New Delhi: Oxford University Press.
———. 1992. Introduction: The Territory of the Anthropology of Pilgrimage. In Alan Morinis (ed.), *Sacred Journeys: The Anthropology of Pilgrimage*. Westport, CT: Greenwood Press, pp. 1–28.
Mullins, Edwin B. 1974. *The Pilgrimage to Santiago*. London: Secker and Warburg.
Murakami Mamoru. 1987. *Shikoku henro reijōki no sekai*. Tokyo: Kyōikusha.
Murray, M. and B. Graham. 1997. Exploring the Dialectics of Route-Based Tourism: The Camino. *Tourism Management*, Vol. 18, No. 8, pp. 513–524.
Nairn, Tom. 1997. A Short History of Knock. In Donal Flanagan (ed.), *The Meaning of Knock*. Dublin: The Columba Press, pp. 7–25.
Nakamura Masatoshi. 1980. Awajishima no junrei: Kōbō Daishi shinkō to jūsanbutsu reijō. *Matsuri*, Vol. 36, pp. 44–64.
Nanda, Meera. 2011. *The God Market: How Globalization Is Making India More Hindu*. New York: Monthly Review Press.
Naquin, Susan. 1992. The Peking Pilgrimage to Miao-feng Shan: Religious Organizations and Sacred Site. In Susan Naquin and Chün-Fang Yü (eds.), *Pilgrims and Sacred Sites in China*. Berkeley, Los Angeles and Oxford: University of California Press, pp. 333–377.
Naquin, Susan, and Chün-Fang Yü. 1992. Introduction. In Susan Naquin and Chün-Fang Yü (eds.) *Pilgrims and Sacred Sites in China*. Berkeley, Los Angeles and Oxford: University of California Press, pp. 1–38.
Nelson, John K. 2012. Japanese Secularities and the Decline of Temple Buddhism. *Journal of Religion in Japan*, Vol. 1, No. 1, pp. 37–60.
NHK (Nihon Hōsō Kyōkai Henshūshitsu) (ed.). 2006. *NHK Shumi yūyū: Shikoku 88 kasho hajimete no Henro*. Tokyo: NHK.
Nishigai Kenji. 1984 *Ishizuchisan to Shugendō*. Tokyo: Meicho Shuppan.

Nishigaki Seiji. 1983. *O-Ise mairi*. Tokyo: Iwanami Shinsho.
Nolan, Mary Lee and Sidney Nolan. 1989. *Christian Pilgrimage in Modern Western Europe*. Chapel Hill: University of North Carolina Press.
Notermans, Catrien. 2007. Loss and Healing: A Marian Pilgrimage in Secular Dutch Society. *Ethnology*, Vol. 46, No. 3, pp. 217–233.
Notoji, Masako. 1990. *Dizunirando to iu seichi*. Tokyo: Iwanami Shinsho.
Oda Masayuki. 1996. Shōdoshima ni okeru utsushi reijō no seiritsu. In Shinno Toshikazu (ed.), *Nihon no junrei: junrei no kōzō to chihō junrei*, Vol. 3. Tokyo: Yūzankaku, pp. 169–193.
Ōishi Mahito. 1989. *Zenkoku shichifukujin meguri*. Tokyo: Midori Shoten.
Okawa Eiji. 2009. *Shōdoshima henro no rekishi to tokushitsu*. Unpublished paper sent by Okawa to author.
Orsi Robert. 1997. Everyday Miracles: The Study of Lived Religion. In David D. Hall (ed.), *Lived Religion in America: Toward a History of Practice*. Princeton, NJ: Princeton University Press, pp. 3–21.
Osada Kōichi, Sakata Masaaki and Seki Mitsuo. 2003. *Gendai no Shikoku henro: Michi no shakaigaku no shiten kara*. Tokyo: Gakubunsha.
Ousterhout, Robert. 1990. Loca Sancta and the Architectural Response to Pilgrimage. In Robert Ousterhoot (ed.), *The Blessings of Pilgrimage*. Urbana and Chicago: University of Illinois Press, pp. 108–124.
Ōzeki Gyōō. 1936. *Shikoku reijō junpai nisshi*. Kyoto: Ritsumeikan.
Ozono Atsuyuki (ed.). 2000. *Zenkoku reijō daijiten*. Tokyo: Rokugatsu Shobō.
Payne, Emily. 2012. Jesus Rises Again (and Again and Again) This Easter in Buenos Aires. *The Guardian*, April 5, 2012, available at http://www.guardian.co.uk/travel/2012/apr/05/easter-religious-theme-park-buenos-aires.
Peters, F. E. 1995. *The Hajj: The Muslim Pilgrimage to Mecca and the Holy Places*. Princeton, NJ: Princeton University Press.
Pigott, Robert. 2010. Are British Muslims Being Priced Out of Pilgrimages? BBC News, November 15, available online at http://www.bbc.co.uk/news/uk-11749511.
Preston, James J. 1992. Spiritual Magnetism: An Organizing Principle for the Study of Pilgrimage. In Alan Morinis (ed.), *Sacred Journeys: The Anthropology of Pilgrimage*. Westport, CT: Greenwood Press, pp. 31–46.
Pruess, James B. 1992. Sanctification Overland: The Creation of a Thai Buddhist Pilgrimage Center. In Alan Morinis (ed.), *Sacred Journeys: The Anthropology of Pilgrimage*. Westport, CT: Greenwood Press, pp. 211–231.
Rambelli, Fabio. 2002. Secret Buddhas: The Limits of Buddhist Representation. *Monumenta Nipponica*, Vol. 57, No. 3, pp. 271–307.
Reader, Ian. 1987a. From Asceticism to the Package Tour: The Pilgrim's Progress in Japan. *Religion*, Vol. 17, No. 2, pp. 133–148.
———. 1987b. Back to the Future: Images of Nostalgia and Renewal in a Japanese Religious Context. *Japanese Journal of Religious Studies*, Vol. 14, No. 4, pp. 287–303.
———. 1988. Miniaturisation and Proliferation: A Study of Small-Scale Pilgrimages in Japan. *Studies in Central and East Asian Religions*, Vol. 1, No. 1, pp. 50–66.
———. 1991. *Religion in Contemporary Japan*. Basingstoke: Macmillan.
———. 1993. *Sendatsu and the Development of Contemporary Japanese Pilgrimage*. Nissan Occasional Papers on Japan No. 17. Oxford: Nissan Institute for Japanese Studies.
———. 1995. Social Action and Personal Benefits in Contemporary Buddhism in Japan. *Buddhist-Christian Studies*, Vol. 15, pp. 3–17.
———. 1996. Creating Pilgrimages: Buddhist Priests and Popular Religion in Contemporary Japan. *Proceedings of the Kyoto Conference on Japanese Studies International Research Center for Japanese Studies, Kyoto*, Vol. 3, pp. 311–324.

———. 1999. Legends, Miracles, and Faith in Kobo Daishi and the Shikoku pilgrimage: A Commentary and Selected Translations from Shinnen's *Shikoku Henro Kudokuki* of 1690. In George J. Tanabe (ed.), *Religions of Japanese in Practice*. Princeton, NJ: Princeton University Press, pp. 360–369.

———. 2001. Reflected Meanings: Underlying Themes in the Experiences of Two Japanese Pilgrims to Europe. In Adriana Boscaro and Maurizio Bozzi (eds.), *Firenze, Il Giappone e L'Asia Orientale*. Florence: Leo S. Olschi, pp. 121–139.

———. 2004. Dichotomies, Contested Terms and Contemporary Issues in the Study of Religion. *Electronic Journal of Contemporary Japanese Studies*, Discussion Paper 3, available online at http://www.japanesestudies.org.uk/discussionpapers/Reader2.html.

———. 2005. *Making Pilgrimages: Meaning and Practice in Shikoku*. Honolulu: University of Hawaii Press.

———. 2007a. Positively Promoting Pilgrimages: Media Representations of Pilgrimage in Japan. *Nova Religio*, Vol. 10, No. 3, pp. 13–31.

———. 2007b. Pilgrimage Growth in the Modern World: Meanings and Implications. *Religion*, Vol. 37, No. 3, pp. 210–229.

———. 2011a. Buddhism in Crisis? Institutional Decline in Modern Japan. *Buddhist Studies Review*, Vol. 28, No. 2, pp. 233–263.

———. 2011b. The Shikoku Pilgrimage Online. In Erica Baffellii, Ian Reader and Birgit Staemmler (eds.), *Japanese Religions on the Internet: Innovation, Representation and Authority*. Routledge Studies in Religion, Media and Culture. New York, and Abingdon, UK: Routledge, pp. 80–100.

———. 2012a. Secularisation R.I.P.? Nonsense! The 'Rush Hour away from the Gods' and the Decline of Religion in Contemporary Japan. *The Journal of Religion in Japan*, Vol. 1, No. 1, pp. 7–36.

———. 2012b. Buddhist Pilgrimage Inventions, Promotions and Exhibitions in Contemporary Japan. Available online at http://blogg.uio.no/prosjekter/plurel/content/buddhist-pilgrimage-inventions-promotions-and-exhibitions-in-contemporary-japan-0.

———. 2013. Promotions, Inventions and Exhibitions: Strategies for Renewal or Evidence of the Secularisation of Pilgrimage and the Decline of Religion in Contemporary Japan? *Beiträge des Arbeitskreises Japanische Religionen*, No. 6, available online at http://tobias-lib.uni-tuebingen.de/portal/bajr/.

Reader, Ian and Paul L. Swanson. 1997. Editors' Introduction: Pilgrimage in the Japanese Religious Tradition. *Japanese Journal of Religious Studies*, Vol. 24, No. 3–4, pp. 225–270.

Reader, Ian and George J. Tanabe, Jr. 1998. *Practically Religious: Worldly Benefits and the Common Religion of Japan*. Honolulu: University of Hawaii Press.

Robertson, Jennifer. 1991. *Native and Newcomer: Making and Remaking a Japanese City*. Berkeley: University of California Press.

Robinson, James. 2012. Shrines and Relics Then and Now. Paper presented at the Pilgrimage 2012 workshop at University College London, March 27, 2012.

Roseman, Sharon R. 2004. Santiago de Compostela in the Year 2000: From Religious Center to European City of Culture. In Ellen Badone and Sharon R. Roseman (eds.), *Intersecting Journeys: The Anthropology of Pilgrimage and Tourism*. Urbana and Chicago: University of Illinois Press, pp. 68–88.

Rowan, Yorke M. 2004. Repackaging the Pilgrimage: Visiting the Holy Land in Orlando. In Yorke M. Rowan and Uzi Baram (eds.), *Marketing Heritage: Archaeology and the Consumption of the Past*. Walnut Creek, CA: Altamira Press, pp. 249–268.

Rue du Bac. nd-a. *The History of the Medal*. Paris: Chapelle Notre Dame de la Médaille Miraculeuse.

———. nd-b. *The Miraculous Medal*. Paris: Chapelle Notre Dame de la Médaille Miraculeuse.

―――. nd-c. *A Light Shining on Earth*. Paris: Chapelle Notre Dame de la Médaille Miraculeuse.
Russell, James Edward. 2011. *Cultural Property and Heritage in Japan*. Unpublished PhD thesis, School of Oriental and African Studies, London, available at http://eprints.soas.ac.uk/14043/.
Saitō Akitoshi. 1988. Kōbō Daishi densetsu. In Hinonishi Shinjō (ed.), *Kōbō Daishi shinkō*. Tokyo: Yūzankaku, pp. 49–61.
Satō Hisamitsu. 2004. *Henro to junrei no shakaigaku*. Kyoto: Jimbo Shoin.
Seki Mitsuo. 1999. Shikoku henro to idō media no tayōka. *Shakagaku Nenshi* (Waseda Shakagakkai), No. 40, pp. 65–80.
Shackley, Myra. 2006. Empty Bottles at Sacred Sites: Religious Retailing at Ireland's National Shrine. In Dallen J. Timothy and Daniel H. Olsen (eds.), *Tourism, Religion and Spiritual Journeys*. London: Routledge, pp. 94–103.
Shikoku Hachijūhakkasho Reijōkai (ed.). 1984. *Shikoku hachijūhakkasho reigenki*. Sakaide, Japan: Shikoku Hachijūhakkasho Reijōkai Honbu Jimusho.
―――. 1988. *Henro: Shikoku Hachijūhakkasho*. Tokyo: Kōdansha.
Shimizutani Kōshō. 1986. *Junrei no kokoro*. Tokyo: Daihōrinkaku.
Shinjō Tsunezō. 1960. *Shaji to kōtsū*. Tokyo: Shibundō.
―――. 1971. *Shomin no tabi no rekishi*. Tokyo: Nihon Hōsō Shuppan.
―――. 1982. *Shaji sankei no shakai keizaishiteki kenkyū*. Tokyo: Hanawa Shobō.
Shinno Toshikazu. 1980. *Tabi no naka no shūkyō*. Tokyo: NHK Books.
―――. 1991. *Nihon yugyō shūkyōron*. Tokyo: Yoshikawa Kōbunkan.
Shinno Toshikazu (ed.). 1996. *Nihon no junrei: junrei no kōzō to chihō junrei*. Tokyo: Yūzankaku.
Shudō Hajime. 1984. *Shima Shikoku reijō meguri*. Osaka: Sōgensha.
Shultz, John. 2009. *Characters on a Page, Characters on a Pilgrimage: Contemporary Memoirs of the Shikoku Henro*. Unpublished PhD dissertation, University of Manchester.
―――. 2011a. Media Transformation, Evangelical Continuity: Enticement for a Japanese Pilgrimage from Woodblocks to Homepages. In Yutaka Tsujinaka and Leslie M. Tkach-Kawasaki (eds.), *Japan and the Internet: Perspectives and Practices*. Tsukuba, Japan: Center for International, Comparative, and Advanced Japanese Studies, University of Tsukuba, pp. 99–113.
―――. 2011b. Pilgrim Leadership Rendered in HTML: Bloggers and the Shikoku Henro. In Erica Baffelli, Ian Reader and Birgit Staemmler (eds.), *Japanese Religions and the Internet: Innovation, Representation, and Authority*. New York: Routledge, pp. 101–117.
Smith, Martyn. 2008. *Religion, Culture, and Sacred Space*. New York: Palgrave Macmillan.
Sox, David. 1985. *Relics and Shrines*. London: George Allen and Unwin.
Statler, Oliver. 1984. *Japanese Pilgrimage*. London: Picador.
Stausberg, Michael. 2011. *Religion and Tourism: Crossroads, Destinations and Encounters*. London and New York: Routledge.
Stephenson, Barry. 2010. *Performing the Reformation: Public Ritual in the City of Luther*. Oxford and New York: Oxford University Press.
Stevens, John. 1993. *Three Zen Masters: Ikkyu, Hakuin, and Ryokan*. New York: Kodansha International.
Stokstad, Marilyn. 1978. *Santiago de Compostela in the Age of Great Pilgrimages*. Norman: University of Oklahoma Press.
Sullivan, Winnifred Fallers. 2005. *The Impossibility of Religious Freedom*. Princeton, NJ: Princeton University Press.
Sumption, Jonathan. 1975. *Pilgrimage: An Image of Medieval Religion*. London: Faber and Faber.
Swanson, Paul. 1981. Shugendō and the Yoshino-Kumano Pilgrimage: An Example of Mountain Pilgrimage. *Monumenta Nipponica*, Vol. 36, No. 1, pp. 55–79.

Swatos, William H. Jr. 2002. Our Lady of Clearwater: Postmodern Traditionalism. In William H. Swatos, Jr., and Luigi Tomasi (eds.), *From Medieval Pilgirmage to Secular Tourism: The Social and Cultural Economics of Piety*. Westport, CT: Praeger Press, pp. 181–192.

Swatos, William H. Jr., and Luigi Tomasi. 2002. Epilogue: Pilgrimage for a New Millennium. In William H. Swatos, Jr., and Luigi Tomasi (eds.), *From Medieval Pilgirmage to Secular Tourism: The Social and Cultural Economics of Piety*. Westport, CT: Praeger Press, pp. 207–208.

Tahara Hisashi and Misumi Haruo (eds.). 1980. *Nihon sairei chizu*, Vol. 5. Tokyo: Kokudo Chiri Kyōkai.

Takada Shinkai. 1985. *Sutete aruke*. Tokyo: Yamanote Shobō.

Tanabe, George J. 2012. Telling Beads: The Forms and Functions of the Buddhist Rosary in Japan. *Beiträge des Arbeitskreises Japanische Religionen*, No. 2, available online at http://tobias-lib.uni-tuebingen.de/portal/bajr/.

Tavinor, Michael. 2007. Sacred Space and the Built Environment. In Philip North and John North (eds.), *Sacred Space: House of God, Gate of Heaven*. London: Continuum, pp. 21–41.

Taylor, Philip. 2004. *Goddess on the Rise: Pilgrimage and Popular Religion in Vietnam*. Honolulu: University of Hawaii Press.

Taylor, William B. 2005. Two Shrines of the Cristo Renovado: Religion and Peasant Politics in Late Colonial Mexico. *American Historical Review*, Vol. 110, No. 4, pp. 945–974.

Tetsudōshō (ed.). 1922. *Omairi*. Tokyo: Tetsudōshō.

Thal, Sarah. 2005. *Rearranging the Landscape of the Gods: The Politics of a Pilgrimage Site in Japan, 1573–1912*. Chicago: University of Chicago Press.

Trainor, Kevin. 1992. When Is a Theft Not a Theft? Relic Theft and the Cult of the Buddha's Relics in Sri Lanka. *Numen*, Vol. 39, No. 1, pp. 1–26.

———. 2007. *Relics, Ritual, and Representation in Buddhism: Rematerializing the Sri Lankan Theravada Tradition*. Cambridge: Cambridge University Press.

Tsukuda Yoshio. 1981. *Nihon zenkoku sanjūsankasho, hachijūhakkasho shūran*. Tokyo: Tsukuda. (private publication)

Turner, Victor and Edith Turner. 1978. *Image and Pilgrimage in Christian Culture*. Oxford: Blackwell.

van der Veer, Peter. 1988. *Gods on Earth; The Management of Religious Experience and Identity in a North Indian Pilgrimage Centre*. London: Athlone Press.

Vaporis, Constantine Nomikos. 1994. *Breaking Barriers: Travel and the State in Early Modern Japan*. Cambridge, MA: Harvard University Press.

Viellard, Jeanne. 1984. *Le Guide du Pèlerin de Saint-Jacques de Compostelle*. Paris: Librairie Philosophique J. Vrin.

Vukonic, Boris. 1992. Medjugorje's Religion and Tourism Connection *Annals of Tourism Research*, Vol. 19, pp. 79–91.

Waller, Gary F. 2011. *Walsingham and the English Imagination*. Farnham, UK: Ashgate.

Watsky, Alexander. 2004. *Chikubushima: Deploying the Sacred Arts in Momoyama Japan*. Seattle: University of Washington Press.

Watsuji Tetsurō. 1961. *Climate and Culture: A Philosophical Study* (trans. by Geoffrey Bownas). Westport, CT: Greenwood Press.

Webb, Diane. 2002. *Medieval European Pilgrimage, c.700-c.1500*. Basingstoke: Macmillan.

Wood, Heather. 1980. *Third Class Ticket*. London: Routledge.

Works, John A. 1976. *Pilgrims in a Strange Land: Hausa Communities in Chad*. New York: Columbia University Press.

Wylie, Bob. 1991. Faith, Hope and Package Tours. *Scotland on Sunday* supplement, June 16, 1991, pp. 18–23.

Yamanoi Daiji. 1987. Zenkōji to degaichō. In Sakurai Tokutarō (ed.), *Bukkyō minzokugaku taikei 3: Seichi to takaikan*. Tokyo: Meicho Shuppan, pp. 227–247.

Yoritomi Motohiro and Toshiyuki Shiragi. 2001. *Shikoku henro no kenkyū*. Nichibunken Sōsho No. 23. Kyoto: Kokusai Nihon Bunka Kenkyū Sentā.
York, Michael. 2002. Contemporary Pagan Pilgrimages. In William H. Swatos, Jr., and Luigi Tomasi (eds.), *From Medieval Pilgrimage to Secular Tourism: The Social and Cultural Economics of Piety*. Westport, CT: Praeger Press, pp. 137–158.
Young, Louise. 1999. Marketing the Modern: Department Stores, Consumer Culture, and the New Middle Class in Interwar Japan. *International Labor and Working-Class History*, Vol. 55, pp. 52–70.
Young, Richard and Fuki Ikeuchi. 1995. Japanese Religion in the 'Hateful Years': Reflections on Pokkuri and Other Geriatric Rituals in Japan's Aging Society. *Japanese Religions*, Vol. 20, No. 2, pp. 167–200.

2. MAGAZINES AND NEWSPAPERS CITED

Chūgai Nippō, June 17, 1988; June 22, 1988; September 9, 1988; October 16, 1990.
Savvy (Magazine), September 2005.
The Guardian, July 31, 1999; September 30, 2002; July 2, 2004; October 16, 2009; November 15, 2010; April 14, 2012.
The Scotsman, April 23, 1990.

3. WEBSITES

Unless otherwise stated, all the sites referred to in this book were extant and available online on January 27, 2013. For sites that were unavailable or inaccessible at this date, I have included either the most recent date at which I accessed them or the date when I first consulted them. Websites are given in alphabetical order.
http://gulfnews.com/business/opinion/haj-vital-to-saudi-economy-1.533412
http://henro-travel.watabi.com/?gclid=CP7J05Wo7KkCFcEd4QodiHejWw (no longer available: last accessed July 6, 2011)
http://itunes.apple.com/jp/app/id434538359?mt=8
http://japanese.joins.com/article/article.php?aid = 103340&servcode=400%A1%F8 code=400&p_no=&comment_gr=article_103340&pn=8&o=a
http://kataragama.org/commercialisation.htm
http://news.bbc.co.uk/1/hi/world/middle_east/4606002.stm
http://news.bbc.co.uk/1/hi/world/south_asia/4494747.stm
http://travel.iyotetsu.co.jp/tour/88/2012/heinichi/index.html
http://travelguides.bmibaby.com/sisp/index.htm?fx=event&event_id=104834 (no longer available; initially accessed February 4, 2008)
http://www.amarnathyatra.org/yatra.htm#top
http://www.bbc.co.uk/news/uk-11749511
http://www.bbc.co.uk/worldservice/programmes/reporting_religion.shtml (no longer available; initially accessed July 2, 2007)
http://www.bernadette-of-lourdes.co.uk/bernadette-of-lourdes.htm
http://www.bl.uk/onlinegallery/onlineex/expfaith/islmanu/pilgcert/033add000027566u000000a0.html
http://www.bunka.go.jp/bunkashingikai/sekaibunkaisan/singi_kekka/besshi_8.html
http://www.centrair.jp/event/ev-title/1180345_3676.html
http://www.chapellenotredamedelamedaillemiraculeuse.com
http://www.culture-routes.lu/php/fo_index.php?lng= en&dest=bd_pa_det&unv=ed
http://www.eurasia.co.jp/nittei/s_europe/special/camino/
http://www.followthecamino.com/
http://www.go2kashmir.com/kashmir-tour-booking.html
http://www.guardian.co.uk/travel/2009/oct/17/free-travel-holiday-budget?page=all

http://www.guardian.co.uk/travel/2010/jan/10/30-new-2010-trips?page=6
http://www.guardian.co.uk/world/2010/nov/14/mecca-hajj-saudi-arabia
http://www.india-pilgrimages.com/spiritual-amarnath-yatra-tours.html
http://www.indiatours.org.uk/kashmir-tour/amarnath-yatra.html
http://www.ippoippodo.com/henro/daiko_junrei.html
http://www.page.sannet.ne.jp/nb_saka/index.html
http://www.jr-odekake.net/navi/saigoku/?kou
http://www.jyuzujyunrei.com/juzu.html
http://www.kokorohenro.org
http://www.kushima.com/henro/
http://www.makemytrip.com/holidays-india/pilgrimage-packages.html
http://www.mandala.ne.jp/88/
http://www.martyrshrine.org/
http://www.my-kagawa.jp/bus/53/
http://www.naruto-u.ac.jp /gp/henro (no longer available; accessed initially July 2008)
http://www.niji.or.jp/home/takesan/yokun.htm
http://www.noe-j.co.jp/snt/santiago/index.html (no longer available; last accessed July 2012).
http://www.ohenro.com
http://www.omotenashi88.net
http://www.pilegrim.info/en/
http://www.pilgrimage-india.com/north-india-pilgrimage/amarnath-yatra.html
http://www1.pref.tokushima.jp/002/01/0801henro/teiansho/1-mokuji.pdf (no longer available; initially accessed April 2008)
http://www.raffles.com/makkah/
http://www.shikoku88.net/tour/gotouchi.html
http://www.shinzakijinsei.com
http://www.shitennoji.or.jp/faq.html
http://www.shokokai.or.jp/21/2140212062/index.htm
http://www.sify.com/finance/even-gods-are-affected-by-global-financial-crisis-news-default-jeguNWdhfjd.html
http://www.suouoshima.com/miyage/ganbare/ohenro.html
http://www.tourisminindia.com/blogs/post/2010/09/22/New-Bharat-Darshan-Pilgrimage-Train-by-IRCTC.aspx
http://www.turgalicia.es/portada-do-bono-iacobus?langId=en_US
http://www.ucanews.com/2012/07/27/indian-pilgrimage-sees-rising-death-toll/
http://www.visitnorway.com/uk/About-Norway/History/The-Pilgrims-Route-to-Trondheim/
http://www.visitsedona.com/article/75
http://www.wf-f.org/OurLadyofLourdes.html
http://www.wheritage.net/shikoku_reizyo88kasyo_to_henromichi.html
http://www.yamato.vc/saigoku33-cyumon/saigoku33-chumon.html
http://www2.kct.ne.jp/~fujita83/
http://www2.kct.ne.jp/~fujita83/sozai/kuma2007.pdf
https://www.cathedral-enterprises.co.uk/kolist/1/Toys+and+Gifts/Bears
https://www.maavaishnodevi.org
https://www.maavaishnodevi.org/new1/index.html
https://www.maavaishnodevi.org/planyatra-registration.aspx
https://www.maavaishnodevi.org/sovenir-shops.aspx
https://www.maavaishnodevi.org/holys_offerings.asp
https://www.pawanhans.co.in/site/inner.aspx?status=3&menu_id=47

Index

accessibility 41–4; *see also* railways; remoteness; transport systems
accommodation and comfort 131–3
advertising *see* promotion and publicity
airport malls 6–8
altruism: as claimed motivation for promoting pilgrimages 90–3
Amarnath, Kashmir, India 21, 41–2, 83–5, 95, 110, 112; danger and 95, 202n11 and n12; merchants and travel agency support of 83–5; online services for 85; package tours of 84–5; political factors in growth of 42–3
Amarnath Shrine Board: and pilgrimage promotion 43
Amish: and non-commodification of religion 80–1
amulets *see* souvenirs
Archbishop of Canterbury: teddy bear souvenirs of 159
asceticism: and origins of Shikoku pilgrimage 65; as not central to pilgrimage 125–34; lack of textual sources affirming importance of in pilgrimage 125
Assisi 21
authenticity: as artificial category 10–11
Awaji: multiple pilgrimage routes and competition on 56–7; promotion of Seven Gods of Good Fortune pilgrimage as tourist resource in 91

Bà Chúa Xú (the Lady of the Realm), Vietnam 23, 132
badges, pilgrim: as motive, as souvenir and commodity 159, 177; British Museum exhibition and 150

Bax, Mart 16–17, 29, 54–5
beads: as souvenirs/motives for pilgrimage 163; *see also Juzu junrei*; souvenirs
Bernadette Soubirous 28, 55
Bijakovići: loses out to Medjugorje in competition for pilgrims 56; Marian apparitions at 55
Bodh Gaya 21, 31–2; allure of for visitors 32; 'rediscovery of' and promotion of as pilgrimage site 32–3, 88
boke fūji (prevention of senility) pilgrimages 66–70
Bronx, New York: Lourdes replica site in 12
Buddhism: pilgrimage used as strategic means of development in 62; *see also* Pure Land; Saikoku; Shikoku
buildings/built landscape: as attracting pilgrims 74–7; *see also* priests; pilgrims
Bunkachō (Japanese Ministry of Culture): and UNESCO applications 173, 179–80, 207n13
bus companies: and formation of pilgrimages in Kyushu 69–70; and in Shikoku 72; *see also* Iyo Tetsu; merchants; Shikoku; transport systems

cable cars: as attraction for pilgrims 44, 129–31; *see also* Hardwar; Shikoku; transport systems
Camino *see* Santiago de Compostela
Canterbury 76; rise and decline of as pilgrimage shrine in medieval England 57; souvenirs at 159

Catherine Labouré 160; *see also* Miraculous Medal: Chapel of Our Lady of the
Centrair (International airport near Nagoya) 6–8
Chichibu 4–6, 197n4; and tourism 102; development of hiking and day trips patterns in 139; pilgrim numbers decline in 6
Chita Hantō 6–7
choice: expansion of as factor in pilgrimage development 128–31; *see also* democratisation; pilgrims
commerce: as integral dimension of religion 81–2, 194–5; as key factor in shaping pilgrimage 110–11; criticised as disjunction from pilgrimage 11–12
commodification: as means of supporting religious practices and institutions 81; new commodities in pilgrimage market 158; role of religious authorities in 80–2; *see also* sacred and profane
competition: as integral to the pilgrimage market 56–9; benefits to pilgrims of 115; between pilgrimages 37–9, 53–7 78–9; between pilgrimages and tourist destinations 188–9
copying ideas from other pilgrimages 75; *see also* competition; Konpira
crowds and noise: as factors in success 44, 80, 128; *see also* pilgrims; remoteness
cultural heritage: as theme in pilgrimage publicity and promotion 169–78; as theme in Shikoku promotion 173–83; *see also* Santiago de Compostela; Shikoku; UNESCO World Heritage status

day-trip pilgrimages 137–9; and casualisation of pilgrimage 137; good weather as factor in 138; reshapes pilgrimage patterns 139
decline in pilgrimage numbers in Japan 6–7; economic impact of decline on pilgrimage locations 87–8; *see also* economic issues; fluctuations; miracles

degaichō (displaying pilgrimage icons at a distant site) 4–5, 15, 16, 186; *see also kaichō*; exhibitions
democratisation: increases pilgrim clienteles 36–7, 93–104; increases scope for ludic behaviour and tourism 101–4; opens pilgrimage up to wider age and gender groups 94–6; *see also* gender; guidebooks; tourism; transport systems
department stores: as sites for pilgrimage exhibitions 1–8; pilgrimages in as authentic 196
Dharmapāla 32
Diego Gelmirez (Bishop of Santiago) 76
disused pilgrimages 194
Dylan, Bob 141, 168

Eade, John and Michael Sallnow 13, 22, 141–2
economic issues: and links between economic flows and pilgrim numbers 35–7, 74, 185, 194; as key factor in pilgrimage development 34–6; benefits of pilgrimage for local/regional communities 86–7; importance for companies 93–4; notion of pilgrimage as local 'crop' 86; economic regeneration: pilgrimage as means of 69–70, 174–83; *see also* Hardwar; Lourdes; Mecca; San Giovanni del Rotondo; Shikoku
Einsiedeln 22, 161
Eliade, Mircea: and problematic division of 'sacred' and 'profane' 29–30
ennichi: dual meanings of 15
Enoshima 103
entertainment 73–6; 101–4; *see also* priests; pilgrims
entrepreneurs *see* merchants; souvenirs
exhibitions: as means of promoting pilgrimages 2, 186; see also *degaichō*; department stores; *kaichō*

fashion: links to pilgrimage promotion 172–3
fluctuations: pilgrim numbers and 6, 17–18; in Santiago 173–6; *see also* economic issues
food *see* gastronomic tours

gastronomic tours: pilgrimages as 171–3
gender 36, 94–6, 99; *see also* democratisation
Glastonbury 33–4; pilgrim wishes reflected at 120
Gold, Anne: and study of Rajasthani pilgrims 46, 113, 115–16, 125, 136
Guadalupe (Mexico) 18
guidebooks 70, 104–10, 136, 172; as encouraging individualised itineraries 105–6; as indicator of changes in pilgrimage 104–10; growing emphasis on entertainment and food in 104–10, 172; online and phone app versions 106; role in creating pilgrim expectations 105–10

hajj : criticisms of commodification in 10, 183–6; democratised and made safer by modern transport 96–8; embracing of comforts in 126, 183–6; rising costs and problems for poorer pilgrims 183–5; status enhancement and 117; *see also* Mecca; Medina
Hankyū Railway Company: and establishment of pilgrimage 90–1; claimed altruistic reasons for 90–1
Hardwar 16–17, 21, 44; as tourist site 102; economic benefits of pilgrimage to town 86; rise to national prominence 44, 99; transformed by railways 33, 44, 99; *see also* cable cars; railways
helicopter tours: and pilgrimage 43, 85, 103
Hello Kitty pilgrimage amulets 158, 166
heritage-isation 183–4; *see also* cultural heritage; Santiago de Compostela; secularising tendencies; Shikoku; UNESCO World Heritage status
hiking: pilgrimage promoted as 188–92; *see also* holidays
hobby, pilgrimage as: 155–6, 191–2
Hokkeji: use of pilgrimage to revive temple 61
holidays: pilgrimages as 131–7; and holy days 16; pilgrimages as holiday destinations 189–92,
pilgrimage featured in holiday brochures 193; *see also ennichi*
Holy Land Experience, Florida: Biblical Theme Park 186–7
Holy Years: as means of pilgrimage promotion 80
home, centrality to pilgrimage process 46–7, 143–7; *see also* souvenirs
Horan, Monseigneur John 40–1
Hoshi Kikaku Public Relations Agency 197n5
Hoshino Eiki 49, 106, 109, 127, 131, 133, 158, 172–4, 200, 204
hot springs 106, 134
Huber, Toni 32–3, 53

identity: as theme in pilgrimage 93, 98–100, 108
Iijima Makoto 107–8, 172
Ikkyū (Zen monk) 82
images of tradition 37–9, 100, 170; *see also* cultural heritage; heritage-isation; promotion and publicity; secularising tendencies
Indian Railways *see* railways
internet: online pilgrimage advertising and publicity 85, 117–19
invention/creation of pilgrimages 8, 49, 66–70, 75–7
iPhone pilgrimage apps 203n22
Ise shrines: entertainment quarters as central to appeal of 133–4; package tours to 94; pilgrimage promoted as means of increasing visitor numbers 61–2, 86; satirical poem about 112
Iyataniji: and removal of leg braces and other miracle reminders 169
Iyo Tetsu (transport company): as agent of pilgrimage development 70–2, 93; attitudes of staff in 93; close relations with Shikoku temples 89, 91–3; role in promoting and increasing pilgrim numbers in Shikoku 92; *see also* transport systems

Jammu and Kashmir government: promotion of regional pilgrimages 42–4
Japan Rail *see* railways
Japan Travel Bureau (JTB) 100; guidebooks produced by 106; *see also* guidebooks

Jerusalem 32, 52, 94, 121–2, 126
Junrei no Kai (Japanese pilgrimage society) 135
Juzu junrei 'Rosary pilgrimage' 163; *see also* souvenirs

kaichō (public display of hidden icons) 4–7, 15, 16, 78, 87, 186, 197n3; as boost to pilgrim numbers 6
Kannon 1–4; 6, 8, 15, 17, 65–6; establishment of pilgrimages to 89; on pilgrimage scrolls 152; ubiquitous nature of 48; *see also* Chichibu; Mogami; Saikoku
Kataragama 9
Kaufman, Suzanne 16–17, 54–6, 136–7, 162–3, 165
Kazan (retired Emperor): and Saikoku legends 1–2, 66
Kintetsu (Japanese department store and railway company): as promoter of pilgrimages 2–3
Knock 9–10, 22, 39–40, 123–4; airport at 40–1; and links to other pilgrimages 124; revival of and promotion as national site 39–41; souvenirs at 10, 143–6
Kōbō Daishi 63, 180; and alms 114–15; as legendary founder of Shikoku pilgrimage 28–9, 48–50, 54; as ubiquitous figure 48; on pilgrimage scrolls 152; souvenirs of 142, 152, 165; *see also* Shikoku
Konpira Shrine 16, 48, 135: buildings and priests 73–5, 87, 102; pilgrim wishes at 120
Korean National Tourist Association: and invented pilgrimage 8
Kōyasan (Mount Kōya) 62–3
Kumano 1, 57, 65–6, 71, 94
Kyushu: prevention of senility pilgrimage in 66–70, 89; as site of cooperation between priests and local bus company 89

labyrinths 52
Lalibela 52
Lochtefeld, James G., 16–17, 21, 86
Lourdes 9–10, 14, 16, 19, 28, 39, 40, 44; ambiguous attitudes to souvenirs at 165; and competitor shrines 55–6; and popular literature and guidebooks and 104–5; authorities' attitudes to miracle claims at 171–2; economic benefits of pilgrimage at 87, 110; factors in rise of 54–6; replicas of 12, 52–3; role of railway and media in promoting 33, 56, 98; souvenirs in development of 162–3
Luther, Martin *see* socks

magazines, travel 107; for young women in Japan 172–3; *see also* media; promotion and publicity
Mahabodhi Society: and transformation of Bodh Gaya 32–3, 88, 100–1; cooperation with Indian Railways 88
Mary, Marian apparitions 28, 39, 160–1; different themes within 203n8; medieval rise in popularity of 57; statuettes and water bottles of 141–2, 146, 149, 167; ubiquitous nature of 49–50; *see also* Einsiedeln; Lourdes; Medjugorje; Miraculous Medal; souvenirs
material dimensions of religion 142–144
Mecca 10; dangers of pilgrimage to in earlier times 94; economic benefits of pilgrimage to 86; luxury hotels, upgraded facilities and destruction of old city 183–6; 'Mecca Opportunity' 183; *see also* hajj
media: and depictions of pilgrimage 56, 98, 109–10, 182–3, 188–92; sponsorship of pilgrimage exhibitions 2, 171; *see also* internet; magazines; NHK
Medina 10; markets in 148
Medjugorje 16, 28, 54–6; competition with Bijakovići 54–5; tourist industry and growth of 85–6
Meitetsu (Japanese department store and railway company): as promoter of pilgrimages 7
merchants 42–3, 56, 83–8; complaints against 11, 85–6; *see also* commerce; transport systems
Miidera (Onjōji): and development of Saikoku 1, 65–6
miniature pilgrimages *see* replicated pilgrimages
miracles, miracle stories: and role in pilgrimage promotion 28–30,

34, 54, 61; contagious nature of 48, 50; decline of and lack of relevance for long-term pilgrimage success 39–41, 169; downplaying of in modern pilgrimages 40, 169–170

Miraculous Medal: Chapel of Our Lady of the (Rue du Bac, Paris) 160–62; medal as souvenir, commodity and sacred object 162; medal used to expand cult 161–3; *see also* souvenirs

miyage (Japanese term for souvenir): etymology of 151; *see also* souvenirs

mizuko kuyō: development of in Shikoku pilgrimage 121–2

Mogami 6, 135

Mori Masato 5, 16, 191

Morzine 55–6; marginalised by comparison with Lourdes 56

multiple performances of pilgrimage: influence on pilgrimage marketplace 122–5; in Japan 122–3; in Vietnam 123

NHK (Japanese national broadcasting agency) 2, 104, 171, 191–2; promotes Shikoku as example of Japanese identity and culture 109–10, 171; promotes Shikoku pilgrimage as hobby 192; sponsors pilgrimage exhibitions 2; *see also* media; promotion and publicity

ordinariness/quotidian nature of pilgrimage 45–8; *see also* home

oshi see under pilgrimage guides

Ōyama 71

package tours 93–8, 101–2; origins of 94–8, 136; *see also* Ise; tourism; Venice

Padre Pio 77, 86, 200n11; *see also* San Giovanni del Rotondo

Padua Cathedral 149–50

panda see pilgrimage guides

Papal indulgences: as stimuli for pilgrimage 79–80

parking facilities: importance of for pilgrimage sites 135

pensions: influence on pilgrim numbers in Japan 35–6

Piano, Renzo 78, 207n22

Picaud, Aimery 113–14

pilgrimage: as cultural property 100; as generic term and universal practice 19–23; as ordinary and quotidian in nature 44–5; as tied to modern developments and technology 109; definitions, academic theories and over-emphasis on Western Christianity in academic studies 13–14, 22–3; importance of Japan for studies of 22–3

pilgrimage boom (*junrei bumu*): concept of in Japan 69–70

pilgrimage guides 62, 70–2, 117; criticisms of 112–14

pilgrimages, interrelationships between 57–8

pilgrimage theme parks 186–7, 192

pilgrim-evangelists 117

pilgrims 112–140; and benefits from market competition and increased choice 115–16, 128–31; and enthusiasm for the marketplace and its comforts/offerings 140; as attracted to noise and hubbub 127–8; as eschewing asceticism 100–1, 125–134; as multiple performers/consumers of pilgrimage 122–5; autonomy of 139–40; carrying home comforts with them 127; complaints of exploitation 11, 112–13; construct stories to gain benefits 113–15; demands by for improved facilities 131–3; desires for side trips and entertainment 133–7; status enhancement and self-promotion 118–19; transactional power and pragmatic orientations of 115–16, 125–8; using multiple forms of transport 129–31; wishes for entertainments and to see other sights 72, 120–2, 135–6

Pope John Paul II 40, 79–80

Preston, James J. 30–3, 39, 41; *see also* spiritual magnetism

priests/religious officials 3, 6, 7, 15, 61–82, 173–4, 178, 189, 192; as understanding the importance of commodification 80–1; complain of pilgrims not praying at temples 156–7; concern over declining pilgrim numbers 7,

174; invent new pilgrimages 66–70; inventiveness of in developing new souvenirs 157–8; role in formation of Saikoku and Shikoku pilgrimages 63–6; role in promoting and inventing pilgrimages 3–7, 61–82
printing press: as factor in pilgrimage development 79–80
promotion and publicity campaigns 4–8; as important for survival of pilgrimages 194–5; as transforming pilgrimage into tourist activity 188–192; in public spaces 1–8; in Shikoku 106–10; publicity materials and 104–10; *see also* media; merchants; NHK
prostitution: and pilgrimage popularity 74–5
Pure Crystal Mountain (Tibet) 52, 200n21
Pure Land, Buddhist 3, 66, 152, 154, 157–8
Pushkar 86, 102; economic benefits of pilgrimage to 86, 102; as tourist destination 102

quietness: as factor in decline 45; as undermining atmosphere of sites 127; *see also* remoteness

railways 88, 98–100; as promoters of pilgrimage and national identity 98–100; French National Railways and Lourdes 33, 56, 88; Indian Railways and pilgrimage 33, 88, 98–9, 190; Japan Rail and pilgrimage development/promotion 91, 100, 103, 158
rebranding of pilgrimage 185–6
regional authorities/governments: and pilgrimage promotion 42–4, 70, 74, 84–5, 87–8, 173–82, 191; as viewing pilgrimage as means of regional regeneration 174
Reijōkai (association of pilgrimage temples): in Kyushu 71; Shikoku 71–2, 93, 159, 170, 173–4; Saikoku 1, 91, 199n5; Shōdoshima 70–1
relics 50, 57; as coterminous with/ acquired as souvenirs 148–51; as means of creating sites/ promoting pilgrimages 77–9; St. Anthony's tongue relic 149–50; theft of relics 78–80; *see also* souvenirs; scrolls
religious officials *see* priests
remoteness: as barrier to pilgrimage success 41–5
replicated pilgrimages 2–3, 12, 50–4, 66, 207n19 and 21; contagious nature of 49–50; *see also* Lourdes; Saikoku; Shikoku

sacred: as assumed quality in pilgrimage sites 28–9, 31; as idealised/ fictitious category 9–11, 29–30, 62; as manifest in souvenirs and other commercial goods 141–6, 160–3, 166–8; as mundane, 'ordinary' and ubiquitous category 47–53, 82, 195; as product of the marketplace 195
sacred and profane: artificiality of concepts and of divisions between 47–53, 143, 160, 166–8, 195
safety: as factor in pilgrimage growth and publicity 94–98; *see also* democratisation
Saikoku pilgrimage 1–8; and 'day trip' tendencies 137–8; as national pilgrimage 34; historical formation 62; legendary founding and merits of 1–2, 29, 48; loses out to Shikoku 37–8, 56; popularity declines 6, 35–9; popularity peak 2; promotional events 1–8, 91; replicas of 49–51, 66; role of guidebooks in shaping 105–6
San Giovanni del Rotondo 77–8; as architectural pilgrimage site 77–78; pilgrimage economy in 86; pilgrimage to boosted by Papal Indulgences 80
sanitisation of pilgrimage 169–70, 187–8; as future of pilgrimage? 192–3
Santiago de Compostela (and Camino/ pilgrims' way to) 10–11, 19, 27, 31, 50, 76, 114; advertised as rural tourism and as holiday location 189–90; advertised to Japanese tourists 190; as holiday experience 178; as site of 'heritage tourism' 176–7; early

dangers of 94; early modern decline and contemporary 'reanimation' 176–8; regional/political and tourist authorities and Catholic Church role in reanimation 175–7; secularising tendencies in 177–8; UNESCO World Heritage status as factor in modern growth 175

Sasaguri 7–8, 88, 156, 198n9; temples cooperate with inns in promotion campaigns 88

Satō Hisamitsu 1–2, 4, 6, 137–8

scrolls 2–3, 151–8, 205n10; aesthetic value of 152–3; as cumulative artefact and replication of pilgrimage 3, 154; as memorial for dead 3; as motivation for doing pilgrimages in Japan 154–7; as ritual object *and* souvenir 154; collection of as hobby 156; completed scrolls available for purchase 205n11; initial meaning of 151–2; Kannon replaced on by Amida to attract new pilgrims 157–8; offered by surrogate pilgrimage services 156–7, 205n11; *see also* souvenirs

secularising tendencies 169–70; 172–3, 177–8, 188–92; as future of pilgrimage? 192–3; religion proclaimed as not needed in pilgrimage 107–9; UNESCO World Heritage applications and 179–82

Sedona 31, 33–4, 120; reinvention as New Age site and engagement of local commercial authorities 33–4; pilgrim wishes reflected at 120

sendatsu see pilgrimage guides

Seven Gods of Good Fortune (*shichifukujin*) pilgrimages 90–91

Shikoku: almsgiving and 114–15; as a hiking tour 172, 191; changing demographics in 35–6, 94–6; cultural heritage and identity as factor in 36–9, 106–10; development of day-trip patterns in 138–9; earlier marginality 34–5; fluctuating periods of decline and growth 34–6; founding legends 28–9; improved facilities in 133; miracles tales in 34; pilgrimage formation 63–4; portrayed as nonreligious 107–8, 172–3; priests worry about possible decline of 174; rise in modern popularity 36–9; spread of replicas of 66; spurred by guidebooks 106–10, 172; temples work with commercial agencies/tourist offices and regional governments 89–90, 106–10, 173–5, 178–83; transport and development of 95–6; UNESCO World Heritage application and campaign 170, 173–4, 178–82, 192 ; *see also* Kōbō Daishi; *Reijōkai*

Shikoku-isation (of Japanese pilgrimage) 18, 59

Shinjō Tsunezō 34–6

Shiva 41–2, 83–5; *see also* Amarnath

Shōdoshima 6–8, 18, 22, 66, 87–8, 157, 194, 198n9, 201n4; declining pilgrim numbers in 7, 18, 36, 39, 44–5; defunct Kannon pilgrimage in 194; difficulty of access and quietness as problem 45; establishment of *Reijōkai* 70

shopping: as integral element of pilgrimage 146–7; *see also* souvenirs

Shri Mata Vaishno Devi Shrine, Kashmir, 18, 43–4; becomes national pilgrimage site/overtakes other local sites 43–4; importance of schedules at 104; sells souvenirs as sacred objects 151, 159–60; supported by regional government 42–4

Shultz, John 116–19, 127, 206n2 and 3; and concept of 'pilgrim-evangelists' 116

snow shakers: as souvenirs and relics 150–1

socks, Martin Luther's 164–5

souvenirs 141–68; ambiguous attitudes to 163–6; as central to pilgrimage 141–6, 166–8; as coterminous with relics and amulets 148–51; as important element in shrine economies 159–60; as memories integrating

228 Index

home and shrine 144–7; as motivation for pilgrimage 145; as reminders and symbols of home 143–7; as sacred 141–6, 160–3, 166–8; competition over 142–3, 159; denounced as tacky/kitsch 9–10, 12, 141–2; importance of new souvenirs 158; sold by shrines/temples 151, 158–60; *see also* Archbishop of Canterbury teddy bears; home; Lourdes; *miyage*; Padua; relics; scrolls; Shikoku; shopping; socks

spiritual magnetism 28, 30–1; problems with the category and its uses 34–44, 59

St. Olaf's Way, Norway: as new heritage/pilgrimage hiking trail 190–1

Suō Oshima: priests revive pilgrimage in, 70–1

superstition: accusations of in pilgrimage 87, 165–6

surrogate pilgrimage (*dairi sanpai*) in Japan 157

swimming/bathing 136

Taiwan 8, 86–7; pilgrimage invented for the Japanese market 8

Tateyama 134

Taylor, Philip 14, 23, 121, 132

Thal, Sarah 16–17, 48, 73–5, 120

Tibetan pilgrims 21, 59; railway travel and changing perceptions of pilgrimage 100–1

timetables: and reshaping of pilgrimage 103–4

tourism: permeability/convergence of tourism and pilgrimage 101–10, 133–7, 188; Shikoku pilgrimage promoted as 'tourist brand' 182

tourist agencies/offices: as cooperating with priests to develop pilgrimages 8, 69–70; as advertising pilgrimages 85, 189

transport systems: as instrumental in developing pilgrimages/increasing access 33–45, 93–104;

as offering increased choice to pilgrims 128–31; enhancing gender and age profiles 35–6, 93–104; impact on pilgrimage 10, 128–31; impact on pilgrim perceptions and experiences 100–1, 137; seductive nature of 98–100, 128–30; transforming local sites into national/international pilgrimages 99; *see also* cable cars; hajj; Hardwar; Lourdes; Mecca; railways; Shikoku

travel industry: uses pilgrimage to boost custom 107–8

Turner, Victor and Edith 8, 13–14, 22, 102

TV dramas 109; *see also* NHK

UNESCO World Heritage status: and pilgrimage 170, 173–82; benefits of status for Santiago de Compostela 175–8; Shikoku and campaigns for 170, 173–4, 178–82, 192

Varanasi 21, 86, and tourism 102; replications of 51–2

Venice: and package tours 94; establishes tourist and complaints offices for pilgrims 94, 113

Vietnamese pilgrims: pragmatic orientations of 121, 132; multiple pilgrimages by 123

Wal-Martisation 18, 59

Walsingham 52, 57, 123, 127; indulgences as means of stimulating pilgrimage to 79

Wittenberg 121, 163–5

Xubi (Santiago pilgrimage mascot) 176–7

Yūben Shinnen 63–4

Zenkōji 48, 87

CPSIA information can be obtained
at www.ICGtesting.com
Printed in the USA
BVHW05s2204020818
523328BV00009B/148/P